UNDRESSING CINEMA

From Audrey Hepburn in Givenchy to sharp-suited gangsters in Tarantino movies, clothing is central to film. Clothes are not mere accessories, but are key elements in the construction of cinematic identities. *Undressing Cinema* focuses on the narrative significance of clothes in film, and proposes new and dynamic links between cinema, fashion and costume history, gender, queer theory and psycho-analysis.

Undressing Cinema explores the difference between the referential relationship of film and fashion, and the notion that clothing, in such films as *The Piano* and *The Age of Innocence*, can be a repressive or expressive statement of sexuality. Discussing new *film noir*, the gangster movie and new black cinema, Bruzzi analyses assumptions about femininity and masculinity and examines the relation-ship between gender and dress in recent cinema: the emergence of the modern *femme fatale* in *Single White Female*, *Disclosure* and *The Last Seduction*; generic male chic in *Goodfellas*, *Reservoir Dogs* and *Leon*; and pride, costume and masculinity in 'Blaxploitation' films, *Boyz N the Hood* and *New Jack City*. The concluding chapters further problematise gender identities through a consideration of drag in films, proposing a radical differentiation between the unerotic cross-dressing of *Mrs Doubtfire* as opposed to the eroticised ambiguity of androgyny in *Orlando*.

Undressing Cinema challenges and reassesses received notions of costume and fashion in film. It radically departs from conventional interpretations of how masculinity and femininity are constructed through clothes and reconsiders the role dressing up plays in the manufacturing of gender, identity, sexuality and desire.

Stella Bruzzi is a lecturer in Film at Royal Holloway, University of London. She has published widely in the areas of cinema and cultural studies and is a regular contributor to *Sight and Sound*.

UNDRESSING CINEMA

Clothing and identity in the movies

Stella Bruzzi

London and New York

First published 1997
by Routledge
11 New Fetter Lane, London EC4P 4EE

Simultaneously published in the USA and Canada
by Routledge
29 West 35th Street, New York, NY 10001

Typeset in Palatino by Keystroke, Jacaranda Lodge, Wolverhampton
Printed and bound in Great Britain by Biddles Ltd, Guildford and King's Lynn

British Library Cataloguing in Publication Data
A catalogue record for this book is available from the British Library

Library of Congress Cataloging-in-Publication Data
Bruzzi, Stella
Undressing cinema : clothing and identity in the movies / Stella
Bruzzi
p.   cm.
Filmography : p.
Includes bibliographical references and index.
(hbk : alk. paper)
1. Costume—Symbolic aspects. 2. Fashion in motion pictures.
I. Title.
PN1995.9.C56B78   1997
791.43'655—dc21   97–7260

ISBN   0–415–13956–2 (hbk)
0–415–13957–0 (pbk)

CONTENTS

Contents

PLATES

Plates

Plates

ACKNOWLEDGEMENTS

Many friends, colleagues and members of my family have helped in different ways and at different stages with the writing of this book. I thank Rebecca Barden at Routledge for her encouragement and guidance on this project, and acknowledge the tremendous help and support I have received from others. I would particularly like to mention Philip Dodd, for having allowed me the space and time to try out in *Sight and Sound* many of the ideas that I have since developed and incorporated here, Millie Simpson for her advice about picture research and Dan Rebellato for his suggestions on various chapters. I would have found it impossible to complete my research without the invaluable resources of the BFI reference library and the assistance of their staff. I also thank the British Library and, for their swift response to specific queries, the Chanel press office and Lisa Brody at Condé Nast.

This book is dedicated with love to Mick.

INTRODUCTION
Clothing and cinema

This book is the last stage of a long and varied journey that began with the first UK screening of *The Piano*. Never having been an ardent fan of conventional 'bodice rippers' or nostalgic fossilisations of a past we never had, I was surprised by my reaction to the costumes. Like most of the audience, I was left moved by the film's sensuous intensity, its engagement with women's history, even its brittleness, its lack of sentimental compassion for the heroine, Ada; but most of all I was moved by the clothes. One sequence, showing Baines (Harvey Keitel) crouched under the piano as Ada (Holly Hunter) is playing, stands out as a turning point in my conversion. In close-up we see Baines's rough, grubby forefinger caress a speck of white skin left exposed by an undarned wool stocking. This gesture is, on one level, a very straightforward signal of Baines's desire for Ada, and Ada registers this through the startled but not unpleased expression on her face in the subsequent shot. Its eroticism, however, as a cinematic image rather than an idea, is created by the multiple juxtapositions of colour and texture: the two skins (one masculine and swarthy, the other feminine and 'white and hairless as an egg'), the heavy blackness of the stocking, and the delicate, if a little perfunctory, edging on Ada's white petticoat. The snatched quotation in parentheses above is from Robert Herrick's two-line poem *Her Legs* (Fowler 1991: 271) which he wrote in 1638 to his muse 'Julia'. Why the words come to mind when thinking of *The Piano* is not simply the pallor of Ada's skin, but the awareness that Herrick, a priest as well as a poet, was a clothes fetishist who translated his unconsummated desires into an attraction for the movement, detail and eroticism of clothes. The scene from *The Piano* replicates the duality of the fetishist: it both gives the costumes a narrative purpose and allows them to exist independently of that dominant discourse. This book is about that independence.

The significant scholarship already available in the area of cinema and clothes has predominantly dealt with the same intersection between women, sexuality and costume found in *The Piano*. The emphasis of this work, from a largely feminist perspective, has gravitated towards period films such as Gainsborough melodramas (Harper 1987, Cook 1996) or to the meaning and production of costume in the era of classical Hollywood (Gaines and Herzog 1990). These texts do not, however, make extensive reference to the theoretical studies of clothes fetishism and the concomitant effect of this sexualisation on the spectator. Even within the discussions of costume and sexuality (for instance Harper 1987 and 1994) there lurks the assumption that clothes, though evocative and complex signifiers, are a means of understanding the body or character who wears them not an end unto themselves. This mandatory bridesmaid status afforded to costume failed to coalesce with my response to cinema where, much of the time, clothes seemed able to impose rather than absorb meaning.

Another key image as I conceived of this book was Alain Delon in Jean-Pierre Melville's *Le Samouraï*. Although the main focus of *Undressing Cinema* is more recent film (1980s and 1990s), the ubiquitous cold, silent, cool gangster of Melville's films retains a certain topicality through having been conspicuously resurrected by Quentin Tarantino in both *Reservoir Dogs* and *Pulp Fiction*. At the end of *Le Samouraï* the hit man Jef (Delon) goes into a bar. In front of the barman (who recognises him as the assassin hired to kill his boss earlier in the film) Jef deliberately, impassively puts on the white gloves he wears for executing a contract killing, stark and bright against the sobriety of his coat and the dinginess of the locale. He then walks over to the pianist, gets out a revolver as if to shoot

i Alain Delon as Jef Costello in *Le Samouraï*
Courtesy of BFI Stills, Posters and Designs

her, but is himself shot in the back first. As he falls to the ground still clasping the gun (which we discover is unloaded), Jef folds his pristine hands across his chest and dies. Throughout the scene (and despite what is going on in terms of action) our gaze is directed towards Jef's inappropriately technical (as opposed to chic) gloves, garments that suggest significance but remain opaque, even after Melville has proffered the explanation, 'White gloves are a tradition with me: all my killers wear them. They are editor's gloves' (Nogueira 1971: 139).

Jef's white gloves once again fail to conform to the idea of costumes as functionaries of the narrative, rather they are spectacular interventions that interfere with the scenes in which they appear and impose themselves onto the character they adorn. Jef is constructed through his costume. The fetishisation or over-valuation of appearance that pervades *Le Samouraï* also raises other fundamental issues concerning clothes and cinema, most importantly the unconventional correlation between masculinity and extreme narcissism exemplified by Delon's fixation on his own reflection. What is of course most surprising about the Delon image is that he is a man. Discussions of costume have tended to exclude men and masculine identities, as if an attention to dress is an inherently feminine trait, despite the recent debates around masculinity and the eroticised male image in the cinema (see Neale 1983) or some recent psychoanalysis-based studies of men and cultural/social identity (e.g. Middleton 1992, Frosh 1994, Leader 1996). Since vanity has now also hit the Anglo-American male population, more recent histories of fashion and its cultural impact (Craik 1994) have considered men as more than disinterested observers.

These questions of gender bring me to the third and final image that helps draw the parameters of this book: the drag queen Felicia/Adam standing on top of the bus crossing Australia in *The Adventures of Priscilla, Queen of the Desert*. Felicia, miming to arias like a camp diva, poses in silver make-up and dress on the moving bus. The camera starts to close in on Felicia's bright face, then pulls out to reveal the excessive, tapered train billowing in the wind and shimmering as its waves catch the sun. There is no straightforward contextualisation for this and the similar scene which occurs later; this is simply, more extravagantly than Jef's oddity gloves, a sequence that functions as a radical narrative interjection. The triumphant image of Felicia is about complicating not cementing the relationship between sex, gender and clothes, and is thus relevant to the analysis of drag and performativity outside cinema (Butler 1990 and 1993, Garber 1993). Felicia's arias, set against the multiple costume changes throughout *Priscilla*, work as a metaphor for the film as a whole, representing as they do the liberation and performative potential of clothes and the fluidities of identity.

These three very different images already imply a broad and eclectic field, but one that contains significant intersections. In order to reflect this intriguing duality, I wanted to do two things: to approach the subject of clothes and cinema

Introduction

in an interdisciplinary way, and to focus the discussions within each chapter on a discrete body of films that most productively exemplify these cross-overs. *Undressing Cinema* does not, therefore, remain closeted within the narrower confines of pure film studies, but suggests links with other fields. Although the emphasis of this book is on representation of clothing and fashion in cinema and the relevance of these to the understanding and interpretation of narrative and images, it also reflects the need to yoke together a heterogeneous and dispersed range of disciplines. Two main axes inform the discussions of specific films in *Undressing Cinema*: the theory, history and art of fashion and costume design, and the debates surrounding the construction of gender and sexuality, primarily in or deriving from psychoanalysis. Within these parameters my intention has been to reassess and challenge some of the assumptions and truisms that have dominated the study of dress, gender and sexuality, and to recontextualise others by applying them to cinema. Running through the discussions in the individual chapters there are arguments posed against received notions of how gender has been constituted in theory and a re-evaluation of the eroticisation and problematisation of the cinematic image through its relationship to clothing.

My fundamental premise, that clothing exists as a discourse not wholly dependent on the structures of narrative and character for signification, is introduced via the two initial chapters. In Chapter 1, the questions raised in relation to the presence of couture designs in cinema pertain largely to issues of spectacle. The foundation for my distinction between designs by costume designers whose role is simply to dress characters and designs made for films by couturiers who have a name and identity beyond cinema is straightforwardly to contrast between those clothes that are intended as spectacle and those that are not. My stress is on work by couturiers renowned for their association with modern cinema such as Jean-Paul Gaultier, Coco Chanel (and the house of Chanel since her death) and Giorgio Armani. Hijacking the tight and prescriptive world of fashion and inserting it into a discussion of cinema threw up many interesting and complicating ideas. The first of these relates to the notion of the spectacular. Whereas Gaultier's designs for *The Cook, the Thief, His Wife & Her Lover* or *Kika* can unproblematically be called 'spectacular' by virtue of calling attention to themselves, Armani's designs for films such as *The Untouchables* and *Voyager* or Chanel's for *Trop Belle Pour Toi!* are more ambiguous in this respect. The inherent contradiction of the latter designs is that they function in a spectacular way whilst not being agents of display, a duality that extends from their ability to prescribe characters' identities or to function in relation to the spectator independently of characters despite remaining visually unextravagant. This duality (both a disavowal and a reference to the function of the spectacular) impinges most obviously on the representation of masculinity (hence the focus on Armani who, for the cinema, dresses predominantly men), whilst it is less expected in relation to the feminine. What evolved out of my examinations of a group of films that deal with this ambivalently defined femininity (*Rear Window*, *Belle de Jour* and *Trop Belle*) were two ideas: first, that clothes do not acquire significance only in relation to the body or character (which is the overriding ethos of most costume design), and second, that fashion is not inevitably produced to render the wearer attractive to the opposite sex. The former contention is the starting point for the notion of clothes as discourse, pursued in various forms throughout the book; the latter is a crucial observation, revisited most extensively during the discussion of *Single White Female*, which casts serious doubt on the theorisation of the feminine image as passive in relation to an active male gaze, as part of the intention behind the all-female dialogue that takes place between female fashion magazines and readers or between fashionable female images and spectators is necessarily to exclude men altogether.

Questions of definitions of gender are tackled from an alternative perspective in Chapter 2's discussion of period costumes and sexuality. Initially with recourse to Freud's essays on sexuality and fetishism and J.C. Flügel's *The Psychology of Clothes*, which is, at heart, a transposition of Freud's ideas on sexuality to the issue of clothing, this discussion explains essentialist arguments for the belief in fixed and segregated genders with reference to dress and fetishism. Flügel's concept of the Great Masculine Renunciation during the nineteenth century (when men renounced the desire for exhibitionism in their own attire and so transferred the effects of display and the sexualisation of the body through clothes onto the increasingly decorative woman) has proved hugely influential. Flügel, after Freud, thus argues for the exhibitionist but passive woman being the embodiment of the man's desire – in short, his fetish; a view that is further substantiated by fashion historians such as James Laver, who consolidates Flügel's notion of the shifting erogenous zone. By subsequently incorporating both historical accounts of fetishism and the debates surrounding cinema's deployment of voyeuristic and fetishistic techniques, the chapter offers analyses of films that both uphold and contest the traditional views. Whilst in an intensely patriarchal film such as *Picnic at Hanging Rock* the representation of women readily conforms to the archetype that the decorative woman is the source of the male's erotic pleasure, both *The Age of Innocence* and *The Piano* offer critiques of this binary, the former by alienating and making strange the past and its objects of fetishism, the latter by indicating how clothes fetishism can be positively appropriated by women. This reconfiguration of fetishism and gender dynamics is another way in which clothing can be seen to construct an independent discursive strategy (thus conforming to Foucault's notion of the entry of sex into discourse) through which one can link, for instance, the secret tight-lacing communications women had with each other across the letter pages of Victorian magazines to modern reassessments of restrictive clothing and fetishism (Kunzle 1982, Gamman and Makinen 1994). Many of these debates are subsequently picked up in the following chapters on gangsters and *femmes fatales*.

Introduction

The second section of *Undressing Cinema* deals with three different modern genres in which clothing makes a significant intervention in the representation and interpretation of identity. The rationale behind grouping together discussions of gangsters, black American cinema and modern *femmes fatales* is to open up the debates around gender, sexuality and appearance begun in the previous two chapters. All the discussions in some way are renegotiations with established stereotypes. For example, what governs and hangs over the shared iconography and mutual veneration expressed by the Franco-American gangster traditions is a constant, ultimately futile striving for a stereotyped, idealised and unattainable image of masculinity. Within this context the gangster's consciously repetitious and self-reflective wardrobe suggests a perpetual need to define and redefine himself against such an image, to create his identity by comparing himself to past icons. These ideas of creating a mythic identity to hold up as an Ideal develop, most significantly, Freud's views on narcissism and Lacan's arguments pertaining to the centrality of the mirror phase and the permanently veiled phallus to the construction of masculinity. Recent American black cinema is likewise informed by a reaction to stereotypes, but is further problematised by the added issue of racial identification. The complexities foregrounded in the analysis of black cinema are of critical importance to this section on gender and genre, as film costume has been regarded largely as a white preserve – despite some of the quintessential clothes movies of all time being black. Certain critics have argued that in the recently revived and reappraised Blaxploitation films of the early 1970s there is a self-conscious acknowledgement and citation of the stereotyped images of blackness centred on exoticism, virility and action (Tasker 1993), a reflexivity, this chapter argues, that leads directly from these black action movies to a 1990s 'ghetto movie' such as *New Jack City*.

An intrinsic element of both these new contextualisations of gender and race archetypes is narcissism. The analysis of gangster films overturns several established assumptions perpetuated by film theory, psychoanalysis and fashion history about men and appearance, notably that men invariably deflect the erotic gaze (Mulvey 1975, Neale 1983) and that their functional clothes necessarily render them unerotic (Laver 1945 and 1969). The conclusion of these debates is that, despite the Great Masculine Renunciation, narcissism and the eroticisation of the male body can exist as correlatives of heterosexual masculinity, even via the ostensibly unspectacular men's suit. These discussions are developed and complicated in Chapter 4 by the issue of race. From the 1940s zoot suiters to 1980s hip-hop fashions and beyond, racial pride has been intricately entwined with excesses of appearance within black culture, so narcissism and exhibitionism, therefore, has been of particular cultural significance to African-Americans. One of the negotiations this chapter has to make is between the film costumes and the creation of subcultural styles (Hebdige 1979, Cosgrove 1989, Tulloch 1993);

whereas the white gangster's style is an appropriation of high fashion, the black gangster's style in 1980s and 1990s 'home-boy' films is anti-fashion that derives from street styles. The notion of an identity governed by race and stereotypes is then questioned by *Waiting to Exhale* which reasserts the relevance of gender (in this case femininity) over race and offers a concluding critique of the outdated view that the more authentically black the hair and clothes styles are, the more ideologically 'right-on' the individual (Mercer 1994).

A comparable preoccupation with the 'natural' as opposed to the 'artificial' has dominated feminist arguments about femininity, a conflict which forms the basis for the reconsideration of the contemporary *femme fatale* in Chapter 5. Here the dilemma centres on the rejection by most feminist commentators, whether in response to the representation of femininity on screen or within a social context, of the image of an overtly sexual, powerful woman as an inevitable construct of patriarchy. Recent feminist writings on women and fashion (e.g. Brownmiller 1984, Coward 1993) have pursued the line adopted by Simone de Beauvoir in *The Second Sex* (1949), namely that the eroticised female figure is necessarily the embodiment of male sexual desires, thus extending many of the debates foregrounded in the analyses of couture and period costume. The established feminist extension of this argument is to perceive women who dress to flaunt rather than disguise sexual difference (as the *femme fatale* does in her stilettos and short skirt) to be colluding in their own oppression. This chapter seeks to counter such feminist notions by expanding upon the idea, proposed during the discussion of fetishism and the costume film, that women's restrictive clothing is not innately oppressive, a contention that requires a re-examination of Riviere's definition of the masquerade and the assumption that this, again, is a tactic for presenting men with the image of women *they* desire. Once more, an issue here is the active, self-conscious use made of a stereotype by a character such as Bridget in *The Last Seduction*, who uses the potential offered by the masquerade (the presentation to the threatened man of an ostensibly unthreatening femininity) to destroy the men around her. Much of this discussion thus extends the examination of the feminine image evolved in Chapter 1 in relation to the spectacular, and also continues the potentially empowering dialogue between feminism and fetishism initiated in Chapter 2. In the final analysis of *Single White Female* there is also a detailed development of the idea that women might not dress with men in mind at all, but rather that women's fashion – and in a cinematic context emphatic femininity – is an exclusory dialogue between a female image and a female spectatorship. The possibility envisaged is that a stereotype can be aggressively reappropriated.

Undressing Cinema is intentionally structured so that the issues raised by the relationship between clothing and the body become increasingly problematised. Whereas all three chapters in the second section of the book deal with a certain correlation between gender and dress, the final section reassesses the validity of that assumption with reference to transvestism. Wearing the clothing of the 'wrong' sex is the most conventionalised method of undermining gender, but on the whole past assessments of transvestism have, rather uncomfortably, bracketed all such mixings and matchings together. The division I have proposed between cross-dressing and androgyny is inspired by a belief that there are essentially two ways in which transvestism has been approached in cinema. Whereas comedies of cross-dressing (*Mrs Doubtfire* proving an exemplary text in this respect) seek to affirm the inflexibility of sexual difference and so leave gender binaries unchallenged, the androgynous image strives to break such oppositions down. Cross-dressing is largely about emphasising the existence of the sex that is temporarily disguised, so we are never left in any doubt that Robin Williams is male despite his feminine attire – indeed his masculinity is inferred even more strongly through its absence. The relationship between body and clothes is treated very differently when it comes to drag. In *The Adventures of Priscilla, Queen of the Desert*, for instance, a similar discrepancy between sex and constructed gender is celebrated not hysterically dismissed. Although cross-dressing can be theorised as a point of radical departure from which to question gender categories (Garber 1993), this disruption of sexual difference only exists on an intellectual level, a result of the troubling comic image having been effectively desexualised.

The blurring of difference that characterises the androgyne is, conversely, more dangerous and destabilising because it incorporates eroticism. Thus, the allure of Little Jo or Orlando is intensified at the moments in either film when the boundaries between body, clothes and gender are least clear, when the image itself conveys doubt and uncertainty, as when Jo hides her female face beneath a wide-brimmed masculine hat. From Virginia Woolf onwards there has, though, been a tendency to perceive androgyny as a perfected, utopian version of femininity, which, with the inclusion of *The Crying Game*, this analysis is keen to dismiss. The significance to this discussion of the uncertain friendship between Dil, the transvestite, and Fergus is that, whilst initially repelled by Dil's 'real' sexuality, Fergus nevertheless spends the remainder of the film redefining his attraction to the androgyne. Drawing together androgyny in fashion, the notion of passing (particularly Butler 1993) and the complex process of disavowal which makes the spectator both recognise and misrecognise the ambivalence of the androgynous image, this final discussion examines the powerful attraction of ambiguity and dismisses the notion that what is more alluring than anything else is the person who passes so successfully that the spectator is 'fooled'. My response to the erotic potential of androgyny is exclusively based on the *cinematic* effect of the image, on the identity being intentionally blurred, and so functions as a discursive, film-based conclusion to the many perspectives cited previously, and in particular to the arguments surrounding the role clothing plays in defining gender, sexuality and desire.

Introduction

A word of warning, though: in 1923, Erich von Stroheim was reputedly relieved of his duties as costume designer on *Merry-Go-Round* for squandering a large portion of the budget on silk underpants embroidered with the Imperial Guard monogram for the Guardsmen extras. Some producers just don't get it.

Part I

DRESSING UP

1

CINEMA AND HAUTE COUTURE
Sabrina to Pretty Woman, Trop Belle Pour Toi!, Prêt-à-Porter

All the films included in this chapter, featuring designs by a diverse range of couturiers such as Jean-Paul Gaultier, Coco Chanel and Giorgio Armani, articulate very different attitudes to the central premise, namely the use of clothes as spectacle and mechanisms for display. A result of having arrived at the distinction between costume and couture design is the belief that clothes can function independently of the body, character and narrative, that through them alternative discursive strategies can be evolved that, in turn, question existing assumptions about the relationship between spectator and image, not necessarily problematised through the use of conventional costumes. Couture's involvement with cinema has an elaborate and fragmented history. From 1931 when Sam Goldwyn offered Coco Chanel one million dollars to design for MGM, high fashion has been brought in to a production to contribute a quality which eludes even the most prolific and proficient costume designers: the glamour of a name. Chanel's reputed disagreements with Gloria Swanson, whom she dressed in *Tonight or Never*, led to her premature departure from Hollywood after barely a year, as, despite proving an imaginative and meticulous costume designer, she was inflexible when asked to tailor her style to the needs of the film or to divest her costumes of the understated chic which had become her couture trademark.[1] Chanel's attitude, exemplified by her 1931 designs for *Palmy Days* for which she made at least four ostensibly identical versions of each dress, slightly differently cut to show the design at its best for a specific movement or action (Leese 1976: 14), was in a subtle way to prioritise the clothes over the narrative, an attitude which runs counter to the traditional ethos of costume design, namely to create looks that complement the narrative, character and stars.[2] The creation of clothes as spectacle is the prerogative of the couturier; the overriding ethos of the costume designer is conversely to fabricate clothes which serve the purposes of the narrative. From the earliest fashion show films of the 1910s to the recent cinematic contributions of Vivienne Westwood (Elizabeth Shue's corsets in *Leaving Las Vegas*) or Jean-Paul Gaultier (*The City of Lost*

3

Children) the issue of couture designs as screen costumes has remained significant. Although discussions of the role fashion plays in film consistently collapse the difference between couture and costume design, the intention of this chapter is to emphasise the distinction and focus on cinema's specific use of couture, in such recent examples as *Kika*, *Pretty Woman*, *Trop Belle Pour Toi!*, *Voyager* and *Prêt-à-Porter*.

The earliest films to feature fashion were cinematic fashion shows, the earliest example to be documented by the costume historian Elizabeth Leese being *Fifty Years of Paris Fashions 1859–1909*. This and subsequent fashion show shorts proved increasingly popular, Pathé, for instance, expanding its coverage in 1911 by producing a series of films devoted exclusively to forthcoming collections. Soon, with Jacob Wilk of World Film Productions' filming of a fashion tour of the USA in 1915 (organised by Mrs Armstrong Whitney), the primitive fashion show film developed into a narrative based genre with definite (if simple) story-lines. As Leese comments, on both sides of the Atlantic 'Fashion films had started out by being simple displays of gowns, then progressed to a story-line built round the display' (Leese 1976: 11). In her discussion of the ways in which the fashion show has been incorporated into features, Charlotte Herzog further distinguishes between films which position a show as essential to the action and those which treat the display of fashion as incidental (Herzog 1990: 136), thereby highlighting fundamentally different motivations for incorporating fashion into narrative film. The narrativised fashion film has clearly survived, and is a form adopted by such later examples as *Funny Face* or *Prêt-à-Porter*, which are both structured around the staged exhibition of fashion on the catwalk. From the late 1920s, Hollywood openly declared its desire to supplant Paris as the leading fashion innovator, a move precipitated by having been left behind after Jean Patou dropped his hem lines in 1929, an innovation that made Hollywood films populated with 'Flapper' dresses (shot up to two years before) look hopelessly *démodé*. The couturier Madame Vionnet introduced the longer bias cut dress also in 1929, a style which was to dominate Hollywood's visions of glamorous femininity through the 1930s, epitomised by Jean Harlow's silver-beaded negligée and 22-inch ostrich feathers in *Dinner at Eight*. As cinema took the initiative in the 1930s and 1940s, the distance between costume and couture fashion was minimised, and Hollywood recruited to its increasingly important design departments several fledgling couturiers such as Howard Greer and Gilbert Adrian, who was brought to work for Cecil B. DeMille and later MGM after allegedly being discovered by Rudolph Valentino and his wife.[3] As the Paris-based couturier Elsa Schiaparelli commented, 'what Hollywood designs today, you will be wearing tomorrow' (Haggard 1990: 6). There are numerous examples from the classical Hollywood period of the effect film styles had on contemporary fashion trends; both Adrian's white, puff-sleeved dress for Crawford in *Letty Lynton* and Edith Head's strapless, violet-encrusted New Look gown for Elizabeth Taylor in *A Place in the Sun*, for instance, spawned a rush of mass-produced imitations,[4] whilst the appearance of Clark Gable bare chested in *It Happened One Night* in 1934 led to an immediate drop in the American sales of men's undershirts of around 30 per cent (Chenoune 1993: 182). Anne Hollander, in her examination of art and clothes, posits that 'dressing is an act usually undertaken with reference to pictures – mental pictures, which are personally edited versions of actual ones. The style in which the image of the clothed figure is rendered . . . governs the way we create and perceive our own clothed selves' (Hollander 1975: 349–50). Cinema, and particularly Hollywood, had a similar relationship with its (largely female) audience in the 1930s, 1940s and 1950s, when spectators swiftly emulated and adopted the styles worn by their favourite film stars in their latest films.[5]

The supremacy of the costume designer as a dictator of fashion and the domination of Head, Adrian, Orry-Kelly and Branton was lessened with the introduction of another French couturier, Hubert de Givenchy, as the major designer for Audrey Hepburn in *Sabrina*, a collaboration which heralded a new relationship between stars and clothes. By the 1950s Edith Head, who was the costume designer for *Sabrina*, readily acknowledged that her role was far less influential in fashion terms than that of the couturier, saying of the gown she designed for Taylor in *A Place in the Sun*, 'People have said . . . that I was a great fashion trend-setter in 1951. That's very funny. My clothes were middle of the road in terms of the current fashion trends' (Head 1983: 97). Head, like many other costume designers, did not create looks that were so fashionable that they would quickly become obsolete. She learnt her lesson

> the hard way. Just after Dior brought out the New Look (in 1947), every film that I had done in the past few months looked like something from the bread lines. With each screening, I was reminded. I vowed that I would never get caught by a fashion trend again.
>
> (Head 1983: 69–70)

Head's relationship with Givenchy became symbolic of the divergence between the respective roles of the costume designer and the couturier. Accounts of how Givenchy came to be assigned the task of creating Hepburn's Parisian wardrobe for *Sabrina* differ; Head herself attributes the decision to the director Billy Wilder, commenting, '(he) broke my heart by suggesting that while the "chauffeur's daughter" was in Paris she actually *buy* a Paris suit designed by a French designer' (Head 1959: 119), whilst others have stated that Hepburn arrived at the initial costume discussion armed with a series of Givenchy sketches to show Head exactly what she wanted (Head 1983: 104). Symptomatic of the friction was the controversy surrounding the 'authorship' of the most innovative design in the film, the black *bateau* neckline evening dress which, to her death in 1981, Head had claimed as hers. Givenchy and even Head's colleagues at Paramount have since

1.1 Humphrey Bogart, Audrey Hepburn, William Holden in *Sabrina*
Courtesy of BFI Stills, Posters and Designs

confided that the dress was too innovative for Head, and had instead been made up from one of Givenchy's original sketches for the film.[6] The demise of the costume designer and inverse rise of the couturier is thus contextualised within the narratives of both *Sabrina* and *Funny Face*. Both films centre on the transformation of Audrey Hepburn from gauche girl to sophisticated gamine, and in both the roles filled by Head and Givenchy are clearly demarcated: whilst Head is given the pre-transformation clothes, it is Givenchy who designs all the show-stopping Parisian fantasies. Since the success of Givenchy's relationship with Audrey Hepburn (whom he dressed off-screen as well) the use of a couturier on a film has become closely aligned with a desire to bequeath to the clothes the kind of star status usually denied to costume. Givenchy and other couturiers since have used films to showcase their designs. Givenchy's signature styles, his strapless, square-necked sheaths in heavy silks and satins, his wraps and trains and his elaborate hats infiltrated every film he worked on with Hepburn up to their final collaboration on *Bloodline*. Film fashions no longer had to remain subservient to narrative and character, and could become much more intrusive, a legacy which, taking in several designers along the way, finds its surest modern expression in the spectacular, innovative costumes of Jean-Paul Gaultier.

Cinema and haute couture

From the late 1950s through to basically 1980, when Giorgio Armani designed Richard Gere's wardrobe for *American Gigolo* and effectively redefined the role of the film couturier, a fluid mutual relationship existed between fashion and costume design. Over these years a film tended towards being a general reflector of outside fashions and trends. There were obviously exceptions, such as Chanel's designs for Delphine Seyrig in *Last Year in Marienbad* which were far more flamboyant than the clothes she had created for Jeanne Moreau in *Les Amants* three years earlier, and Paco Rabanne's space-age look for Jane Fonda in the final sequence of *Barbarella*, both of which are examples of fashions being created for films that, although they bore some relation to the trends of the day, were nevertheless non-functional flights of fancy. Over this period costume design started certain notable trends, usually pertaining to street rather than high fashion, such as Marlon Brando's 'slob look' of flying jacket and white T-shirt in *The Wild One* (which he reputedly provided himself, in an era when this was no longer expected of male stars) and James Dean's tortured adolescent in similar T-shirt and wind-cheater in *Rebel Without A Cause*. With the ascendancy of European cinema in the early 1960s, there arrived a more harmonious relationship between couture and street styles – the appropriation of haute couture glamour by a landmark film such as *La Dolce Vita*, or the throwaway use of a Dior day dress on Jean Seberg in *A bout de souffle*. Films of the mid-1960s such as *Darling* and *Two For the Road* brought in the by now common practice of 'shopping' rather than designing film costume, of buying in designer off-the-peg items. The latter (another Hepburn/Givenchy collaboration) trawled the ready-to-wear collections of designers such as Mary Quant, Yves Saint Laurent and Givenchy himself.[7] Apparent through the 1960s, therefore, is a growing desire to treat haute couture (and perhaps spectacular costume designs in general) with less reverence and more irony, a tendency exemplified by the quintessentially 1960s André Courrèges-inspired costumes by Hardy Amies for *2001: A Space Odyssey*. As Amies was at the time the Queen's favourite designer, his costumes are particularly unexpected. The very notion of couture styles being synonymous with art and pure exhibitionism was questioned and mocked by Saint Laurent's exquisitely mundane wardrobe for *Belle de Jour*, a film whose attitude to unexceptional but very expensive clothes still resonates in the designs of the markedly unflamboyant cinema work of modern couturiers such as Cerruti, Armani and the house of Chanel, who dressed Carole Bouquet in *Trop Belle Pour Toi!*.

As a troublesome epitaph to the ability of film fashion to inspire particularly bland contemporary trends, there is the work of Ralph Lauren on two highly influential films of the 1970s, *The Great Gatsby* and *Annie Hall*, both of which testify to the designer's obsessive nostalgia for a bourgeois past of leisure wear and natural fabrics in pale shades. As one writer says of Lauren's wardrobe for Robert Redford as Gatsby, the fact that the suits worn in the film (set in the 1920s) could have been worn in 1974 without causing comment, is a reflection on the moribund state of male dress (McDowell 1992: 96). The costumes are also, for all the suave ease they evoke, a sad reflection on the misuse of couturiers in cinema as subsidiary costume designers who subsume their styles to the narratives and characters. Since then, even the less extrovert designers (Armani being the strongest example) have begun to restate their presence as dictators of fashion outside cinema, a re-evaluation which has likewise reinstated the element of display into couturier film designs. Nino Cerruti, another prolific men's couturier who has worked on several films, has identified his intention to manufacture a look that is 'common', to subtly infuse reality with invisible style (Irvine 1995: 157), indicating that clothes can be items of display in cinema without being spectacularly extrovert. Certain fashion writers have related the rise in prominence of all technicians and stylists involved in cinema during the late 1970s and 1980s (including fashion designers) with the demise of the classic era star (Butazzi and Molfino 1986: 19–20), but it may be more appropriate to simplify matters by equating the emergence of the design movie with the 1980s' idolisation of the label. In an age when 'shopping' a film falls within the remit of the costume designer, the involvement of the couturier in film is far from standardised.

The most interesting debates surrounding the involvement of fashion in film still centre on the questions of exhibitionism and art; whether clothes should perform a spectacular as opposed to a subservient visual role in film; and whether those same costumes should remain functional intermediaries to narrative and character, or stand out as art objects in themselves. Peter Wollen makes the distinction between Hollywood's 'play safe' attitude to fashion, and the predominantly European art cinema tradition that made fashion into 'an integral part of the overall look of the film which was genuinely treated as another art-form in its own right; incorporated into the cinema but not reduced to an ornament or an accessory' (Wollen, P. 1995: 13). Into the latter tradition, for which the starting point is taken as Chanel's work on *Last Year in Marienbad*, Wollen places the costume designs of, for example, Jean-Paul Gaultier. In his analysis Wollen expresses the rather contentious and elitist attitude that fashion as art is 'good', and that only extravagant designs can be classified as 'art'. This emphasis on artistry recalls the origins of couture designs; as Anne Hollander suggests, 'In the middle of the nineteenth century the French invented, fostered, and spread the idea of the dress designer as an original genius, like a painter – someone totally responsible for his creations' (Hollander 1993: 351). The outmoded attitude, expressed by Wollen, that only the spectacular can be art, and that 'good' fashion designers necessarily create designs for display and effect will be contested later with reference to Yves Saint Laurent and Armani.

As mentioned above, Jean-Paul Gaultier is one of the couturiers who also design for film and who Wollen classifies as an 'artist'. When working for film

Gaultier, a designer whose signature styles off the screen have been radical, spectacular garments such as his early 1980s male skirt and the 1986 'Cone Dress', often creates costumes anew, rather than lend or adapt existent lines. He has seemingly approached his film work (which to date includes *The Cook, the Thief, His Wife & Her Lover, Kika, My Life Is Hell, The City of Lost Children* and *Prêt-à-Porter*) as if it were art, saying, for instance, that cinema has afforded him the opportunity of letting his imagination run wild and has, in turn, proved 'food for my fashion' (Irvine 1995: 157). His involvement in cinema projects is also often greater than that of many other couturiers, designing entirely original costumes for all one hundred characters in *The City of Lost Children* and one-offs for the protagonists in *The Cook, the Thief* often for negligible financial rewards.

Gaultier's designs for Greenaway's *The Cook, the Thief, His Wife & Her Lover* are wildly eclectic. Helen Mirren's caged cobweb dress and the waitresses' corsets bear the trademarks of past Gaultier collections, whilst elsewhere his reference points are a heady blend of 1960s 'space age' fashions, Cavalier uniforms, seventeenth-century Cardinals' robes and modern business suits. Although the items for the leads (except Alan Howard's clothes as 'the lover') are specially designed one-offs, many of the other costumes are from Gaultier's regular

1.2 Helen Mirren and Michael Gambon in *The Cook, the Thief, His Wife & Her Lover*
Courtesy of BFI Stills, Posters and Designs

9

ready-to-wear collection, the extras reputedly having been 'let loose amongst his rails and told to deck themselves out in whatever they would wear to a swanky restaurant' (Maiberger 1989: 159). Gaultier, belying Wollen's suggestion that 'artistic' costume designers seem to find their inspiration from outside rather than inside mainstream cinema, includes several touches of traditional Hollywood glamour in his *The Cook, the Thief* costumes, particularly the long gloves, whipped hair and yards of chiffon used for Helen Mirren as Georgina. The self-conscious affiliation with an existent film tradition is further signalled by Mirren's cape with its collar of dark, upright feathers that frame her face, a direct reference to the much copied feather cloak designed by Chanel for Delphine Seyrig in *Last Year At Marienbad*.[8] Gaultier's costumes for *The Cook, the Thief* are tightly aligned with the film's highly formalistic narrative structure. Greenaway's film (like many of his others) is structured around the idea of a procession: the clear separation of the interconnecting rooms (the restaurant, the kitchens, the rest room) along a horizontal axis, the evenly paced tracking shots following the action, the positioning of the characters (at table and elsewhere) in straight lines, and the division of the narrative into seven consecutive days. The insistence of this pattern is repeated on the level of costume, most notably in the co-ordination of costumes with the dominant colours of the lighting and *mise-en-scène*, so that clothes change colour (whilst maintaining the same design) as the characters move from room to room. Greenaway identifies the essence of the decor and the costumes as being vulgarity, commenting, 'The people in the film are part of a swaggering society and wear clothes to identify themselves and set themselves apart' (Bergan 1989: 29). The costumes here are characterised by their looked-at-ness; changes are motivated purely by the requirements of the overall design rather than the narrative, and thus they fulfil a star-like role, processing through the film as arbitrary signs which precede rather than follow character.

Gaultier's costumes are deliberately intrusive, and thus instrumental in defining the spectator's responses to a film. Pedro Almodóvar's *Kika* juxtaposes several styles and couturiers with just such an intention in mind; of using costume to impose rather than reflect meaning built up within the characters and narration. Almodóvar refers to his film having 'the structure of a collage or a very radical puzzle' (Strauss 1996: 127), indicating again that display-orientated couture functions best in a narrative environment where consistency, conformity and invisibility are not paramount concerns. The designers credited during the title sequence are Jean-Paul Gaultier, who designed (specially for the film) the costumes for Victoria Abril as Andrea, the exploitative presenter of a gruesome television 'reality show', who alternates between vamp and robot, and Gianni Versace, who loaned the film items from his current collection, notably Kika's gaudy, clashing, optimistic frocks. Two couturiers, therefore, are employed to create the distinctive signature looks of the two protagonists.[9]

Cinema and haute couture

Andrea hosts a television show comprising video footage shot by herself of murder, rape and other lurid events, and is, as Almodóvar describes her, the embodiment of the corrosive horrors of television's titillating predilection for voyeuristic and exploitative entertainment. Her function is thus largely symbolic, a connotation which informs Gaultier's costumes. As the television personality, Andrea has two looks: the militaristic Martian for her roving filming trips and the futuristic vamp for her studio pieces to camera. The former, in military green decorated with chrome, is a rich amalgam of the functional and the expressionistic (clearly referencing the robot in Fritz Lang's *Metropolis*), overlaid with militaristic and technological trimmings such as multiple zips, epaulettes studded with video controls, flip up shades, heavy-duty boots and a moulded helmet onto which her video camera is mounted. Andrea presents herself to the characters she videos and stalks as just another persistent, story-hungry journalist. Her look, however, particularly in any dialogue scene, acts as a disruptive, jarring force, and contradicts, by its obtrusiveness, the presumption that snuff television is invariably captured by an unobtrusive camera and 'stringer'. To this overall symbolism are added anarchic details which alternately fetishise and alienate Andrea. The militaristic costume's most overtly fetishistic features are the breastplate lamps protected with industrial meshing, which function as a makeshift lighting system (used by Andrea during her final interrogation of Nicholas [Peter Coyote]).

The alienating function of Gaultier's costumes for Andrea is made explicit in the studio sequences through the wild discrepancy between her heightened glamour and the horror of the 'real life' filmed extracts she introduces. During one transmission Andrea introduces a report on a self-flagellating and mutilating religious ceremony for her 'Bloody Ceremonies' slot. The dominant dynamic of this scene is clearly the collision between Andrea's appearance and the potential effect of the subject matter. Andrea, deploying all the coquettish poise of the traditional television host, is dressed in parody evening wear: a tight, mutilated red velvet dress over a loosely crocheted black vest, her hair scraped back Flamenco style and her legs and arms (to the length of elegant evening gloves) swathed in surgical bandages which offer a particularly gruesome and direct link with the ritual being screened. The provocative Gaultier costumes for these scenes serve an ambivalent function: on the one hand they are metaphors for (in Almodóvar's view) the exploitation of ghoulish television, and on the other they render Andrea inappropriately glamorous. Andrea's costumes are not merely distancing devices but exaggerated, conventionalised mechanisms for making the female form into an objectified spectacle. During her first broadcast Andrea wears another distressed black and red velvet dress, this time with two plastic breasts exploding through the ripped fabric, stalking the stage and kicking her train out of the way like an adept cat-walk model. Gaultier's costumes are both pure aesthetic displays and perversely functional, a complex blend often found in his real couture designs.

1.3 Victoria Abril wearing Jean-Paul Gaultier in *Kika*
Courtesy of Ronald Grant Archive

Andrea's costumes are thus an interesting development of the 'star costume' or single item of spectacular couture, used to make one character stand out visually from the others. A classic example of this sartorial convention is Howard Greer's fancy-dress ball costume for Katherine Hepburn in *Christopher Strong*, which he agreed to make despite having left Hollywood by 1933 to open his own couture house. For most of Arzner's film Hepburn dons utilitarian and masculine clothes, but for the ball (which we do not see) she wears a shimmering, luminous silver dress, cape and skull cap with fine, virtually imperceptible antennae bouncing off it. The same mechanism is adopted in many of the Givenchy/Audrey Hepburn films, particularly *Funny Face*, which hardly disguises the fact that it is a prolonged cat-walk show. The clothes in these instances intrude on, dominate the scenes they are couched in.

1.4 Victoria Abril and Man in *Kika*
Courtesy of BFI Stills, Posters and Designs

Not unlike the early fashion show shorts, Gaultier's costumes for Victoria Abril in *Kika* are pure spectacle. Although contextualised within a more formal framework, they are not wholly motivated by either character or narrative. An anomaly suggested by the alienating way in which costumes function in *Kika* is that the more sensational clothes become, the less they signify the beauty and desirability of, in this instance, the female characters who wear them. This contravenes directly the traditional interpretation of adornment as something which accentuates and complements the feminine, but is somehow symptomatic of how *couture* as

13

opposed to the generic *fashion* operates in cinema. A useful comparison to make, which also serves to highlight the different agendas of couture and fashion, is between Bertrand Blier's *Trop Belle Pour Toi!* and Garry Marshall's *Pretty Woman*, two recent films overtly preoccupied with the representation of femininity through an elaborate and expensive wardrobe. Both films focus on a central female figure who is persistently named as beautiful, but whereas Carole Bouquet's Chanel-clad perfection in *Trop Belle Pour Toi!* is established from the start and thus exists independently of her or the ensuing action, Julia Roberts's comparable perfection is created, Cinderella fashion, through the course of the film and so exists only as a causal, dependent response to the narrative itself. There is a further distinction to be made between the two protagonists' beauty which pertains directly to the difference between the specific signification of couture and the general connotations of fashion. Whereas couture acts as a barrier to identification and intimacy in *Trop Belle Pour Toi!*, fashion in *Pretty Woman* does the reverse.

Pretty Woman is an intentionally formulaic romance, constructed around the improbable match between a hooker (Vivien) and a rich businessman (Edward) which deliberately announces itself as a fairy-tale: Vivien is likened to Cinderella, for example, and is rescued at the end by Edward on the 1990s version of a white charger, a white limousine. As Robert Lapsley and Michael Westlake have observed, the film's reflexivity diverts 'the contradiction faced by the spectator who is no longer able to believe in romance . . . yet at the same time wishes to do so' (Lapsley and Westlake 1992: 28). In *Pretty Woman* the dream is expressed through clothes. A woman acquiring sexual confidence and a man through the appropriation of a new wardrobe is a well-established cinematic convention. Charlotte in *Now Voyager*, for example, conducts her courtship with Jerry dressed entirely in the clothes of a woman we never see. In *Pretty Woman* there is a similar transaction between clothes and female identity, and a similar awareness that the woman is at her most alluring when wearing clothes that do not belong to or are new to her. The basis for the successful fairy-tale driving *Pretty Woman* (Vivien after all gets her man) is the ease with which Vivien adapts to her new wealth and Rodeo Drive wardrobe.[10] Coco Chanel is reported as having said, 'If a woman walks into a room and people say, "Oh, what a marvellous dress", then she is badly dressed. If they say, "What a beautiful woman," then she is well dressed' (Craik 1994: 83). Chanel's stated aim is to construct a wardrobe that projects its beauty onto the woman wearing it; a woman, therefore, must inhabit, be appropriate to, be at one with her clothes if she is to be found attractive. All the admiring glances shot at Vivien from men throughout *Pretty Woman* (in the street, in the hotel lobby) abide by such a rule, as the film is at pains to prove that, far from being mutton dressed up as lamb after her trips to Rodeo Drive, she is a natural who was waiting to be discovered. The number of times Edward and Bernie, the hotel manager who befriends her, attribute the term 'special' to Vivien is testament to this.

The slippage between personality and clothes ensures that, on their own count, the clothes are not particularly 'special', but rather function as a symbolic visual shorthand for desirable femininity, volume (the number of options, changes, bags and boxes) being of far greater significance than style. The wide but not extravagant black hat, the slim-fitting pale dress buttoned down the front, the white gloves to half-way up the forearm, the polka-dot dress with matching hat trim, are deliberately unexceptional metonyms for tasteful elegance. The majority of the negative critical responses to *Pretty Woman* concentrated on the film's fixation with wealth, exchange and consumerism.[11] Within this one can discern the further connotation that what really makes Vivien 'pretty' (and this is the film's most potentially interesting comment on femininity) is her capacity to spend copious amounts of money on clothes. It is significant, though, that the money she spends is Edward's. The traditional economic exchange between men and women when clothes are the currency is characterised by the man spending on behalf of the woman in order to buy her. As Herzog concludes, 'If men are buying women, then women are buying clothes to get bought, or just to get a man, period' (Herzog 1990: 158). The supposed attraction of this commodification of women through clothes is exemplified by the Rodeo Drive spending spree sequence, swathed in the lush tones and insistent beat of the Roy Orbison track, 'Pretty Woman'. From the moment Edward dangles his gold credit card in front of Vivien's nose, through the orgiastic trying on and purchasing montage, to her contented, overladen return to the Beverly Wilshire Hotel, this whole sequence is cut like a pop promo celebrating the art of shopping.

One film *Pretty Woman* clearly resembles is *Sabrina*, which constructs a similar fairy-tale around the parallel between a woman changing her clothes and increasing her sexual (and economic) status. There are, however, important differences which inform the relationship between identity and costume. Whereas clothes in *Pretty Woman* are homogenised, making no significant distinction between couture and non-couture items, the pieces of couture design in *Sabrina* perform a different expositional and symbolic function to those which are not. The contrast between couture and fashion can best be made by comparing the two pivotal outfits used in each film to illustrate the woman's sartorial transition: the ballgown Hepburn wears to the Larrabee ball in *Sabrina*, and the red gown Roberts wears to the opera in *Pretty Woman*. Selected wardrobes for *Pretty Woman* are by Cerruti 1881 (principally Richard Gere's suits), but the red, off-the-shoulder gown is designed by the costume designer, Marilyn Vance-Straker. Hepburn's ball gown is created by Givenchy, not the film's costume designer Edith Head. Vance-Straker's dress of silk chiffon with silk-back satin crepe overlays is showy but conservative and derivative, recalling principally Yves Saint Laurent – his 1959–60 and 1981–2 rouched, torso-hugging couture evening dresses or the red Rive Gauche off-the-shoulder cocktail gown shown in Spring 1985 which has a similar 'V' neckline. There also appear to

1.5 Richard Gere and Julia Roberts in *Pretty Woman*
Courtesy of Ronald Grant Archive and
Audrey Hepburn and William Holden in *Sabrina*
Courtesy of BFI Stills, Posters and Designs

be echoes of Bruce Oldfield's red velvet Tulip Dress of 1986 and Caroline Roehm's 1980s trapunto-stitched satin bustiers with dart necklines.[12] As Edith Head has intimated, costume designers must remain 'middle of the road' (Head 1983: 97), they are not, as Vance-Straker confirms, 'doing fashion – we're doing characters, building energy, portraying a slice of real life' (Vance-Straker 1991: 15). Gaines sums up the imperatives facing the costume designer when she says, 'costume assimilates bodily signifiers into character, but body as a whole engulfs the dress' (Gaines 1990: 193).

This process of assimilation and denial of identity is only one factor in *Sabrina*, as Hepburn enters in her 'lovely dress with yards of skirt – way off the shoulders' to the admiring stares of all the men – and women – at the ball. One point of focus is Hepburn, but the other is the Parisian gown, innovative in its mixture of lengths and shapes, juxtaposing a tight above-the-ankle dress, a long, trailing train and a strapless bodice. Significantly, the other young women at the Larrabee ball are wearing standardised, 'middle of the road' New Look gowns. Hepburn's design is set apart by the detail, the floral embroidery on the white chiffon, the dark tasselled trim and dark lining that round off the train, the weight of the fabric apparent as Hepburn moves, and the fact that it creases. Whilst conventional ideas about costume stipulate that they should serve the narrative and refrain from being spectacular, Givenchy's gowns for *Sabrina* intentionally create a visual diversion.

In *The Fashion System*, his exhaustive dissection of the semiology of fashion, Roland Barthes suggests distinctions between the real, the written and the imaged garment that is useful for cinema's oscillating dialogue with couture. Barthes identifies 'three different structures, one technological, another iconic, the third verbal' for each item of fashion. The reader of a fashion magazine (to keep to Barthes' model) assumes that the common reference point of a photograph and the accompanying words 'are united in the actual dress they both refer to', but in reality there is only an equivalence between the different structures, not a complete identification (Barthes 1963: 4–5). Similarly, both couture and non-couture costumes for film are only equivalent, as they diverge in both their relations to the spectacular and in their affiliations to the dominant narrative. The majority of film costumes are 'real' in that they are given meaning only in terms of how they pertain to and are informed by character and narrative, are depen-dent on contextualisation for significance and do not impose meaning. Therefore the red dress in *Pretty Woman* carries the meaning: '*Vivien* is pretty'. Iconic clothes serve a proclamatory function in film, they collide with the sequences in which they are placed because they carry an alternative, independent meaning that is not necessarily subservient to or even compatible with that of the dominant narrative. 'Iconic' and 'spectacular' are not interchangeable terms when applied to couture costume, although they frequently intersect, as in Hepburn's grand entrance to the Larrabee ball in *Sabrina*, where all the connotations of Paris, Givenchy and stylistic difference converge on the one dress. The Givenchy gown impacts on Hepburn rather than vice versa: 'Hepburn is pretty because of her dress'. The essence of iconic clothes is that they have an independent, prior meaning; they function as interjections or disruptions of the normative reality of the text.

A pattern that emerges among certain films in which the iconic and the real are segregated is that they construct or impose a distant, unreal feminine ideal that could be termed 'too beautiful'. In such films as *Rear Window*, *Belle de Jour* and *Trop Belle Pour Toi!*, the role of couture clothes or the haute couture industry are fundamental components in the characterisation of Lisa, Severine and Florence. In the first scene of *Rear Window*, Lisa (Grace Kelly), who works at the exclusive end of the New York fashion trade, arrives in an evening dress 'right off the Paris plane' at the apartment of her partner Jeff (James Stewart), an intrepid photojournalist. Kelly's dress is intentionally spectacular, contrasting a tight black top half cut to a plunging V both front and back and a full white tulle and chiffon three-quarter length skirt embroidered with black sequins in sprig patterns coming down from the waistline.[13] Lisa ostentatiously does a twirl to show the creation off, to a defiantly disinterested Jeff who dedicates his time, while she glides around the apartment fixing the dinner delivered from '21', to enumerating their incompatibilities. Hitchcock initially goes to great lengths to establish our identification with Jeff's point of view, repeating twice the soft-focus, slow-motion shot of Lisa stooping to kiss Jeff on the lips. The spectator's position, however, is soon declared to be at odds with Jeff's, and the problem is the iconic status of the dress. Paradoxically, despite the emphasis on Lisa's beauty, this opening scene is the low point of their relationship. As the vulnerable, deflated Lisa serves the lobster dinner, tentatively enquiring of Jeff what he thinks of it, he wearily replies, 'Lisa, it's perfect – it's always perfect'. She is perfect to a fault, she is too beautiful.

Where the fashionable, too beautiful woman is concerned the issues of identity and identification become problematised, as the focus has shifted away from the woman herself to the art and spectacle of her clothes. Lisa is the embodiment of feminine perfection and yet (until she enters the masculine murder mystery narrative motivated by Jeff) she is the woman rejected by her lover. Lapsley and Westlake argue that Hollywood's 'supposedly perfect beings are so many versions of *la femme*, the nonexistent figuration of the *objet a*, that by concealing castration can within the male fantasy make good the lack' (Lapsley and Westlake 1992: 36). The beauty of Lacan's idealised woman thereby functions as a barrier masquerading the reality that underneath the surface there is nothing, that 'all these beautiful women are simulacra' (36). Lapsley and Westlake's analysis then reverts to the conventionalised view that the representation of and identification with the idealised woman is dictated by male fantasy, so that 'those women deemed beautiful function to mask the lack in the Other and support the illusion of sexual

1.6 Grace Kelly and James Stewart in *Rear Window*
Courtesy of BFI Stills, Posters and Designs

rapport, while those considered unattractive become the objects of the male aggression resulting from disappointment at the lack in the Other' (36). Films overtly preoccupied with fashion establish a very different relationship between the idealised female image on the screen and the spectator. Not only is the audience for fashion traditionally female, and so the assumption that the dictating fantasy is male a tendentious one, but it is the clothes more than the woman that render her perfect and become the point of identification. Because this feminine discourse could be seen as one that excludes men (as illustrated by Jeff's feigned interest in the detailed description Lisa offers of what her early evening cocktail partner was wearing), the version of *la femme* offered in *Rear Window* or *Belle de Jour* and *Trop Belle Pour Toi!*, although presenting women as simulacra, use clothes as distancing devices whereby the presumed bond between beauty and sexuality or desirability is displaced.

Grace Kelly's perfection in *Rear Window* is identified through an excess of glamour – a peculiarly intrusive and noisy costume detail being her multi-stringed pearl bracelet with clanking gold lockets and hanging medallions; conversely, the equivalent beauty of Catherine Deneuve and Carole Bouquet in *Belle de Jour* and *Trop Belle Pour Toi!* is characterised by an absence of the spectacular. The defiantly unsensuous couture in both films complicates the questions raised so far about fashion as art, and contradicts the common equation between women's fashion and sexual display – and the concomitant correlation between spectacular clothes and femininity. Richard Dyer has related certain types of sensual fabrics such as chiffon, silk and satin to available, desirable female sexuality (Herzog 1990: 156); the sort of brothel iconography that in the cinema has, for example, been associated with 'bombshells' like Jean Harlow. It is easy, therefore, to elaborate upon this and to align the selling of the dress with the selling of the body it adorns, to propose, as Herzog does, that the look directed at the clothes on display is analogous to the look directed at the body, and to presume, again, that this desiring look is male (157). And yet, the costumes of both Catherine Deneuve in *Belle de Jour* and Carole Bouquet in *Trop Belle Pour Toi!* sever these traditional ties between the woman's body and clothes and have very little to do with making a sexual proposition except in the most ambiguous of ways. The couture element of both wardrobes is instrumental in disengaging the characters Severine and Florence from the discourse of femininity and beauty created around the male subject. In both cases couture garments do not signify desire except in relation to class and exclusivity and do not conform to the conventionalised notions of sartorial femininity identified by Dyer. This is one result of including couturier designs (by Yves Saint Laurent and Chanel) to define the female protagonists, for (as discussed above in relation to *Sabrina* and *Pretty Woman*) such costumes possess an independent identity which imposes itself on the characters. There is a complex discussion to be had, therefore, about the role of understated couture in the elusive portrayal of women who are 'too beautiful'.

Coco Chanel once commented, 'Le Scheherazade c'est facile. Une petite robe noir c'est difficile' [The Scheherazade look is easy. A little black dress is difficult] (Carter 1980: 56), so identifying the labour and artistry that goes into crafting simplicity. Chanel invented the *Garçonne* look, masculinising women's clothes by using trousers, polo jumpers and cuffed shirts with cuff links, whilst still retaining and emphasising femininity through the addition of accessories such as large gilt chains, pussy-cat bows and delicate tipped sling-backs. Throughout her career, but most prominently after her relaunch in 1954, Chanel has become associated with an almost perverse attention to unobtrusive detail, an affectation exemplified by the delicate silk linings with contrasting braid trimmings on her classic, soft Linton tweed suits of the late 1950s and 1960s. Such designs typified Chanel's opposition to the styles (which she loathed) typified by Dior; the overblown, ultra-feminine New Look which, as illustrated by *Rear Window* and *Sabrina*, put the decoration on the outside. Yves Saint Laurent, though less streamlined than Chanel, similarly created certain collections that were fervently anti-spectacular. Critics were quick to point out his debt to the ethos of Chanel, most conspicuously shown in his 1960s daytime box suits and use of white collars on wool dresses.[14] Deneuve as Severine is dressed exclusively by Yves Saint Laurent, and

Bouquet as Florence by the house of Chanel.[15] Both women have long histories of being 'too beautiful'. Bouquet succeeded Deneuve as Buñuel's 'French woman' when she performed the role of the similarly iconic, idealised woman in *That Obscure Object of Desire* (Bouquet 1990: 64); she then, in 1988, took over from Deneuve as the face of Chanel No. 5. In addition, Deneuve has been Saint Laurent's muse and close friend for decades and has frequently modelled his clothes, on one occasion against a projected still of herself in *Belle de Jour*. On screen, both are used as icons whose sexuality is signalled through clothes and an association with fashion.

In *Belle de Jour*, Deneuve in effect models a Saint Laurent 'capsule wardrobe' of the time in her red tweed afternoon suit, black coat and hat, matching wool-knit hat and polo neck, low-slung patent court shoes and plain dark dress with white collar and cuffs. The film prioritises her clothes and plays on their exclusivity, blending them into the surreal narrative about a bored bourgeois housewife who is frigid with her husband but has an active, sado-masochistic fantasy life and works in a brothel in the afternoons. Moments of personal crisis (when, for instance, Severine fears her husband Pierre is about to find out about her secret daytime job) are deflected onto close-ups of her shiny shoes pacing to and fro, an overdetermination of her accessories which is representative of

1.7 Catherine Deneuve in *Belle de Jour*
Courtesy of BFI Stills, Posters and Designs

the sado-masochistic denial suggested by Deneuve's entire wardrobe. Deneuve's sexuality, unlike Jean Harlow's, is not conveyed through a wardrobe of sensuous silks, furs and feathers; rather her attractiveness is marked by a severity, a lack of sensuality, ornamentation or flamboyance in her wardrobe: all sharp lines, fastened buttons and perfect co-ordination. This lack is only partly linked to Severine's sexual repression when with her husband and the concomitant impulse to destroy her immaculate appearance during her vivid fantasies. There is also the way in which the clothes are signalled as beautiful, as when a client and the other prostitutes at the brothel heap admiration on Severine's self-consciously, absurdly unremarkable beige dress, fondling the jersey fabric, glancing at the label and complimenting Severine on her style. The object of their praise is couture, the exclusivity of the clothes which, in turn, define Severine's ambiguous sexuality.

The alienating effect of the perfect simplicity of couture is examined at length in *Trop Belle Pour Toi!* in which, again, the image of the central woman is characterised by cool, elegant sartorial understatement. Blier's ironic polemic is based on a straightforward inversion: a wealthy husband (Bernard/Depardieu) is married to a staggeringly beautiful woman (Florence/Bouquet) but falls in love with his plain secretary (Colette/Balasko) and is finally left without either. *Trop Belle* is an essay on the oppression and the oppressiveness of beauty. As Florence is introduced (after a brief flash-forward showing Bernard's affair with Colette)

1.8 Carole Bouquet and Gerard Depardieu at their wedding in *Trop Belle Pour Toi!*
Courtesy of BFI Stills, Posters and Designs

she has in her thrall the guests around a dinner party table, all captivated by her delivery of a formless, pretentious monologue, the ostensible subject of which is femininity. We hear Florence's voice as she begins, with the ponderous diction of someone who does not have to fight for attention: 'Imagine a woman always trying to be more feminine, easier on the eye, more desirable, forever seeking to go beyond the bounds'. Accompanying this is a strange shot, through the glass table-top, of her knees framed by the light folds of her yellow dress. At a measured, emphatic pace that mimics the way she talks, the camera glides up past the gold-buttoned front of the dress towards Florence's face, her eyes cast down as if she herself is wrapped in the beauty of her words. A comparably steady tracking shot then sidles past the faces of the individual guests, all mesmerised, not by the dialogue, which gets progressively less intelligible, but by the perfect woman who names and performs herself. Bernard, the husband, merely observes the parties embroiled in this empty exchange with incredulity. Florence is femininity distilled, identified only through and by her beauty. When later the film cuts to a flashback of her wedding speech, Florence is shown apologising for being 'too beautiful': 'beauty doesn't mean much, I'm a woman just like any other'. But in her beaded Juliet cap and square-necked lace dress, with her perfect poise and double-edged modesty she does not believe what she is saying and neither does anyone else. Beauty, though, is the only language Florence knows, and when she confronts the 'homely' Colette about the affair by telling her she is ugly and lacking in class she asks with disbelief, 'Surely it wasn't love at first sight?'. Upon finding out about Bernard's infidelity, she discovers the fragility of her identification with a superficial and intangible ideal.

In her self-identification with this, abstract notion of femininity, Florence assumes she is perfect. She is necessarily shallow and empty by virtue of being consciously defined by her appearance, but this hysterical transferral of her subjectivity onto her image is presumed to conform to what is ultimately required of women under patriarchy. Fashion, which is at the centre of this representation, is marketed and consumed in a gender-specific way; whilst women's fashion magazines are aimed at and absorbed by women, men's fashion magazines are read by men. Likewise, early fashion-show films assumed a female spectatorship, and many early Hollywood producers (Sam Goldwyn, for example) recognised the impact fashionable costumes had on the numbers of women going to the movies. This relationship is replicated in a film such as *Prêt-à-Porter*, in which the final catwalk shows develop a running dialogue between the largely female models and the three female fashion editors, a dynamic that strongly suggests that the discourse of women's fashion excludes men, or that women interpret the femininity constituted through the amalgamation of clothes and the female body differently from men. The assumption, therefore, which pervades the use of display mechanisms in films such as *Pretty Woman* – that women dress up for men –

can be disputed. Herzog tentatively questions this presumption in her discussion of the fashion show in film. She develops John Berger's observation that a woman is taught to see herself from two points of view, 'the surveyed and the surveyor', and argues that 'the spectator to whom women address themselves is not just a man but also a woman' (Herzog 1990: 158), but then fails to develop the questions this observation raises about the complexities of looking, and disappointingly ends with a classic misunderstanding:

> The point here is that a woman looks at herself and at other women *as a man looks at her*, but the male perspective is assimilated into what she thinks is her own critical eye.
>
> (my italics; 158–9)

This attitude is heterosexist and demeaning to the female spectator, and fails to recognise arenas (such as fashion) where the active gaze is not *ipso facto* male. The act of looking at a garment, whether in a magazine or on the screen, frequently has nothing to do with sexual desire (for the wearer of the garment at least) and much more to do with an attraction to clothes. Fetishism thus encroaches on this rapport between fashion and spectator as a contradictory impulse that de-eroticises the body. Fashion is thus an exclusory device, an interloper into the traditionally male-orientated relationship between the viewer (male or female) and the female image. The 'too beautiful' woman is not, as traditionally perceived, a symbol of lack, but a symbolic rejection of the spectator whose desire for her is predicated on the collapsing of the difference between body and clothes. It is possible, there-fore, as is implied in *Rear Window*, that men, in turn, reject women who identify themselves through fashion. As this pattern is repeated in *Trop Belle Pour Toi!*, an alternative is posited to the notion of *la femme* articulated above: that it is the woman who is considered unattractive who masks the lack in the Other, not her beautiful counterpart.

According to classical psychoanalytic theory the hysteric is a woman articulating and confronting femininity as it is designated by men on the surface of her body; the hysteric who transfers these traumas on to her clothes could be viewed as the logical, socialised extension of this. The hysterical element of Bouquet's appearance is manifest in the tortuously polished and exclusive anonymity of the clothes that have been selected to represent her; they are not spectacular, sensuous metaphors for desirability but the most recognisable and thus oppressive of twentieth-century fashion uniforms. The burden of Florence's fashionable beauty is that it has been divested of any idiosyncrasy or meaningful personalising mark. She moves effortlessly from one suffocatingly elegant Chanel outfit to another; if it is not the little black dress then it is the red cardigan jacket with gilt buttons or the pale cashmere jumper over the discreet black skirt, not a hair out of place or an accessory uncoordinated. The hysterical symbolism of Florence's too beautiful clothes is most conclusively conveyed through the imposition of multiple and arbitrary costume changes. A distinguishing feature of this film (and others by Blier) is the illogical switching between different times and layers of narrative, conditioning the spectator to view each scene as a symbolic unit, not a causal link in a sequential structure. In one scene Florence alternates, without motivation, between a black 'sweet heart' evening dress and her wedding outfit. It is the Chanel house style, therefore, that imposes coherence and which functions as Florence's only consistent defining feature. *Trop Belle Pour Toi!* is a treatise on oppression, on the unlikely torture of excess, whether this is Florence's studied Chanel wardrobe, the stifling Schubert soundtrack (which an exasperated Bernard rails against throughout) or the heavy intimacy of Bernard's physical relationship with Colette. All are unrelenting impositions over which the characters have no control.

The minimalist aesthetic of the Chanel and Saint Laurent clothes in *Trop Belle* and *Belle de Jour* is grounded in a paradox: that deliberately unspectacular fashion can still function in a spectacular way. Within this reorganisation of the expected relationship between couture and display resides the further preoccupation with femininity and dress. Contrary to what is usually implied in feminist writings about fashion and costume, the motivation behind an excessive attention to women's clothes is not necessarily to sexualise women or make them more desirable, particularly when the attention is lavished on the least flamboyant of clothes. Although this would have at first seemed unlikely, the argument could be extended further to suggest that the clothes in *Trop Belle*, in all their understatedness, function as devices for intervention to the extent that Gaultier's costumes do, though they employ very different signs. This again raises the issue, first mooted by Chanel when she extolled the complex virtues of the 'petite robe noir', of the art of anti-display fashion.

The elitism of a commentator such as Wollen, who only acknowledges artistry in the spectacular, most readily excludes men's film fashion and couture, which is seldom showy. Wollen is inevitably dismissive of the work of Giorgio Armani, whose basic motivation, he suggests, 'has been to design clothes in which the wearer will feel secure against embarrassment, against sticking out like a sore thumb. . . . Armani wants people to feel comfortably well-dressed in his clothes, elegant, attractive, but never eccentric' (Wollen, P. 1995: 13–14). Wollen's dismissive analysis disregards the double meaning of classic fashion, namely that even the least extravagant item of clothing is spectacular because it can be recognised as exclusive. This is not brazen but fetishistic fashion. An alternative view of Armani to Wollen's is expressed by Craik, when she identifies him as one of the recent menswear fashion designers (alongside the ostensibly wilder Gaultier, Galliano, Kenzo, Kawakubo and Yamamoto) who have 'deliberately pushed the limits of men's fashion by proposing new radical looks' (Craik 1994: 200). Armani's style stems, the designer himself believes, from an Italian as opposed to a French or British couture ethos, namely to create fashions which are 'logical, rational and wearable' (Armani 1986: 398), characteristics which mark the specific innovation most readily associated with him, the informal, liberated jacket design for both men and women. Having entered the fashion industry as assistant to Nino Cerruti in 1961, Armani launched his solo career in 1970 by designing menswear, and it is in the nebulous intersection between masculinity and narcissism that Armani's muted radicalism is represented.

Armani has designed costumes for, among others, *The Untouchables*, *Streets of Fire*, *Voyager* and, most recently, *Stealing Beauty*. The moment which, for better or worse, has become synonymous with Armani's involvement in film is the sequence in *American Gigolo* when Julian (Richard Gere), the high-class gigolo of the title, is getting ready to go out cruising. Dressed so far only in a pair of grey trousers, Julian swaggers and shuffles to the beat of a bland pop music track, rifles through a copious collection of Armani-labelled jackets, ties and shirts, assembles alternative combinations on the bed and finally, having decided on the right ensemble, admires himself in the mirror. Most of the disproportionately serious scholarly interest in *American Gigolo* pertains to its representation of male sexuality,[16] equating the care Julian takes over his clothes with his job, his narcissism, his latent homosexuality, his femininity; in short, with everything except fashion. Men's clothes have usually been interpreted as unproblematically functional (a belief that is queried at greater length in the discussions of gangsters), and male costumes as an irrelevance. For much of the classic Hollywood era, for instance, male actors were expected to supply their own costumes, Clark Gable's 1935 contract with MGM specifying that the studio would provide only period costumes. In the dressing scene from *American Gigolo*, a man is presented communing with his clothes, a rarity in itself, as the 'what shall I wear' scenario has traditionally been a female preserve. Throughout the film Julian moves with the easy, hip-thrusting swagger of a catwalk model, his gestural repertoire always that of the person who is displaying clothes, as in the scene when Michelle (Lauren Hutton) comes to his apartment and he self-consciously opens out his jacket by resting his hands on his waistband in a rather classic mail-order menswear pose. For all the interest in Julian's sexuality, *American Gigolo* is a clothes movie; the objects of fetishism are not Julian but what he wears. As the camera pans back and forth along the line of light jackets, silk shirts and knitted ties before Julian tries them on, the erotic fascination is with the clothes, the gentle folds on the lining, the harmonious juxtaposition of shade and fabric.

The British costume designer Lindy Hemming (responsible for *Four Weddings and a Funeral*) has commented that couturiers want to preserve their house look whilst working on film character pieces (Goodridge 1994: 14). Designing for a film is, for a couturier, an ambiguous process of maintaining a balance between self-promotion and immersing the designs in the film. Why Armani is of greater

1.9 Sean Connery in *The Untouchables*
Courtesy of BFI Stills, Posters and Designs

interest to this debate than, for example, the more prolific Nino Cerruti (who to date has contributed clothes to some thirty-nine films)[17] is that, despite his costumes not being readily identified by their outrageousness as Gaultier's are, he takes more risks and retains a stronger identity even when working within the confines of costume. Armani's most infamous collaboration to date was with Marilyn Vance-Straker on Brian de Palma's *The Untouchables*, for which he

27

produced the majority of the costumes for all the significant characters except Robert de Niro as Al Capone. The tension between Armani and Vance-Straker was over design control, Vance-Straker protesting that Armani really wanted overall responsibility (Goodridge 1994: 13), a tension that is, to a certain extent, acted out on the clothes themselves, particularly the loud, very un-Armani ties that were demanded (Furnival 1990: 14).

In *The Untouchables*, set in 1930s Chicago, Armani uses two, virtually contradictory, tactics to deal with period reconstruction. The first, used for the secondary characters such as Capone's gangsters, is to adopt a limited range of sartorial bywords for the 1920s/1930s mob milieu, such as felt hats and loud accessories. Capone's men conform very much to the image of the cliché cinema gangster, but their tie pins and pocket handkerchiefs are the requisite period indicators to reassure the audience that this is an 'authentic' reproduction of an era they recognise. The second, applied to the 'Untouchables', is to elide the differences between the styles of the 1930s and 1980s, and to dress them eclectically and loosely in garments that shuffle easily between the two periods, such as Eliot Ness's full-cut, single-breasted, unbelted raincoat. Ness (Kevin Costner) is dressed predominantly in plain grey/blue usually pin-stripe three-piece suits which, whilst nevertheless passing for credible reproductions, significantly lack the 1930s embellishments retained for the gangsters. Particularly in the fashioning of Malone (Sean Connery) and Stone (Andy Garcia) Armani then subliminally cites his own design trademarks of soft fabrics and unstructured casual chic. Malone is characterised by his grey chunky-knit cardigan, his relaxed tweed jacket and his cap, none of which are presumably intended to seem exclusive to the 1930s. Even more ambiguous are Stone's light brown blouson jackets (one suede, the other leather) and his matching leather waistcoat, which is backed with pale wool rather than the more traditional silk; all of which display styling, fabric and colour links with prevalent contemporary Italian fashions (particularly the coupling of leather jackets and red scarf).

Armani's relaxed assimilation of his own designer identity into ostensibly authentic period costumes emerges evocatively in the wardrobe he designed for Walter Faber (Sam Shepard) in Volker Schlöndorff's *Voyager*. As far as Armani's contribution is concerned, the film is an imaginative scavenging of the sartorial archives. As he did with the 'Untouchables', Armani lends Faber an easy universality by downplaying the inflexible over-emphasis of the late 1950s demonstrated in the costume designs of the other characters who are uniformly clad in items, such as bright Hawaiian shirts and bright, full, tight-waisted skirts. There are two dominant design tactics employed for Faber: one is to impose coherence on his wardrobe by creating a run of a few 'capsule' items which adopt the same style but appear in various different colours (the most persistent being his range of light-weight trousers, all with a large, right-side back pocket and his Trilbys); the

1.10 Sam Shepard in *Voyager*
Courtesy of BFI Stills, Posters and Designs

other is to develop items which take as their starting point an authentic 1950s style. Faber has, for instance, a collection of loose silk shirts with two large breast pockets, a style that ostensibly echoes the 1950s fashion for baggy synthetic shirts. This type of shirt, however, in early 1990s cinema became the ubiquitous sartorial sign of middle-class, intellectual chic, whether in Hollywood or Europe, whether on men or women, and so is never going to be simply an authentic 1950s item. Armani freely cites and expands upon the fashions of the time, including, for example, Faber's *rive gauche*-inspired black polo neck (cut a little more generously than it would have been at the time), a garment which has had many transmutations and carries with it various associative meanings — of creativity, informality, austerity — and is an unconventionally seductive item which frames and enhances the features of the face. Having established Faber's eclectic universality, on a

29

couple of occasions items are then inserted into the repertoire that retain only the most tenuous engagement with 1957, such as the formal splayed-collar shirt which was a hugely influential Italian design of the late 1980s/early 1990s, and his casual black jacket with beige under collar. Faber's eclectic wardrobe is thus appropriate to his itinerant traveller's existence.

Even in Armani's period designs there is an inherent ambivalence whereby the functionalism of the clothes is set off by their modern stylishness, a relaxation of the differences between contemporaneity and period which also creates a point of identification with the characters. The homogeneity of Giorgio Armani's style, though unspectacular, is distinctive, and the 'Armani look' has an eponymous identity which transcends the designer's own creations and has become a byword for a certain type of man.[18] In this, he also permits his own identity to be stamped onto the costumes he produces, and so, like Chanel or Yves Saint Laurent, creates spectacular costumes (in that they are interjections into the narrative) utilising the paradoxical means of anti-display couture. The contention that such clothes still retain a spectacular function is particularly pertinent to men's fashion, which is conventionally presumed to be anti-declamatory. Craik, for example, refers to recent male fashions as having 'celebrated the body itself and played down the decorative attributes of clothing and body decoration' (Craik 1994: 197), as if the actual garments are devoid of significance except in their relationship to a new-found male body narcissism, and she concludes, 'The revival of the peacock may be some way off yet' (203). In the cinema work of Giorgio Armani it is possible to detect a use of couture clothes based on an intrinsic, subtle fetishism of detail, a desire to highlight the qualities of the clothes themselves, an emphasis which does not prioritise the body or character wearing them.

This discussion began by making reference to the fashion show in film, the presentation of clothes for display and the creation of narratives around them. The function of bodies in such a context is to move in such a way as to enhance and show off the clothes. The role of fashion-show models, from the earliest *demoiselles de magasin* used by Gagelin, Charles Worth's employer, in the 1860s (Craik 1994: 76), to the contemporary catwalk models has been to subordinate themselves to what they are wearing. Catwalk or runway models were selected for specific attributes, not necessarily those of the photographic model; they 'had to be supple, move well, and have a sense of rhythm in order to bring the clothes they were modelling to "life"'(Craik 1994: 79). Several couturiers have specified the need to design for (and on) models rather than dummies. Chanel always designed in 3-D rather than by drawing, and Yves Saint Laurent comments, 'I cannot work without the movement of the human body. A dress is not static, it has rhythm' (Duras 1988: 128). The interaction between body and clothes is essential to fashion, but the balance between the two is not constant. Apparently assuming that the dominant element is the body, Elizabeth Wilson starts *Adorned in Dreams* by asking why clothes which are not on bodies are 'eerie' (Wilson 1985: 1–2). In his discussion of Erté, Barthes, using more violent terms, similarly contends, 'It is not possible to conceive a garment without the body . . . the empty garment, without head and without limbs (a schizophrenic fantasy), is death, not the body's neutral absence, but the body decapitated, mutilated' (Barthes 1973: 107). Barthes' suggestion is that dress has no intrinsic value without a body to adorn, and the prioritisation of the former over the latter has traditionally been viewed as either inappropriately aesthetic or as indicative of the superficiality and frivolity of fashion. Quentin Bell, for example, censoriously declares, 'In obeying fashion we undergo discomforts and distress which are, from a strictly economic point of view, needless and futile' (Bell, Q. 1947: 13). The reverential, often flimsily uncritical films made about designers cement such a view. With the exception of Wim Wenders' reflective essay on Yohji Yamamoto *Notebook on Cities and Clothes* (which is as much a rumination on film-making as it is on couture), designer biopics (such as Martin Scorsese's *Made in Milan* which follows Giorgio Armani, or Douglas Keeve's *Unzipped* about Isaac Mizrahi) are relentlessly self-congratulatory testaments to the opinion that *haute couture* has no intrinsic moral or social value.

Seeming to take as its premise the view that an interest in fashion is morally and intellectually indefensible (despite the director's reputed love of couture [Jacobs 1994–5: 1]), Robert Altman's sprawling, enjoyable and sympathetically inconsequential *Prêt-à-Porter* functions as an extended critique of the Paris ready-to-wear collections. Altman's target is the ridiculous in *haute couture*, the needlessly spectacular; so Armani, it is said, was omitted for not being ridiculous enough (although several of the costumes were incongruously designed by the even more classic Nino Cerruti).[19] *Prêt-à-Porter* emphasises the unwearability of high fashion, its total lack of functionalism and its inappropriateness to daily use, juxtaposing the collections of real designers (such as Issey Miyaki, Jean-Paul Gaultier and Gianfranco Ferré for Dior) with the fictional shows, so as to maximise the trivialisation of the former through their proximity to the latter. Within this framework the film develops a polemic around the tension and dichotomy between clothes and the body, structured around the inevitability of nakedness and an intransigent distrust of those who over-identify themselves with their dressed appearance. There is a perpetual cycle of undressing and re-dressing that runs through *Prêt-à-Porter*, as many of the characters lose, strip off or swap their clothes for others. Sergio (Marcello Mastroianni), for example, has to find a new set of clothes after falling in the Seine, and in a hotel lobby absconds with the suitcase of the American journalist, Joe Flynn (Tim Robbins), who happens to be several inches taller than him. With his portable sewing machine Sergio then sets about altering the length of Flynn's loud but classic sports journalist's separates, whilst Flynn is condemned to the anonymity of casuals and a bathrobe, and spying his clothes on someone else on television. The romantic elevation of nakedness is, in this particular strand of *Prêt-à-Porter*'s web, manifested in the ensuing sexual relationship between Flynn and another American journalist, Anne Eisenhower (Julia Roberts), who has likewise lost her baggage and is, to boot, booked into the same hotel room. Bereft of clothes (and hence social status), the two are relieved of the burden of conformity and spend much of the film in bed. A parallel story in which clothes and identity are exchanged is that of Major Hamilton (Danny Aiello), whose partner (Teri Garr) appears sporadically through the first half of the film on an extended shopping binge for large designer clothes. These clothes, it turns out, are for Hamilton to attend a transvestite convention in classic Chanel. Whilst Hamilton is treated with tenderness, the characters the film appears particularly to despise are those who express a fear of nakedness, such as the three mutually suspicious, mutually dependent magazine editors (Regina, Sissy and Nina). The three women are in competition to secure a contract with the fashion photographer Milo (Stephen Rea), and in their eagerness stoop to flirtation and grovelling: Regina (Linda Hunt) gets down in all fours, Sissy (Sally Kellerman) flashes Milo her breasts and Nina (Tracy Ullman) undresses down to her underwear. They all subsequently find themselves captured on Milo's spy camera. Letting down their facade is the ultimate shameful compromise, and one with which the three women cannot cope. Nina's panicked reaction is the most inappropriate as, having been photographed by Milo in her underwear, she rushes from his bedroom and clutches first for the most frivolous and useless garment of all: her ornate but insubstantial Philip Treacy hat.

Altman, like Bell, Barthes and numerous others, cannot see the point of fashion and is certainly not inclined to elevate it to the status of art. The intention behind his topsy-turvy, multi-narrative film is thus to prove fashion's inadequacy by highlighting its inversion of a functionalist system of value. The repetitive parade of catwalk shows are served up as lavish, empty farces, a succession of ephemeral, frothy gestures simply vying with each other to be the most spectacular and thus, under the film's rules, the silliest. This invalidation of couture is expressed by the actor Richard E. Grant who plays Cort Romney (CR), a fictionalised male version of Vivienne Westwood (who also designs CR's collection for the film). As preparation for the shoot Grant attended Westwood's real Paris show and comments, 'The weirder clothes elicit the most positive response and whilst it is all obviously original and flamboyant, I cannot fathom just where or when such gear could be worn. This is clearly beside the point, but the point of it all is *what*?' (Grant, 1996: 288). Although in terms of visual styles the extravagance of the costumes exhibited comes close to conforming to the categories of fashion as art discussed earlier in this chapter, they are not rendered special but spectacularly trivial by being shown to excess. The volume of clothes on display in *Prêt-à-Porter* (and the implication of waste and frippery) is used as a gauge of fashion's insubstantiality and ugliness.

The clothes/nakedness thesis is concluded, as is the film, with Simone Lo's show, in which her models walk naked rather than dressed along the catwalk; the ultimate invalidation of fashion. As the same crowd which has attended all the previous shows rise to their feet in admiration, the obvious allusion is to 'The Emperor's New Clothes', and the film's target the complacency of people who simply value something because someone else does. Jacobs misunderstands this statement as being representative of Altman's desire to strip fashion of its mystique and prove that, 'without their fancy clothes they're (the models) just like us' (Jacobs, 1994–5: 4). Altman's gesture is altogether more complex than this, for rather than confronting simply the industry's vacuousness, he is confronting the fragility (as he perceives it) of our reliance on clothing for identity and safety. At the end of Joe Orton's black farce *What The Butler Saw*, in which all the characters who can least handle it end up without their clothes on, Rance says, 'Let us put our clothes on and face the world'; Altman's exposé is likewise of those who see life as a protracted, nightmarish flight from nakedness. The action of *Prêt-à-Porter* has been punctuated with the inane observations of the television journalist Kitty (Kim Basinger) who now, with Simone Lo's waving, naked models still lapping up the applause behind her, is lost for words: the language of clothes can find no way of theorising nakedness. As Kitty tenders her spontaneous resignation, her assistant Sophie (Chiara Mastroianni) takes over the microphone and declares, 'Simone Lo has just shown us a celebration of fashion in the profoundest sense of the word', echoing Vivienne Westwood's sentiment, 'fashion is eventually about being naked' (Wilson 1985: 215). Both statements are inherently antagonistic to the positive attributes of fashion, as both suggest that the underlying rationale for clothing is the discovery of nakedness.

This last inversion of Altman's fictitious (but Cerruti 1881–designed) Paris couture scene functions as an affirmation of the supremacy of the body over clothes, the reinstatement of the 'natural' which has been lost under the endless fabricated layers. Flügel concludes *The Psychology of Clothes* with a similarly utopian possibility that

> dress is, after all, destined to be but an episode in the history of humanity, and that man (and perhaps before him woman) will one day go about his business secure in the control both of his body and of his wider physical environment, disdaining the sartorial crutches on which he perilously supported himself during the earlier, tottering stages of his march towards a higher culture.
>
> (Flügel 1930: 238)

The arguments proposed in this chapter have attempted to counter those of Barthes, Bell, Wilson and Altman who all, in their very different ways, argue for clothes to be considered relevant only in relation to the body. Discussions of costume have similarly stressed this correlation. Gaines, for example, asserts that, 'in the discourse on costume, dress, like an expression of emotion, seemed to grow out of the mysteries of the body (Gaines 1990: 187), continuing, later in the same article: 'Costume assimilates bodily signifiers into character, but body as a whole engulfs the dress. . . . Thus it is that costume is eclipsed by both character and body at the expense of developing its own aesthetic discourse' (193). The differentiation between costume and couture designs has been an essential means of challenging these widespread beliefs that clothing in cinema does not possess an aesthetic discourse or that it cannot function independently of narrative and character. The argument has also been with those who believe that clothing can only be disruptive within a narrative film if overly spectacular (Gaines 1990, 192–3). The independent alternative offered by fashion in particular necessitates a reversal of the normative clothes/body relationship that understands the former to be subservient to the latter, and allows for clothes to be the objects of the spectatorial gaze and to be admired or acknowledged in spite of the general trajectory of the film. This notion of clothing's distancing, disruptive potential is to be returned to in several guises through the book, as fetishism in the following chapter and as adjuncts of generic stereotypes in the discussions that make up Part II.

2

DESIRE AND THE COSTUME FILM
Picnic at Hanging Rock, The Age of Innocence, The Piano

Costume dramas, despite their continuing popularity, have rarely elicited anything other than rather derogatory or cursory attention (although see Harper 1994, Cook 1996). A variety of reasons has been proffered for this by those, largely feminist, critics more favourably disposed to the genre, principally that the costume film is aimed at a largely female spectatorship, and so, like the melodrama, has not merited serious consideration from male writers. A charge frequently levelled at historical romances is that (unlike, presumably, comparable pieces of men's cinema) they sideline history and foreground far more trivial interests in desire, sex and clothes. Behind the genderisation of the costume film lies the further implication, expanded upon by Sue Harper when she discusses costume in the Gainsborough melodrama (Harper 1987), that the films possess a covert, codified discourse that centres on the clothes themselves. It is this notion of an alternative discourse that will be explored further in this chapter and developed into a discussion of a group of modern films that focus specifically on the fetishistic value of history and historical clothes.

Recent films as diverse and distinctive as *Daughters of the Dust*, *Sommersby*, *The Piano*, *Orlando*, *The Age of Innocence* and *Sister My Sister* are symptomatic of a resurgence in costume films, a renewed interest that extends the parameters beyond the stifling daintiness of the Merchant-Ivory canon and the saccharine reworkings of Jane Austen. The latter are what Alan Parker dubbed 'the Laura Ashley school of film-making'. There are two principal charges levelled at costume films: that they lack authenticity and that they are frivolous. Pervading much of the existing critical writing given over to the costume film is a sceptical distrust of the films' motives, their prioritisation of bourgeois ideals and their conservative, nostalgic view of the past. Andrew Higson and Tana Wollen, for example, talk of the British heritage films and television 'screen fictions' of the 1980s (*Chariots of Fire*, *A Room with a View*, *Brideshead Revisited*) as vacuous, uncritical and superficial, to be unfavourably compared with such interrogative contemporaneous screen ventures as *Distant Voices, Still Lives* and *Boys From the Blackstuff* (Wollen T. 1991, Higson 1993 and 1996). The strength of such arguments are obfuscated by a dogmatic lack of discernment, a refusal to acknowledge the differences as well as the similarities between films that employ period costumes, as if the costumes themselves, Delilah-like, possess a disempowering capacity to divest any film they adorn of its critical, intellectual or ironic potential. The crucial issue, and one which will be returned to in various guises throughout this book, is whether to look at or through the clothes.

Films such as *Howards End* or Ang Lee's *Sense and Sensibility* look through clothes, as the major design effort is to signal the accuracy of the costumes and to submit them to the greater framework of historical and literary authenticity. Costume films that, conversely, choose to look at clothes create an alternative discourse, and one that usually counters or complicates the ostensible strategy of the overriding narrative. When costumes are looked at rather than through, the element conventionally prioritised is their eroticism. This might be another reason for the costume film's relegation to the division of the frivolous, for it is their emphasis on sex and sexuality (such as the British costume romances of the 1940s) that appeals most to a female audience. In her discussion of the *Englishwoman's Domestic Magazine* of the 1860s, Margaret Beetham introduces a distinction of particular relevance to this examination of costume films. Beetham suggests that the *Englishwoman's Domestic Magazine* 'was caught up in several different economies and discourses', that it supported both women's growing demands for political, civil and economic rights over the decade, but nevertheless continued to publish 'sensation' fiction that focused purely on feminine desire and sexuality (Beetham 1996: 71–2). Whereas the economic discourse is no doubt perceived by most to possess intrinsic worth, the sexual discourse is more frequently dismissed as escapist fantasy. When, for example, Alison Light examines the popularity of women's historical fiction she voices her concern that a preoccupation with fantasy obscures a novel's moral, social or political message (Light 1989: 69). In a previous discussion of recent costume films I suggested a distinction could be made between the 'liberal' and the 'sexual' models adopted by women film-makers working within the genre. The 'liberal' model (exemplified by such films as *My Brilliant Career*, *Rosa Luxemburg* and *An Angel at My Table*) seeks to map out, via the lives of emblematic or iconic historical personalities, a collective women's cultural and political history. In these films clothes are merely signifiers to carry information about country, class and period. The 'sexual' model, on the other hand, (exemplified by *The Piano* and *Sister, My Sister*, for example) foregrounds the emotional and repressed aspects of past women's lives and maps out an alternative but equally genderised territory that centres on the erotic. In these films the clothes themselves become significant components of a contrapuntal, sexualised discourse (Bruzzi 1993: 232–42).

Desire and the costume film

Throughout her discussions of British costume films Sue Harper rejoices in their wilful disregard for historical accuracy in favour or a sexier escapism. In Gainsborough melodramas such as *The Wicked Lady* or *Jassy* Harper identifies a closeted 'costume narrative' in which the inauthentic period clothes are loaded with ambiguity and furtive desire, playing out 'contradictions between the verbal level of plot and scripts, and the non-verbal discourses or décor and costume' which the (largely female) audiences could 'decode' (Harper 1987: 167). At times the costumes operate metonymically, as in the 'vulval symbolism' Harper identifies in the use of fur, folds and velvet in some of the women's costumes in *The Wicked Lady* (Harper 1994: 130). Too often period costumes are presumed to signify sexual repression as opposed to the presence of an active sexual discourse. One of the intentions of this chapter is to develop previous discussions of the sexualisation of costume and to propose that, through their use of historical costumes, *Picnic at Hanging Rock*, *The Age of Innocence* and *The Piano* create a transgressive, erotic discourse which exists both despite and because of the ostensible moral restrictiveness of the times in which they are set. At the heart of this dynamic ambivalence is an interest in the fetishistic attraction of clothes themselves, which is the basis for a covert dialogue between character and character and character and spectator comparable to that discovered in the use certain films have made of *haute couture*. From the moment *The Age of Innocence*, for example, represents the exclusive milieu of late 1800s New York through an exquisite, close-up montage of accessories and sartorial detail, it is apparent that it is demanding a different level of engagement from its spectators than the traditionally disengaged heritage film.[1]

Fetishism has, primarily through the application of psychoanalysis, been considered by Christian Metz, Laura Mulvey and others an influential and significant notion for understanding the eroticism of mainstream cinema. The intention of this chapter is to position costume within the debates about how gender difference and conventions of appearance inform the way in which we look by focusing on clothes and their (often implied) relationship with the body, a particularly pertinent issue when considering the supposed repressiveness of the last century. *Picnic at Hanging Rock*, *The Age of Innocence* and *The Piano* offer divergent perspectives on fetishism, and in many ways chart how approaches to sexual fetishism in general have progressed since the 1880s when the term was first applied to the 'perversion' of substituting an inanimate object for the sexual object. *Picnic at Hanging Rock*, for instance, conforms closely to Freud's hugely influential interpretation of fetishism as a male perversion through which the woman becomes a symbol of masculine desire, whilst *The Piano*, in offering a representation of the past from a clearly feminine perspective, posits the notion that fetishism is not exclusively applicable to men. Campion's film suggests that superficially restrictive clothes function as equivocal signifiers, acting both as barriers to sexual expression and as the very means of reaching sexual fulfilment. In both recent BBC Austen adaptations there were indications that female characters (and spectators) do fetishise the male body through the clothes that adorn it. In the opening episode of *Pride and Prejudice* Eliza's desire for Darcy is conveyed through a horizontal pan following the look from her eyes to Darcy's crotch, whilst in *Persuasion* the final liberation of Anne's previously repressed desire for Wentworth is described through a close-up of the Captain's stitched white gloves clasping her accepting hand. The power of clothes fetishism is that it exists on the cusp between display and denial, signalling as much a lack as a presence of sexual desire, through which it is especially relevant to films that depict a past, less ostensibly liberated age. As Louise J. Kaplan comments, '[a] fetish is designed to keep the lies hidden, to divert attention from the whole story by focusing attention on the detail' (Kaplan, L. 1993: 34), an allusion to fetish as narrative tool that is pertinent to film, as, likewise, is Robert Stoller's definition of a fetish as 'a story masquerading as an object' (Stoller 1985: 155). In all three films the fetish is, at some stage, the object or detail masking the whole story, but whereas in *Picnic at Hanging Rock* the story is left mysterious, by the time we get to *The Piano* it is unveiled.

Period clothes are not always transparent and are capable of being deeply ambiguous. To the fashion historian James Laver the crinoline, despite its 'solid and immovable' tea-cosy shape (Laver 1995: 184), is a complex and perplexing agent of seduction:

> The crinoline was in a constant state of agitation, swaying from side to side. It was like a rather restless captive balloon, and not at all, except in shape, like the igloo of the Eskimos. It swayed now to one side, now to the other, tipped up a little, swung forward and backward. Any pressure on one side of the steel hoops was communicated by their elasticity to the other side, and resulted in a sudden upward shooting of the skirt. It was probably this upward shooting which gave mid-Victorian men their complex about ankles, and it certainly resulted in a new fashion in boots.
>
> (Laver 1945: 52–3)

The more traditional view of the crinoline was as a metaphor and a metonym for women's oppression, condemned by more moralistic commentators as a garment which was 'as good a device for impeding movement as could well be devised' (Bell, Q. 1947: 90–1), and by feminists as a fashion whose 'whole style trembled with meek submissiveness' and reflected the dutiful wife's growing confinement to the bourgeois home (Wilson 1985: 30). The fundamental difference between these divergent opinions on the hooped contraption that dominated western women's fashion for over twenty years from 1856 is fetishism. Laver, for example, is not just an anti-functionalist commentator on fashion but one who, even inadvertently as above, conveys through his meticulous and excitable writing the erotic allure of garments, fabrics and accessories. He explains, in *Taste and Fashion*, how Victorian mothers like his own had to momentarily release their children's hands whilst crossing the road 'in order to gather their voluminous skirts from the ground to prevent them trailing in the mud. As they did so there was the rustle of innumerable silk petticoats underneath, and even a glimpse of lace frill' (Laver 1945: 199). The ostensible motive for the description (the mothers' sensible actions) is rapidly forgotten, and Laver's focus transferred to the underlying point of interest (the sensuality and movement of the women's clothes). A similar division between functionalism and fetishism pervades what is loosely labelled 'the costume film', where clothes usually exist as empty historical signifiers but can more imaginatively become essential components of a film's erotic language. Because the nineteenth century's fashions (for both sexes) appeared to embody what Foucault terms modern puritanism's 'triple edict of taboo, non-existence, and silence' (Foucault 1976: 5), they are fertile ground for fetishism; prohibition possessing an allure that laxity does not.

It was Krafft-Ebing in *Psychopathia Sexualis* (1886) who first used the term 'fetishism' in a sexual and criminal sense, and the term was subsequently adopted by Binet in 'Le fetichisme dans l'amour' (1888) and most notably by Freud. Foucault's reading of fetishism in *The History of Sexuality* was as 'the model perversion' which 'served as a guiding thread for analysing all other deviations' (Foucault 1976: 154), and if one turns to Freud's early writings on the subject in 'The sexual aberrations' the reason for such an assertion becomes apparent. In his first of the *Three Essays on Sexuality* written in 1905 Freud sets up a polemic, outlining what is 'aberrant' against an intentionally prescriptive and narrow sense of what constitutes 'normality', namely heterosexual, penetrative sex. Why fetishism is so important and why, therefore, 'no other variation of the sexual instinct that borders on the pathological can lay so much claim to our interest as this one' (Freud 1905: 66) is because, more clearly than the other aberrations, it simultaneously obstructs and substitutes the 'normal' sexual act. At this point Freud's emphasis is on the object choices of the fetishist, on the 'unsuitability' of the inanimate objects or the 'inappropriateness' of the part of the body substituted for the sex. Freud, like others since (for example, Gamman and Makinen 1994), identifies stages of fetishism, the situation only becoming pathological, he argues, when the fetish goes beyond being something the individual needs 'if the sexual aim is to be attained' (such as a particular hair colour, a visible naked foot, a piece of material) and actually allows the fetish to supplant that aim and become 'the sole sexual object' (Freud 1905: 66–7). Although he is already writing in terms of the fetish as symbolic (analogous to the anthropological fetish thought to embody a deity), this idea is not fully developed. By his 1909 paper 'On the genesis of fetishism' Freud has extended his argument, incorporating Krafft-Ebing's association of the fetish object with the subject's first conscious sexual impulses to explain the peculiarity of certain object-choices. It is also in this essay that Freud categorically argues for fetishism as a male perversion focused on the selection of substitutive objects that serve to repress and deny the sight of his mother's 'castration'. The essay then clearly suggests how, through an interest in fashion, women become both passive fetishists and a complete, imaginary fetish offered up for male contemplation:

> half of humanity must be classed among the clothes fetishists. All women, that is, are clothes fetishists. . . . It is a question again of the repression of the same drive, this time however in the passive form of allowing oneself to be seen, which is repressed by the clothes, and on account of which the clothes are raised to a fetish.
>
> (quoted in Ganman and Makinen 1994: 41)

As historians of the period have noted, fashions of the nineteenth century not only accentuated but elaborated and constructed gender difference, and, as Elizabeth Wilson puts it, 'woman and costumes together created femininity' (Wilson 1985: 29). If, therefore, this notion of femininity is pursued, then the clothed woman mirrors the male ideal of femininity and becomes the fetish that masks and embodies his fears of castration; a castration which, because of how the Freudian fetish operates, is simultaneously denied and acknowledged.

This is given clarification by Freud in his 1927 essay 'Fetishism' in which he comments that the (male) child, having 'perceived that a woman does not possess a penis', did not simply, through fetish substitution, 'retain the belief that women have a phallus' but rather retained that belief whilst having 'also given it up' (Freud 1927: 352–3). It is the knowingness of this ambivalent state which is most appropriate to how fetishism operates in costume films, for Freud does not equate fetishism only with repression but introduces the more conscious, deliberate notion of 'disavowal'; so 'yes, in his mind the woman *has* got a penis, in spite of everything; but this penis is not the same as it was before' (Freud 1927: 353). To explain the idiosyncrasy of many notably unphallic fetishes Freud suggests that the choice of object is dependent not on the similarity to the penis but to the original traumatic moment of perceiving the woman (mother) to be 'castrated'. Hence shoes, feet, underwear and substitutes for female pubic hair such as fur or velvet are fixated on because 'it is as though the last impression before the uncanny and traumatic one is retained as a fetish' (354). Freud understands the act of acquiring a fetish quite unmetaphorically. The shoe, for example, can be chosen because it was the last thing the 'inquisitive boy [peering] at the woman's genitals from below, from her legs up' (354) remembers before his traumatic realisation. This is obviously greatly facilitated by a wider skirt, which is what gives Baines's action in *The Piano* of snooping up Ada's hoops as she plays her piano such a blatant eroticism. Both disavowal and affirmation of the female 'lack', Freud concludes, went into the construction of the fetish, which 'signified that women were castrated and that they were not castrated' (356). To return to Foucault's comment that fetishism is the 'model perversion', it is now starkly apparent why: Freud's reading categorically defines man as the sexual subject and the fetish-choice as driven by the fear of his own castration. Like the perverse Chinese custom which legitimised the mutilation of the female foot so that it could be revered as a fetish, it seems, as Freud concludes, that 'the Chinese male wants to thank the woman for having submitted to being castrated' (357).

This fashionable foot-binding custom is more painful, perhaps, but no more contradictory than other prevalent nineteenth-century fashions such as tight-lacing, also conventionally understood, in that most patriarchal of times, as affirming the importance of clear gender delineations. A significant aspect of fashion's evolution can be seen as a continuation of Darwin's theories of difference, motivated by politics rather than necessity as J. C. Flügel suggests in his chapter on 'The Ethics of Dress' in *The Psychology of Clothes*:

> There seems to be (especially in modern life) no essential factor in the nature, habits or functions of the two sexes that would necessitate a striking difference of costume – other than the desire to accentuate sex differences themselves.
>
> (Flügel 1930: 201)

Going against Darwin, Flügel believes that the 'logical' response to the post-industrial flaunting of gender would be to abolish 'unnecessary sex distinctions in costume' altogether (201). He is, however, resigned to the fact that the 'majority' desire titillation and eroticism from clothes, and see distinctive dress as a means of stimulating sexual instincts. A consistently forceful argument used to explicate the divergence between men and women's fashions is that femininity has been emphasised for the express purpose of making women erotically appealing to men: 'for man in every age has created woman in the image of his own desire. It is false flattery of women to pretend that this is not so' (Laver 1945: 198). In a later book, *Modesty In Dress*, Laver develops this notion by identifying two polarised principles: the hierarchical and the seductive. The former is applicable to men because 'a man's clothes are a function of his relation to society' whilst the latter pertains to women because 'a woman's clothes are a function of her relation to man' (Laver 1969: 173). As Simone de Beauvoir acerbically comments in 1949, excessively feminine clothes have nothing to do with glorifying or emancipating women, but are devices of enslavement that make them prey to male desires (de Beauvoir 1949: 543).

The eroticism that dominated women's nineteenth-century fashions was perhaps more subtle and ambiguous than this implies. Flügel perceives there to be a fundamental paradox in women's clothes, that whilst they ostensibly function to emphasise morality and modesty they in effect arouse desire. As examples of this one could cite Laver's excitement at imagining the movements of the crinoline, or his equally ardent support of the small waist, corset and the deep Bertha *décolletage* which 'emphasised the impression of something very precious emerging from a complicated wrapping, as a flower emerges from the paper which encloses its stalk' (Laver 1945: 146). Perhaps unsurprisingly James Laver is neither a fan of more liberated or masculine clothes on women nor a supporter of overtly erotic fashions, maintaining that the naked body is not as appealing as the clothed one, and that a woman in suspenders is less alluring than a woman sporting a crinoline. Fetishism (as opposed to eroticism) is founded on tension, distance and imagination, and is dependent on symbolic rather than actual association between the subject and the object of (his) desire. It is precisely *because* the crinoline says 'touch me not' that Laver finds it seductive (52).

In costume films interested in sexuality (above nostalgia and history telling) the contrast between the obtainable concealed body and the means of enforcing that concealment (namely the clothes) is seen to heighten expectation and arousal. The shiny black boots in *Diary of a Chambermaid*, the Amish cap in *Witness*,[2] the lock of hair in *Golden Braid* or the scrap of dirty lace in *Picnic at Hanging Rock* are personal fetishes, inappropriate substitutes as Freud would deem them for the unobtainable woman they represent. Important to all these instances of the fetishisation of the woman and of the man's desire is the notion of difference, contrast and, most significantly, distance. Just as Christian Metz posits that distance rather than proximity is essential to the voyeuristic impulse, that 'all desire depends on the infinite pursuit of its absent object' (Metz 1975: 60), so the erotic effect of fetishised articles of clothing is essentially related to their metaphoric value. The underlying implication for fashion is that an idealised (male conceived) image of femininity acquires symbolic effect by having been constructed through costume, and that the greater the divergence between the 'natural' body and the 'unnatural', distortive clothes the greater the sexual stimulation.

This is a predominantly masculine view of the workings of clothes fetishism, and there obviously exist arguments and cinematic examples which counter it. In *Sister My Sister*, by comparison, the fetishisation of particularly articles of clothing, household objects and food is expressive of an exclusively female repressed sexuality. The codification of desire in this much later film uses a similar displacement tactic to Freudian male fetishism (the substitute of an inanimate object for a living object-choice) but only pertains to the sexualities of the various female characters. The strenuous affirmation of hierarchical sexual difference and the conceptualisation of elaborate detail and ornamentation as essential to fabricating women's attractiveness to men remain, however, the sexual mechanisms operative in a highly masculine fantasy film such as *Picnic at Hanging Rock*, an adaptation that embellishes the already insistent fetishism of Joan Lindsay's original 1968 novel.

Desire and the costume film

Picnic at Hanging Rock is the story of a fictional murder mystery that took place on St Valentine's Day 1900. Most of the schoolgirls of Appleyard College go on a picnic at Hanging Rock, a group of them want to explore the rock further and three of them (including the pivotal character Miranda) are never found, whilst Irma, who is found, cannot remember anything of what occurred. A particularly Freudian reading of fetishism, which stresses the significance of sexual difference and the importance of the 'normal' sex act, is deeply relevant to Weir's tumescent, adolescent fantasy, to its heterosexism (with its sharp gender delineations) and to its fundamental preoccupation with the transition from childhood to adulthood and thus the point of sexual awakening.

As women's exhibitionism in fashion has been understood to be for the enjoyment of men or at least as a means of ensuring their attention, so the same controlling gaze has been attributed to the male spectator looking at the fetishised, iconic female form on the screen. Whether this is through demystification or over-valuation of the woman as Laura Mulvey suggests, the fetishisation relegates her to the passive role of bearer of male desires, thus dissipating the threat her very 'castrated' presence evokes. The girls in *Picnic at Hanging Rock* are subjected to both 'the investigative side of voyeurism' Mulvey identifies in Hitchcock's work and become 'the ultimate fetish' produced by von Sternberg, as often in Weir's film 'the powerful look of the male protagonist. . . . is broken in favour of the image in direct rapport with the spectator' (Mulvey 1975: 311). *Picnic at Hanging Rock*'s conception of fragmented, transcendent and superficial female beauty is only partially provoked by narrative necessity. Much of the film's fetishism is contained within hiatus sequences divested of any plot function in which the spectacle of beatific schoolgirl sexuality is simply offered up for display. Just as Mulvey only refers to a male spectator, so Weir only addresses a masculine erotic gaze.

Picnic opens with just such a hiatus sequence in which the pupils, preparing for their St. Valentine's Day excursion, are presented to us as direct objects of fetishism. The film's mystery is sustained by elliptical dialogue, narration and images which, like Miranda's quivering opening piece of voice-over ('what we see and what we seem are but a dream – a dream within a dream') lend it a teasing, ornate vacuity. Like the expressionistic montage sequences of the classic 1930s Hollywood gangster films, the beginning of *Picnic at Hanging Rock* offers a symbolic condensation of the issues and iconography that are more conventionally enacted through the narrative, in this instance the idealisation of femininity through clothes and feminine sexuality. The girls and their romanticised French teacher are dressed exclusively in frail, pristine white (with the exception of the 'deviant' Sara who has blue sleeves)[3] and are ritualistically preparing themselves not just for the day but for womanhood. Hence the dreamy reading aloud of Valentine's messages, Irma and Miranda's sensuous face-washing in front of self-scrutinising mirrors and, most fetishistically of all, lacing each other into corsets. It is the hyperbolic self-consciousness of this montage sequence that makes it so obviously symbolic, with the abundance of flowers, soft focus and golden light; an excessive fusion of the mechanics of fetishism and the fetishising potential of the cinematic apparatus. As if we needed prompting into cleaning our own glasses to further enable us to enjoy the ensuing spectacle, one girl is shown polishing *hers* immediately after the line of giggling, whispering schoolgirls has performed its corset-lacing routine. From the outset, the girls' sexuality is defined as being for an unspecified but omnipresent phallus, metonymically represented by St Valentine, but also contained within the film's masculinisation of the voyeuristic and fetishistic impulses. In keeping with Lacan's notion of the phallus as something lost, forever out of reach, but nevertheless pursued as if it were attainable, there is a coalescence throughout *Picnic at Hanging Rock* between direct and indirect fetishism, between the real and the veiled. For example, before setting off on their final ascent up Hanging Rock, the girls reverentially, slowly remove their stockings and shoes: for the rock, the spectator and the unspecified phallus. There is a direct alignment at a point such as this between the active, consuming spectatorial gaze, the phallic rock (which has already been identified as such through a laboured series of low-angle shots) and the veiled phallus governing the girls' actions from the start.

The direct fetishism scenes in *Picnic at Hanging Rock* are frequently 'rites of passage' sequences in which we, the spectators, are voyeuristically engaged with the girls' progress towards maturity. There are several such rituals that have marked the transition from girlhood to womanhood through the use of clothes, most of which, like the acquisition of deforming shoes, uplifting bras and sculpting corsets or girdles, have involved extreme physical restriction. The significant ritual of *Picnic at Hanging Rock* is that of the pupils lacing each other into their corsets, an action that signals both confinement and liberation. This activity further differentiates between those who are ready for sex and those, notably the plump and uncorseted Edith, who are not.[4] Crucial to these fashions is the tension between pain and pleasure; as David Kunzle comments, 'The state of being tightly corseted is a form of erotic tension and constitutes *ipso facto* a demand for erotic release, which may be deliberately controlled, prolonged and postponed' (Kunzle 1982: 31). Kunzle, who was the first to call for a radical reassessment of the corset's relationship to female sexuality, noted that many of the advocates of tight-lacing in the mid-1800s were sexually assertive women, and that the majority of the corset's sternest critics were conservative men who felt threatened by this clandestine expression of desire. Tight-lacing (or the excessive constriction of the waist by means of a corset) was a deeply ambiguous phenomenon. Whilst the corset, particularly by feminists, has been traditionally interpreted as a tyrannical garment of oppression, there are well-documented examples of tight-lacing as a popular nineteenth-century erotic pursuit. Fetishistic correspondence in innocuous sounding Victorian women's magazines such as *The Queen* and *The Englishwoman's Domestic Magazine* was rife, as readers, often vying with each other for the smallest waist, offered 'advice' on how to lace more tightly. In the correspondence pages of domestic magazines there are ample examples of women using tight-lacing for auto-erotic pleasure, describing, for instance, the light-headedness which follows the deliberate interruption of their circulation. Although it is presumed (even by Kunzle) that such tight-laced women are to be found desirable by men (Kunzle 1982: 43), it is strikingly apparent that many correspondents derive the greatest pleasure from the narcissistic contemplation of themselves in restrictive undergarments. During the 1860s–1880s it was primarily men who documented the reasons why tight-lacing was reprehensible, for instance the doctors who alerted adults to the direct use of corsets for masturbatory satisfaction among pubescent girls (170–1, 218–22). A more moderate view of the 'corset controversy' than Kunzle's is offered by Valerie Steele who argues that 'most accounts of very small waists represented *fantasies*' (Steele 1985: 163), and that the vast majority of corsets in fashion museums suggest that the real average size of the Victorian and Edwardian waist was several inches wider than the 'perfect' 11 inches aspired to by readers of *Englishwoman's Domestic Magazine*. According to Steele, therefore, the idea of a tight-lacing epidemic rather than the reality of one is what excited male and female readers alike.

A preoccupation with lacing and restriction is, however, a pervasive force through *Picnic at Hanging Rock*. As if signalling its own interest in fetishism, the major departures the film makes from the original novel are the moments (such as the opening montage) which dwell on the latent perversity of the pupils' sexuality and not on the narrative. In the book there is a cursory mention of a 'padded horizontal board fitted with leather straps, on which the child Sara, continually in trouble for stooping, was to pass the gymnasium hour this afternoon' (Lindsay 1968: 131). Although bizarre, this is not presented as a sadistic instrument of torture, which is roughly in keeping with the times, as such correctional contraptions were, in 1900, considered old-fashioned but not perverse. In the film, however, the treatment of Sara is overloaded with perversity, and the shame of the teacher who has administered this punishment is likewise underlined, as she guiltily cowers behind a chair when Mademoiselle and Irma interrupt the dancing lesson. Identified from the start as the deviant pupil, she is systematically, though subtly, punished throughout the film. Because, it is insinuated, Sara is in love with Miranda, she is not allowed on the picnic, she is prevented from reading out one of her love poems, and now she is strapped up.

Of persistent interest to historians has been the gender and identity of the addressee of the nineteenth-century fetish correspondences. Was it, perhaps, men who got a sexual kick out of hearing about and disapproving of women tight-lacing or whipping their horses? A similar ambiguity resides in *Picnic at Hanging Rock*.

Whereas Sara can be likened to the problematic, sexually active girls who discovered devious means to practice auto-eroticism and thus implicitly deny the importance to their sexual development of the male, Irma, it is made clear, survives the tragedy of St Valentine's day to enter into an exclusively heterosexual womanhood. Whilst it is titillatingly confirmed that she, the only girl to be found alive, is sexually 'quite intact' and only superficially injured, Irma was discovered on the rock clothed but minus her corset. Kunzle quotes an Australian poem of 1890 telling of an adolescent girl who equates the pain of love with the pain of wearing a corset, and who, on the threshold of marriage, summons the 'iron-clad corset, as befits the chaste woman' asking for her companion to 'pull and heave on the laces, that the bridally enhanced body be truly ethereal'.[5] If the painful corset is a sign of virtue and maturity, it is little wonder that the fully recovered Irma (the problematic goings-on with her corset having represented her rite of passage) should return once more to Appleyard College dressed in an intensely adult scarlet cape and feathered hat, visually differentiated from the other school-girls still clothed in virginal white by colour and an ostentatiously adult hour-glass figure.

The most categorical example of the female functioning in *Picnic at Hanging Rock* to provoke both diegetic and extra-diegetic male desire is the aptly named Miranda. As she disappears up the rock she waves back at the French mistress who remarks, looking down at a reproduction in her art history book, 'now I know that Miranda is a Botticelli angel'. Thus identified with an imaginary, idealised vision of beauty, Miranda becomes the film's ultimate, mysterious fetish. The film cements this through the repeated use of a slow motion image of Miranda waving to Mademoiselle (and, by implication, the adoring enraptured spectator) before turning away and disappearing forever. As *Picnic at Hanging Rock* uses clothes as one of the ways of differentiating between the girls who are on the brink of womanhood and those who are not, so it clearly demarcates the masculine and the feminine. It could be argued that, with so many women looking admiringly at Miranda, this is a film that throws into question the assertion that the active erotic gaze is necessarily male. Likewise, if one takes into account the possibility that pain can be pleasurable, there is also the subversive suggestion that women can derive fetishistic enjoyment from such oppression. It is primarily the character-isation of the two adolescent males Michael and Bertie (likewise on the cusp of adulthood) that counters such a positive feminist reading. As mentioned earlier, in costume films interested in fetishism, distance and gap is significant to the relationship between clothes and desire. A film such as *Picnic at Hanging Rock* creates a mysterious, sexual world based on several enforced but never coherently explained oppositions: between clothes and bodies, spectator and narrative, people and landscape, desire and sex, male and female. Sexual difference is even represented through the use of two distinct types of music: a whimsical, feminine

2.1 Miranda (Anne Lambert) emerging from a rock in *Picnic at Hanging Rock*
Courtesy of BFI Stills, Posters and Designs

and indeterminate pan pipe tune for the girls, and a strident, soaring track which builds to a definite crescendo for the boys. Distance is the basis for fetishistic fantasy, perpetually denying and affirming the underlying desires through an elaborate interplay between metaphor, metonym and sexual object. The fetishist's ultimate fantasy (even if it may be Freud's) is not to dispense with the fetish and unravel the mystery, but to retain (and perhaps embellish) the ambiguity. We do not wish Miranda to be explained, she is a shared fetish, the figure onto which our desires are projected. She, like the ever-veiled phallus, remains beautiful by virtue of being unfound and unexplained.

In *Picnic at Hanging Rock* such fetishistic ambiguity is expressed via the pleasure/pain dynamic as it pertains to the significant males in the film, the spectator and the eroticised clothes. Michael, an English gentleman staying with his uncle and aunt, never meets but falls deeply in love with Miranda after seeing her only once. In one of the film's 'male-bonding' scenes Michael and Bertie, a servant, watch the four girls heading for Hanging Rock cross a stream, their white dresses gleaming in the sun. Whilst Bertie makes crude comments about their legs and hour-glass figures, Michael becomes painfully smitten, haunted by the frozen image of Miranda, an image that the spectator, once again, is given in softened, slow close-up. Michael's obsession with the film's unobtainable (and hence perfect) object is for him tortuous, for us titillating, an ambivalence exemplified by his return to the rock, in a last desperate attempt to find Miranda. Throughout *Picnic at Hanging Rock* the language of desire has been the language of clothes, and in Michael's actions the transferral of attention from actual femininity to unsuitable substitutes for the sexual object is complete. In another show of male camaraderie, Bertie discovers Michael, after his night-time search of Hanging Rock for the lost girls, slumped in a catatonic trance. As the masculine music soars Michael, now transferred to the back of a buggy, holds out his trembling clenched fist towards Bertie who wrests from it a tiny scrap of lace (an exchange again not in the book). We are subsequently shown, in close-up, the frail piece of material nestling in Bertie's palm, its delicacy and whiteness symbolically contrasted with his soiled, rough skin. Without having it explained why, this improbable bit of insubstantiality is, ultimately, what propelled Michael into his catatonia, what leads Bertie to find Irma and what must suffice as the film's symbol for the impenetrable mystery of what occurred on the rock. In such a hyperbolic and hysterical film the absent object remains tantalisingly opaque, nearly sending Michael mad, but serving to preserve the spectator's fantasy of enigmatic femininity 'perfectly intact'. What has been created here is an exclusively male fantasy in which representation, symbolism and narrative converge to evoke the (adolescent) male obsession with the female sexual object. The female is both central and absent, 'the enigma the hieroglyphic, the picture, the image' (Doane 1991: 18). The only viable position for the female spectator is as an enigma-identifier; to desire to be the absented object with whom everyone is infatuated: in short, to desire to be the fetish.

Rather than being primarily an example of fetishistic behaviour as *Picnic* to a certain extent is, *The Age of Innocence*, in its treatment of the image as well as the narrative, is a total fetishistic experience. The absenting of particularly women's sexuality and desire is the mainstay of melodramatic romanticism, making the entire film-watching experience into a deeply fetishistic enterprise. Melodramas of necessity manipulate detail, visual style and music to convey emotions the characters are not permitted to express, thus films such as Ophuls' *Letter From an Unknown Woman*, Sirk's *All That Heaven Allows* and Scorsese's *The Age of Innocence* (which, the director readily acknowledges, is indebted to the sumptuous though claustrophobic melodramatic tradition [Christie 1994: 10–15]) become fetish objects in themselves. *The Age of Innocence* is the clearest example to date of Scorsese's fetishisation of cinema history. Technically the film has several past reference points: there's some of the 'romance and tragedy' of Ophuls' camera, some 'pure Eisenstein stuff' in the editing, and the Soviet technique of using shade and light to focus on the important part of an image. There is also the conscious involvement of some of the most experienced cinematic craftspeople, such as Saul and Elaine Bass who had been designing title and credit sequences for over forty years, and Elmer Bernstein who wrote 'the closest to a traditional Hollywood score I have ever worked with' (Christie 1994: 14). Melodramas are narratives of allusion, Ophuls' romantic tracks, cranes and pans, for example, bearing contradictory functions: to create a point of identification with the characters' emotions whilst at the same time substituting for them and signalling their repression. The intensity of the desire is deflected onto the film image itself, and is eloquently understood through distance not closeness. *The Age of Innocence* is likewise about gaps and lack. Newland Archer (the film's – although not the book's – undoubted subject) falls in love with the married but estranged Countess Ellen Olenska whilst he is engaged to her cousin May Welland. Social convention bars Newland from marrying Ellen, so he weds May. The essence of melodrama is that being in a perpetual state of loss and longing is a more delicious experience than consummation, a tantalisingly torn state preserved in *The Age of Innocence* largely through Michael Ballhaus' camera and lighting and Thelma Schoonmaker's editing; so just as Newland at the end wants to hold onto his idealised image of Ellen rather than see her again, we are fulfilled by the sensuality of the film, its roaming camera and slow dissolves. Because the ultimate object remains obscured and so much is left understated, fetishism also dictates that part of the enjoyment of reading or watching a piece of period romanticism is filling in the blanks. Again Scorsese uses a lush filmic style to do this, as in the instances when measured costume drama sequences dissolve into violent red or yellow that engulf the whole screen; sudden eruptions of passion and desire that, as they are flaunted, become just as rapidly repressed.

Dressing up

This degree of image fetishism is carried over into the narrative and *mise-en-scène*, as *The Age of Innocence* is built around detail. Most of Scorsese's films are obsessed with ritual and social codes, with how his male characters particularly perceive themselves to be defined (and confined) by their environments. It is the gap between reality and expectation that, in films like *Taxi Driver* and *Raging Bull*, prompts the extreme physical outbursts of Travis Bickle or Jake La Motta. In *The Age of Innocence* a comparable pain is evoked by an accentuation rather than diminution of the formalities and social niceties. The presentation and precision of the rituals that dominate 1870s upper-class New York society become, in Scorsese's adaptation, tempting cinematic renditions of Freud's notion of fetishistic disavowal, in particular the repeated ritual of dining. However tantalising and excessive the food, no sooner does one ornate course appear on the table than it dissolves elegantly, effortlessly into the next, seldom to be consumed and never to be enjoyed. The one dinner that is seen to be consumed (at Archer's family home) is, significantly, a badly cooked test of endurance. Whereas one's suspicions about fetishism and eroticism in *Picnic at Hanging Rock* might be that it is really a case of 'The Emperor's New Clothes' in which a fascination with costume betrays a fascination with emptiness, *The Age of Innocence* is more grandiloquently poignant in this respect, as the details are the brittle surface which both suppress and convey emotion. As Edith Wharton puts it in the original novel, 'They all lived in a hieroglyphic world, where the real thing was never said or done or even thought, but only represented by a set of arbitrary signs' (Wharton 1920: 55). The pleasure in the text is being able to read those signs, to feel the intensity of the suppressed instinct conveyed through the many closely observed, ritualistic actions the adaptation focuses on such as letters being passed, cigars being clipped or hands being slipped into gloves. The potency of the metaphoric language is that the spectator is both aware that such actions and objects possess a significance beyond themselves and their immediate function, but ultimately excluded from their exact, codified meaning. This equivocal function of the imaginary sign is prominent in *The Age of Innocence*'s use of costume detail, most notably the clothes of the ostensibly transparent, straightforward May. When identifying with Newland's patronising gaze (as we are constrained to be at the Beaufort Ball at which May announces their engagement), May is presented as an innocent cocooned in lace, muslin and organza against a complex world. There are, however, moments when costume detail is employed to suggest May's disguised strength, for example when she triumphantly manoeuvres her heavy train out of the door, having told Newland she is pregnant and thus thwarting his desire to elope with Ellen. Here, May's bustle-encased lower body, as Pam Cook implies, could be seen to function as a 'powerful image of male terror in the face of the maternal body' (Cook 1994: 46). A far less comprehensible – but more evocative and sensual – use of May's clothes as signifiers occurs when the delicate fibres of her lace-encrusted summer dress are punctured by the point of the pin she has been given for winning the archery competition. The penetration of the strands of cloth function as an abstracted image of repressed violence.

The past is made strange in *The Age of Innocence* through an obsessive attention to minutiae and authenticity, as if the spectator has been invited to observe the meticulous dissection of late nineteenth-century manners, cuisine, and clothes in order to both revel in them and recognise their role as signifiers of that society's extreme superficiality. The fetishised object thus simultaneously represses and renders visible the implied desire. As Scorsese comments about Wharton's technique, 'what seems to be description is in fact a clear picture of that culture built up block by block – through every plate and glass and piece of silverware, all the sofas and what's on them' (Christie 1994: 12). The notion of re-examining the past through the present is important to all the films being discussed in this chapter (an awareness, perhaps of differentiation is central to their fetishisation of that past), and this is the case on several levels in *The Age of Innocence*. Both Wharton and Scorsese are outsiders looking in. Wharton had gone into exile in Europe and wrote the novel in 1920 about the 1870s New York of her childhood, and Scorsese, from a background far removed from that of the characters, had never before attempted a straight costume drama. This juxtaposition between old and new informs the film, and the primary site on which we see the tension being acted out is Gabriella Pescucci's luxurious costumes. A scene such as the one in which Newland kneels down to kiss Ellen's embroidered shoe exemplifies the film's preoccupation with making the codes of the past strange. As it exists in the novel, Newland's gesture of suddenly stooping to kiss the 'tip of the satin shoe that showed under her dress' is odd but engagingly impulsive (Wharton 1920: 156). There exists, however, a chasm between imagination and realisation, and as a described passage in a book, Newland's arcane kiss can be freely imbued with whatever abstract desire the reader likes. The representation of the scene in the film is obviously less suggestive and more concrete, and the spectator is constrained to acknowledge the strangeness of the past, compelled to confront the outmoded awkwardness of the gesture rather than fantasise it into romantic abstraction.

Newland kissing Ellen's shoe offers an analysis of fetishism (its reality, its mechanics) rather than an immersion in its implied eroticism, and in its oddity the scene is illustrative of the fundamental distance between Scorsese and his subject matter. This is an audacious scene that does not comfort us with a bygone universal romanticism (where the dress is different but the language of love remains the same), but rather confronts us with a form of expression so outmoded that it is almost embarrassing to observe. Although the most obvious thing to say about *The Age of Innocence* is that it is a love story (and in that respect universal), Scorsese's adaptation focuses resolutely on the unsuitable object. The film's use of melodramatic excess highlights the painful loss and absence of what could so easily

2.2 Daniel Day Lewis and Michelle Pfeiffer in *The Age of Innocence*
Courtesy of BFI Stills, Posters and Designs

have been. Whilst the fetishism in *Picnic at Hanging Rock* is titillating and somehow a substitute for empty fantasy, in *The Age of Innocence* it is resonant with the sense that, at another time, distance would not have been necessary. In the back of a carriage from the station Newland and Ellen snatch two precious hours together; he passionately unbuttons her glove and kisses her exposed wrist, an action that is filmed with the same slow, sensuous dissolves as is much of the would-be love story. The pity is unbearable: pulling all the stops out for *this*?

Picnic at Hanging Rock and *The Piano* both imply that restrictiveness can be exciting. *The Age of Innocence* suggests that living by a strict nineteenth-century code can only be stultifying. Newland Archer is immured by the conventions that surround him, symbolised to an extent by the monotonous uniformity of his clothes. This is very much Scorsese's take on Wharton who is more resolutely critical of her protagonist, portraying him as complicit in his entrapment and not purely a victim of circumstance. At first Newland appears oblivious to the weight of convention, a lack of awareness delicately signalled during the second sequence (the Beaufort Ball) by the table of neatly laid out and labelled white evening gloves to which he blithely adds his own. Men are defined through their conformity and Newland, before he falls in love with Ellen, is quite content to comply. As the film progresses the distanciation between masculine conventionality and Archer's desire increases, until he is smothered rather than complemented by the formality of his heavy, layered clothes. One sequence evokes with particular poignancy the repression of male individuality by conformity. After Newland and Ellen have managed a brief meeting they part, the camera (carrying the inevitability of distance) retreating cruelly from Ellen with every jump cut.[6] This snatched moment is the prelude to a scene that at first appears to possess no direct narrative function, and indeed is not in the book. In slow motion a sea of grey-suited men walk towards the camera accompanied by Michael William Both's melancholy song 'Marble Halls' ('But I also dreamt which charmed me most/That you loved me still the same'), all clutching identical bowler hats threatened by the battering wind. Although Newland then emerges from the crowd holding tightly onto his bowler, so linking this scene with the narrative proper, the potency of this image is that it can remain an abstract metaphor for fearful, unthinking male conformity, 'the conformity of men who've learnt to keep it all under their hats' (Taubin 1993: 8). Like the sudden, violent bursts of screen-drowning colour or the involuntary moan Newland emits in the previous scene as Ellen touches his hand, desire throughout *The Age of Innocence* is fleetingly permitted to surface in order to be instantly bottled up under hats and under convention.

The representation of Newland Archer suggests that sartorial conformity corresponds to emotional repression, that he can be 'read' through his clothes. In one of the most influential accounts of how masculinity has been expressed through clothes, Flügel described what he termed 'The Great Masculine Renunciation',

2.3 Daniel Day Lewis as Newland in *The Age of Innocence*
Courtesy of BFI Stills, Posters and Designs

when 'Man abandoned his claim to be considered beautiful' (Flügel 1930: 111). The argument posited by Flügel for men's clothes becoming utilitarian, austere and uniform in the nineteenth century is increased democratisation since the French Revolution, 'the fact that the ideal of work had now become respectable' (Flügel 1930: 112) and thus that man was, as a result, defined more by his social than his personal role. Flügel then conflates sartorial and psychological changes in a significant statement about how the masculine ideal is symbolised by physical appearance, commenting:

It is, indeed, safe to say that, in sartorial matters, modern man has a far sterner and more rigid conscience than has modern woman, and that man's morality tends to find expression in his clothes. . . . modern man's clothing abounds in features which symbolise his devotion to the principles of duty, of renunciation and of self-control. The whole relatively 'fixed' system of his clothing is, in fact, an outward and visible sign of the strictness of his adherence to the social code.

(Flügel 1930: 113)

Newland Archer has bought into this code of denial and fraternity: he works as a lawyer and wears his bowler hat. But just as the attention on obsessively researched surface details in *The Age of Innocence* serves to deflect attention onto what is *not* visible, so Newland's renunciatory stiffness serves to accentuate his potential for passion.

The romantic necessity of unfulfilment is expressed verbally by Countess Olenska in the shoe-kissing scene when she says 'I can't love you unless I give you up', but it is evoked filmically through the subjectification of Archer who, right at the end when he is offered the chance to see Ellen again, declines to meet her and bridge the gap between imagination and reality. As with every act of fetishism, distance preserves the mystery. So Newland would rather imagine the past Ellen than meet the present one, and as he closes his eyes a rapid montage culminating in the Ellen he remembers turning round and smiling at him flashes across the screen. Archer is playing a game with himself which he's played before: if she turns around he will go to meet her; if she does not, he will walk on by. As Amy Taubin suggests, *The Age of Innocence* is about 'the suffocating anxiety of waiting for the sign on which one believes one's life depends, wanting it to come and at the same time fearing it' (Taubin 1993: 9). Fetishism keeps the danger of change at bay.

Both *Picnic at Hanging Rock* and *The Age of Innocence* make use of the fetishistic transferral of desire for the woman onto her clothes as both the symbols and the masking agents for this fear of change. In this they are both masculine films, although *The Age of Innocence* is self-reflective in its representation of fetishism, as if offering a commentary on its peculiarity. Primarily through their portrayal of the male characters, both films emphasise the significance (if a safe convention-alism is to be maintained) of distance, the clothes and narrative separations functioning effectively as barriers. Newland Archer realises his loss, but Michael in *Picnic at Hanging Rock* is an exemplary pathological, Freudian fetishist who keeps a voyeuristic distance between himself and Miranda.[7] Freud comments in 'Touching and Looking' that '[t]he progressive concealment of the body which goes along with civilisation keeps sexual curiosity awake', and that a 'normal' endeavour would be to 'complete the sexual object by revealing its hidden parts'

(Freud 1905: 69). Clearly Michael cannot go beyond scopophilia and so is exclusively confined to fetishising his fantasised object-choice.

If the man cannot (or does not want to) go beyond the level of civilised concealment, the woman inevitably becomes the passive representation of his active sexuality. A playful example of this imbalance can be found in the verses to Julia by the seventeenth-century poet and priest Robert Herrick. His poems convincingly posit the notion that distance is more erotic than closeness, and emphasise the attraction rather than the sadness of over-valuing the inappropriate substitute for the sexual object. Even in a poem such as 'The Nightpiece, To Julia', in which Herrick finally imagines a union with his ideal love, his focus are her what Freud would term 'unsuitable' feet:

> Then Julia let me woo thee,
> Thus, thus to come unto me;
> And when I shall meet
> Thy silvery feet,
> My soul I'll pour into thee.
> (Fowler 1991: 275)

Herrick suggests that conventional consummation is not so devoutly to be wished after all, as his verse resonates with a desire for an image of woman so objectified that the mythic Julia's identity is lost beneath 'that liquefaction of her clothes' (Fowler 1991: 276). Julia's clothes are not substitutes for her absent body but signifiers of Herrick's desire. 'Delight in Disorder' conveys the intensity of Herrick's imaginatively active though repressed sexual longings through the freedom and immorality granted the clothes not the completely absented muse, as it is the dress that possesses a 'sweet disorder', the lace is 'erring', the cuff 'neglectful', the petticoat 'tempestuous' and the shoestring 'careless' (Fowler 1991: 257–8). Needless to say Herrick never gets his Julia, but the suspicion is that he is quite satisfied with observing her mischievous clothes. As he writes in 'Art above nature: To Julia' after praising again the tempting 'wild civility' of her appearance:

> I must confess, mine eye and heart
> Dote less on nature, than on art.
> (Fowler 1991: 274)

There is a sense, therefore, that Herrick is not just making do with the glittering and the vibration of Julia's clothes, but that his erotic gaze wants to be fixed on them. It is mistaken to hold, as Steele does, that, despite everything, it is Julia and not her clothes that are Herrick's true object-choice. Steele maintains, with reference to Herrick's Julia poems, that 'the desire for the body can be partially transferred onto clothes, which then provide an additional erotic charge of their own. But ultimately it is the wearer who is 'sweet' and 'wanton' (Steele

1985: 42). Julia is a muse, an impossible, unattainable ideal, and so her clothes and not her are the substitute phallus; they are what the poet desires – and what he makes his reader desire.

Flügel concludes his section on 'The Great Masculine Renunciation and its Causes' with the observation that

> in the case of the exhibitionistic desires connected with self-display, a particularly easy form of conversion may be found in a change from (passive) exhibitionism to (active) scoptophilia (erotic pleasure in the use of vision) – the desire to be seen being transformed into the desire to see.
>
> (Flügel 1930: 118)

And so the man does not renounce his exhibitionism at all but experiences the pleasures of 'vicarious display' (Flügel 1930: 118) through the desired woman, an active, if displaced, sexuality very apparent in Herrick's verse. In this belief, Flügel is in agreement with Darwin when he comments in *The Descent of Man* that, 'In civilised life man is largely, but by no means exclusively, influenced in the choice of his wife by external appearance' (Darwin 1871: 873). The sexual effect of display has thus been transferred to the woman. What occurs in *The Piano* in terms of fetishism (a clear indication that this film is in part a critique of both Victorian sexuality and the manner in which it has been interpreted by Flügel, Freud and others) is less to do with elaborate distanciation manoeuvres, and more to do with expressing direct desire and trying to have sex. This seems to be the intention behind the many archetypes and stereotypes that are reconsidered through the narrative in which Ada, a mute Scottish woman, has been packed off to New Zealand with her daughter Flora to marry a local landowner Stewart, but instead falls for his neighbour, George Baines. Whilst giving him piano lessons and winning back her instrument, Ada enters into an elaborate striptease whereby she exchanges and removes items of clothing in return for keys. In its re-examination of voyeurism, fetishism, striptease and hysteria, *The Piano* adopts clothes and their relationship to sexuality and the body as primary signifiers. There is a matter-of-factness in the clothes-dialogues between Ada and Baines that indicates any fetishism in this film is fetishism as a means to an end, namely intercourse. Campion herself has commented on being able to explore the physical side of a relationship in a way that Emily Brontë, for example, could not, and of being able, in the 1990s, to be 'a lot more investigative of the power of eroticism' (Campion 1993: 6). *The Piano*'s complex sensuality is informed by this eclecticism, being in several ways a re-examination of and a counter-argument to the conventional views of nineteenth-century sexuality. The film is deeply methodical in this respect, taking traditional mechanisms of desire and modes of articulation in order to question and subvert them, and, essentially, to give twentieth-century feminism a voice in situations where in the past such an intervention has not occurred.

The potential sexuality and sensuality of clothes is overtly explored in *The Piano*, as both costume and the body appear linked in this film to a complex feminist displacement of the conventionalised objectification of the woman's form via scopophilia and fetishism. It is not only Ada who is caught up in this radical exploration, although her fierce independence is essentially manifested by her repeated refusal to conform to the designated role of the pacified and distanced image of woman contained by the voyeuristic male gaze. This is where Stewart would have her, but the film strips him of this traditional power by refusing to align his look as the on-screen voyeur with ours. *The Piano* offers, in its representation of Stewart, a feminist re-contextualisation of Flügel. It is almost as if Stewart deliberately conforms to the ideas (or ideals) of The Great Masculine Renunciation. He is the archetypal nineteenth-century colonial husband bound by a burdensome sense of his position within patriarchal history, a character who is socially defined, obsessively aware (but not in control) of his territory, his whiteness and his role as head of the household. The problem is that Stewart inhabits a feminised not a Darwinian world to which he cannot see how to adapt because it is so manifestly correlated with Ada, his transgressive wife who creates alternative discursive strategies to counter his intended subjugation of her. Voyeurism, for example, as it is presented within the narrative, is not a pleasurably active pursuit but one born out of desperation and isolation. Stewart is forever (comically at times) portrayed as the outsider, isolated within a feminist framework by his dependency on scopophilia. He is consistently identified with an act of looking that is estranged rather than normative; squinting through a camera lens, or spying on Ada and Baines having sex through cracks in the timber and the floorboards. He is thus emasculated rather than empowered by his possession of (only) the look, as the tropes of traditional masculinity are gradually ridiculed. The misguidedness of Stewart's unthinking appropriation of convention is neatly illustrated in his costumes, which Janet Patterson deliberately made too small for Sam Neill 'to make him look uncomfortably uptight', adding that 'particularly in the scene when he first goes to meet Ada, his clothes are not a good fit' (Patterson 1993: 9). That the representation of Stewart is ironic is established in the opening sequence in which he checks his reflection and clumsily flattens his hair before meeting Ada for the first time. The would-be patriarch is the film's outsider looking in, being mimicked by his Maori helpers strutting around in top hats calling him 'dry balls'.

Stewart's masculine counterpart is Baines who, having discarded the ideology and the clothes of the European colonialist, has 'gone native'. This, again, is an example of *The Piano* intentionally bringing a 1990s consciousness to bear on a nineteenth-century narrative. Whereas Stewart is dressed in the monochrome uniform of repression, Baines formed a strong relationship with the Maoris and appropriated a look which closely resembles theirs. There is an easiness about

Baines, illustrated by the rich blue dyes, thick weave and authentic whale-bone buttons of his costume, and the Maori-esque markings on his face.[8] Baines symbolises the presence of the dangerous, erotic Other, the force that in the context of traditional repression narratives conventionally remains implied but concealed. A significant precursor to Baines is the man influenced by the wayward gypsy figure in several 1940s melodramas such as *Jassy*, *Blanche Fury* or the quasi-melodrama *Duel in the Sun*. The dangerous sexuality of Gregory Peck in *Duel in the Sun* or Stewart Granger in *Blanche Fury* is signalled through their ostentatious adoption of a gypsified look. Thus Granger's wearing of a red polka-dot necker-chief he has bought from a gypsy woman becomes a metonym for his rebellion against social and sexual norms. These, of course, are the men both the female characters and the audience are attracted to and identify with, in part because sexual, erotic clothes are conventionally viewed as feminine. In the terms adopted by Flügel, Baines has reclaimed 'the principle of erotic exposure' (Flügel 1930: 110–11), apparently (by the 1850s) the sole prerogative of women, and revived male narcissism. Whereas the conventionalised interpretation of gender differ-ence, as it has impinged on dress and physical appearance, is of the woman as object of display onto whom subjective male sexuality has been displaced, in *The Piano* the power relationship is inverted, as it is Baines who first presents himself naked to Ada thus, peacock-like, putting himself on display. In his

2.4 Holly Hunter and Maori women in *The Piano*
Courtesy of Ronald Grant Archive

appearance, Baines, with his Maori tattoos, hybrid clothes and unkempt hair, repeatedly functions to confront Stewart not with his supremacy but his lack.

Stewart's lack is further accentuated by his exclusion from sex, the gender conventions again being subverted to enforce this are grounded in the film's use of clothes as ambiguous signifiers for femininity. Ada's oppressive and austere Victorian costumes are made to function both for and against her, and are both internal and external signifiers of her desire and her social position. The most poetic example of this is the final, perplexing image of the drowned Ada tied to her piano, encased in her billowing skirts.[9] Dressed largely in black with an austerely authentic lampshade bonnet, Ada superficially embodies the archetypal nineteenth-century wife. James Laver, for example, declares the mid-nineteenth-century bonnet to be 'a sign of submission to male authority' (Laver 1969: 123). Unlike Baines, however, who does not keep his radicalism under his hat, Ada (via her conventionality) embodies the potential of clothes as an oppositional discourse not reliant for signification (even through a positive appropriation of difference) on any pre-established patriarchal models. The complexity of this situation is captured in the juxtapositional image of Ada posing for wedding photographs in a dress she has simply flung over her day clothes, without even attempting to fasten the back. The sartorial collisions here signal her clear rebellion against her designated position.

A similar duality informs the representation of clothes elsewhere in *The Piano*, for example Ada's cumbersome crinoline that both constricts her movements (as when she is negotiating the New Zealand mud) and works in support of her (as when it prevents Stewart from raping her). Clothes in *The Piano* function as discursive strategies for talking about sex, gender and the existence of desire underneath the veneer of conformity. In this the film's use of costume is reminiscent of Michel Foucault's analysis of sex and the expression of sexuality in *The History of Sexuality*. Foucault offers a revolutionary thesis for understanding the outcome of administered censorship of the articulation of desire from the eighteenth century onwards. Far from imposing censorship as the authorities had assumed, the measures that were brought in to prohibit sex and curtail the public acknowledgement of it brought into being 'an apparatus for producing an even greater quantity of discourse about sex' (Foucault 1976: 4–5). Sex was thus 'driven out of hiding and constrained to lead a discursive existence' (33), and although western laws of prohibition were enforced, they had the contradictory effect of drawing 'Western man . . . to the task of telling everything concerning his sex'(23). Silence, as Foucault maintains, is not 'the absolute limit of discourse' as there is no 'binary division to be made between what one says and what one does not say' (27). Instead, the discursive existence of sex led to the teasing paradox that, in striving to consign sex 'to a shadow existence', modern societies 'dedicated themselves to speaking of it *ad infinitum*, while exploiting it as *the* secret

(35). The dialectic between intention and this 'putting into discourse of sex' (12) is given narrative representation in *The Piano*. Stewart, in an attempt to deny sex, attempts to repress Flora's sexuality by making her scrub down the tree trunks she (following the more expressive Maoris) has been rubbing herself against; whilst Ada and Baines, in defiance of such social regulation, evolve a sexual 'clothes language' that transgresses the presumed boundary between silence and discourse.

The eroticism of striptease, which plays on the proximity and difference between clothes and the body, has seldom been disputed; as one writer on fetishism puts it, 'the moment we invented clothing we also invented the possibility of striptease' (Brand 1970: 19). In this nineteenth-century context, the clandestine dialogue between Ada and Baines is a case of the putting into discourse of sex. Rather than repressing or camouflaging sex, the oppressive Victorian clothes become the very agents through which desire is made possible. Unlike either *Picnic at Hanging Rock* or *The Age of Innocence* in which similarly prohibitive costumes substitute the unobtainable sexual object and signal its absence, in *The Piano* (and Freud would have approved) they and their fetishistic potential act as preludes to the consummation that does occur. More so than the other films (excepting the wrist-kissing scene in *The Age of Innocence*) the fetishistic emphasis in the Ada/Baines exchanges is on the juxtaposition of clothes and body. The forbidding Victorian woman's garments become elaborate mechanisms for getting closer to her, as when Baines, crouching under the piano, raises Ada's hoops and feels with his rough fingertip the spot of flesh exposed by a hole in her worsted stocking. If such contact was simply initiated by the man this would indeed remain a rather artful but traditional striptease, but the woman's active participation in this clothes dialogue is what renders it unconventional. The striptease sequences in *The Piano* conform to how several writers have viewed female fetishism as more interested in forging links between the fetish and the desired sexual object. Brand, for example, in reference to a case from the 1890s in which a widow became fixated on her dead husband's gloves, comments that the direct association between the fetish and the desired (in this instance) man 'is typical of the female psyche which tends always to fix on one person and for whom sexual symbols are relatively unimportant save in their ability to bring the lover closer' (Brand 1970: 67).[10]

The Piano, enforcing a simple inversion of the normative process, addresses the question of what happens when the agent of the gaze is female and its object is the male body. It is in the film's representation of Ada's desire that *The Piano* adopts comparably fetishistic stylistic techniques to *The Age of Innocence*, notably the use of luscious golden light and fluid camera movements for the sequences that focus on the bodies of both Stewart and Baines. There are two such scenes in *The Piano* which most notably demonstrate female desire of the male body (for the film is unquestioningly heterosexual) and the subsequent feminisation of that body as the conventional scopophilic roles are reversed. One positions Ada as the subject of the eroticising gaze and shows her stroking Stewart's body as he lies half asleep. The contextualisation of this action emphasises, on a literal level, Ada's control over Stewart. The exchange also carries the more abstract connotation that Ada, through her relationship with Baines, has discovered an attraction for the male body. An example of the reversal of the traditional voyeuristic dynamic in which the intermediary figure of Ada is dispensed with occurs as the naked Baines is presented dusting and caressing the piano (which is, by its direct association with her, a fetish substitute for Ada). This image of the private, naked Baines who is classically unaware of being looked at, directly confronts the spectator-voyeur with an unconventional representation of masculinity as the object of the female gaze. Baines (in what is a feminist inversion of Laura Mulvey's theorisation of the voyeur/object male/female relationship) is placed 'in direct erotic rapport with the (implicitly female) spectator' (Mulvey 1975: 311). For most of the film Stewart and Baines are oppositional images constructed as the expressions of Ada's desire; the sensualisation of Stewart's body is, therefore, unexpected because it uses many of the same features as the scenes between Ada and Baines, most notably the erotic play between garments and exposed flesh. Furthermore, Stewart's nakedness, like Baines's, is bathed in a lusciously sensuous orange light. *The Piano*, particularly in the two scenes in which Ada caresses Stewart,[11] has set down a radical challenge to the normative gender organisation exemplified by *Picnic at Hanging Rock*.

As Ada is demonstrably capable of fetishism and of possessing the active, scopophilic gaze the traditional paradigms with which the discussion of fetishism and *Picnic at Hanging Rock* started need to be reassessed. A demonstrable piece of women's cinema such as *The Piano* (Campion herself eschews the attribution 'feminist') challenges the conventional male assumptions about fetishism as articulated by Freud and psychologists such as Flügel and Krafft-Ebing who developed and extended his ideas. Freud's understanding of fetishism was motivated by a desire to explicate male sexuality, and as such saw women as passive fetish objects who stood for and expressed a libido which was exclusively male. Peter Weir's *Picnic at Hanging Rock* is a male fantasy which continues this patriarchal tradition in which Miranda and the other girls are the eroticised substitutes for the veiled phallus. This view of fetishism as pertaining only to the active male sexual drive is questioned by a fashion commentator such as Kunzle who, in his discussion of the secret dialogues between women concerning tight-lacing, refutes the belief that women are not fetishists. If one further links Kunzle's argument to that posited by Foucault in *A History of Sexuality*, then the possibility of clothes as sexual discourse becomes solidified. Such a discourse is predominantly aligned with a female sexuality and point of identification, as official histories of sexuality have tended to disregard active, feminine eroticism and to likewise view women's clothes as representative of a passive, repressed pattern of desire. Gamman and Makinen, for instance, question the statistical evidence (used by Freud, Krafft-Ebing and others) which suggests that women are not active fetishists, asking '[c]ould the importance that is attributed to fetishism be because it is located so firmly on the protection and valorisation of the phallus?' (Gamman and Makinen 1994: 103). From a feminist perspective, Gamman and Makinen counter Freud's theory that a fetish is the substitute for the mother's castrated penis, although, as I have indicated, his model holds true for certain male-orientated fantasies such as *Picnic at Hanging Rock*.

The sexualisation of costume, from 1940s historical melodramas to *The Piano*, similarly stems from an acknowledgement that such a pattern of female fetishism exists and can be articulated. In a broader sense, however, all three films discussed in this chapter respond positively to fetishism because of its inherent, complex ambiguity. The attraction for Wharton (and Scorsese after her), for example, is towards distance, difference and the simultaneous avowal and disavowal of eroticism. The overriding preoccupation with detail in *The Age of Innocence* derives from a fascination with the power of displacement and metaphor, and the concomitant emphasis on what is left unstated rather than what is stated. In *Harper's Bazaar* Wharton once remarked:

> I have often sighed, in looking back at my childhood, how pitiful provision was made for the life of the imagination behind those uniform brown facades, and then have concluded since, for reasons which escape us, the creative mind thrives best on a reduced diet, I probably had the fare best suited to me.
>
> (Scorsese and Cocks 1993: 183)

The clothes discourse in *The Age of Innocence* and *The Piano* is reliant on the imagination, on the power of allusion over statement. In this, the use of period costume resembles the ostensibly dissimilar function of couture designs in films. Both groups of films put in place an alternative, independent dialogue between costumes and the spectator. Subsequent chapters will examine more specific ways in which such a discourse has been continued and expanded.

Part II
GENDER

3

THE INSTABILITIES OF THE FRANCO-AMERICAN GANGSTER
Scarface to *Pulp Fiction, Casino, Leon*

Throughout the gangster genre clothes are equated with status, money and style. In the opening scene of *Little Caesar*, two small-time crooks dream of becoming big-time gangsters. Joe turns to Rico and muses, 'Gee, the clothes I could wear!'. Clothes are also over-valued objects of fetishism, which symbolise the gangster's identity. In Jean-Pierre Melville's *Le Doulos*, Jean loses a fragment of his trench-coat as it gets stuck in a car door, and the piece of cloth turns out to be a vital police clue. Even such apparently innocuous damage to the gangster's appearance signals his vulnerability. The trait that distinguishes the screen gangster from the majority of other masculine archetypes is his overt narcissism, manifested by a preoccupation with the appearance of others and a self-conscious regard for his own. The fixation on style and superficiality that characterises the gangster genre as a whole is particularly evident in the reflective relationship between the American and French traditions, the mutual scavenging, cross-referencing and straight copying that has been perpetrated since the French cinema of the 1950s began to express its fondness for Americana (itself a fetishism of detail). The ultimate focus of this discussion is the gangster film today, but, in such an intro-verted and self-conscious genre, the look of Martin Scorsese's Mafia movies, or the postmodern eclecticism of *Reservoir Dogs*, *Pulp Fiction* and *Leon* needs to be contextualised in terms of history and generic evolution. The Franco-American context, for instance, is important to both Tarantino and Besson: Tarantino makes specific reference to the films of Melville, Godard and Truffaut, and Besson, after making chic crime films like *Subway* and *Nikita* in France, has set *Leon* in New York and is currently working on a remake of *The Driver*. Walter Hill's *The Driver* is, in turn, a remake of a French thriller of the 1960s, Jean-Pierre Melville's *Le Samouraï*. This limited sequence of films attests to one important area of overlap between the French and American crime film traditions, namely the number of copy-cat texts that have been made. To name but a few: *A bout de souffle* has been remade as *Breathless*, *Nikita* as *The Assassin*, *The Killing* as *23h58*. There are also, in

67

these films and others, specific allusions to the other country's tradition, such as the appearance of French actress Isabelle Adjani in *The Driver* and Butch's French wife in *Pulp Fiction*, or the use of American women in both *À bout de souffle* and *Le Samouraï*, none of which serve any narrative purpose. Similarly inconsequential to the action but significant to the iconographic framework of these gangster films is the predilection for citing details from past films. The extreme close-up of 'The Wolf' ringing Jimmie's doorbell in *Pulp Fiction*, for example, echoes the three-edit sequence showing Charles Aznavour likewise ringing a doorbell in Truffaut's *Tirez sur le Pianiste*, whilst Silien's brief visit to his stables at the end of Melville's *Le Doulos* recalls the final shot of Huston's *The Asphalt Jungle*. The individual film-makers, therefore, are keen to perpetuate the self-consciousness of the genre, and, to be inferred from this mutual veneration, even Roger Avary's shambolic American in the Paris heist film *Killing Zoë*, is an essential narcissism that informs most aspects of the genre's overall development. The clothes and identity of the gangster have evolved along similar lines to the genre as a whole, the definitive screen gangster look having been constructed with the major Hollywood pictures of the 1930s and 1940s, ironically critiqued and cited in the French films of the 1950s and 1960s and shown to be disintegrating in the 1980s and 1990s.

Men's dress is usually considered to be innately stable and to lack the 'natural tendency to change' of women's clothes, displaying instead, by virtue of being functional rather than decorative, a tendency to 'stereotype itself' and 'adopt the uniform of a profession' (Laver 1945: 185–6). There is also, therefore, the suspicion with which flamboyant male dressers like dandies and dudes have traditionally been viewed, because 'real men' are not supposed to be narcissistically preoccupied with their clothes and appearance. As Jennifer Craik affirms, men's fashion has been a contradiction in terms:

> Accordingly, the rhetoric of men's fashion takes the form of a set of denials that include the following propositions: that there is no men's fashion; that men dress for fit and comfort, rather than for style; that women dress men and buy clothes for men; that men who dress up are peculiar (one way or another); that men do not notice clothes; and that most men have not been duped into the endless pursuit of seasonal fads.

> (Craik 1994: 176)

The most repeated assumption about men's clothes held by fashion historians and writers such as Flügel, Quentin Bell or Laver is that men worthy of the name are not interested in fashion, and that the non-expressive uniformity which has by and large characterised male dress codes since the early 1800s is the result of a belief that 'overt interest in clothing and appearance implied a tendency towards unmanliness and effeminacy' (Breward 1995: 171).[1] Men's allegiance to functional and more professionally orientated dress codes is conventionally presumed to attest to an overwhelming impulse to conform, to blend in with the crowd as Newland Archer does in his grey suit and bowler hat in *The Age of Innocence*. Darian Leader begins the psychoanalytic ruminations of *Why Do Women Write More Letters Than They Post?* with just such an observation, claiming:

> While most men like to be included in generalisations, many women don't. This fact is well known to retailers: if you want to sell a coat to a man, you can tell him that everyone in the City or on Wall Street is wearing it, but if you want to sell it to a woman, it is better to say, on the contrary, that no one is wearing it.
>
> (Leader 1996: vii)

Vanity in a man also came to signify evil and degeneracy (the most obsessively narcissistic gangster is often the most violent), until the acceptance of style-conscious men in the 1980s which problematised everything. Masculine attire, traditionally characterised by consistency, functionality and durability, is exemplified by the suit. Supposedly symbolic of traditional manliness, this ubiquitous garment, as one writer suggests, 'denotes holding back personal feelings, or self-restraint, and focusing energy on achieving organisational goals, or goal-directed behaviour' (Rubinstein 1995: 58). It is interesting that, unlike restrictive feminine clothing, readily taken to be shimmering with furtive erotic potential, comparably limiting masculine dress is perceived to be blandly straightforward: the suited man is dependable, the dandy is not.

Such puritanism, and the normative disassociation of men from narcissistic self-admiration, has similarly controlled too many discussions of the desexualised representation of men in cinema. Laura Mulvey's prescriptive assertion, 'According to the principles of the ruling ideology and the psychical structures that back it up, the male figure cannot bear the burden of sexual objectification. Man is reluctant to gaze at his exhibitionist like' has remained hugely influential (Mulvey 1975: 310). In the early 1980s Steve Neale, in his essay 'Masculinity as spectacle', applied Mulvey's arguments concerned primarily with the eroticisation of the female form in mainstream cinema to the representation of men, suggesting that the explicitly erotic look at the male body is deflected and disavowed within classical narratives through the use of action and other legitimising tactics, so 'We are offered the spectacle of male bodies, but bodies unmarked as objects of erotic display' (Neale 1983: 18). Neale's conclusions arise from a similar adherence to rigid gender boundaries as Mulvey, culminating in the claim that only the 'feminised' man (not a category that is adequately explained) 'is presented quite explicitly as the object of an erotic look' (18). The notion of the desexualised male body is a firmly held but flimsily proven truism that can be contested, from the perspectives of both fashion and representation, with reference to the figure of the gangster. So many screen gangsters invite comments about their appearance, show themselves off, openly admire each other's clothes and are obsessively consumed by their own image, as to question such opinions about male representation. However, neither do these gangsters, in any meaningful way, lapse into the category of the 'feminised' man, and although they are men of action, they are also men of fashion.

When considering the costumes of the screen gangster the spectator is struck by this ambivalence, that here are characters who have both cultivated an aggressively masculine image and are immensely vain, and whose sartorial flamboyance, far from intimating femininity or effeminacy, is the most important sign of their masculine social and material success. The screen gangster's narcissism has an actual reference point in the attitudes to clothes of their real-life prototypes, which is subsequently transferred to the attention paid to costume detail in the films. Robert de Niro, for instance, stipulated that he wished to be dressed, when playing Al Capone in *The Untouchables*, by Capone's old tailor, and even demanded the same Sulk and Son silk boxer shorts. As genres go, gangster films are notably defined by superficiality and attention to detail. Colin McArthur divides the 'recurrent patterns of imagery' that permeate the genre into three categories, two that concern the iconography of the gangsters' milieux and the technology (such as cars and guns) at their disposal, and one that surrounds 'the physical presence, attributes and dress of the actors and the characters they play' (McArthur 1972: 23–4). Extending even to Leon, there is a pronounced consistency in terms of appearance, the gangster persona having been developed and refined, particularly since the mutual homages of the French and American traditions began, into an outwardly stereotypical role.

In *Mythologies* Roland Barthes comments:

> Myth does not deny things, on the contrary its function is to talk about them; simply, it purifies them, it makes them innocent, it gives them a natural and eternal justification, it gives them a clarity which is not that of an explanation but that of a statement of fact.
>
> (Barthes 1957: 156)

Barthes' idea of myths being created through the process of speech and identification is borne out by the development of the mythologised gangster. The gangster's identity, or rather his imagined identity, is created out of, to use Jacques Lacan's discussion of the ego, 'the superimposition of various coats borrowed from what I will call the bric-a-brac of its props department' (Lacan 1954–5: 155). Each screen gangster is defined, largely iconographically, against his predecessors and, more importantly, is shown to be consciously striving to emulate that mythologised ideal by obsessively judging how he looks in front of an actual mirror or through the approval of others. In this the distinguishing clothes a gangster wears are (with few exceptions) mandatory. So, for example, when Henry in *Goodfellas* returns home in his first flashy suit and the camera pans slowly up his body, his horrified mother inevitably exclaims, 'My God, you look like a gangster'. The myth of the gangster is proclaimed and codified by the way he dresses, the suit, hat, accessories and trenchcoat being the most common identifying marks of his status. As McArthur suggests, the gangsters' square outline 'is an extension of their physical presence, a visual shorthand for their violent potential' (McArthur 1972: 26). When considering the interrelationship between clothes and art history Anne Hollander remarks, 'One might say that individual appearances in clothes are not 'statements', as they are often called, but more like public readings of literary works in different genres of which the rules are generally understood' (Hollander 1975: xv), a notion that is pertinent also to cinematic genres with their rules and perpetual modifications. The 'rules' that assist the mythologisation and are translated from one film to the next usually facilitate the easy and immediate identification of the composite screen gangster, a figure who wants recognition as a gangster and, as so many of them say, to stand out.

This desire to conform to an already established model that will be instantly identifiable to characters and spectators alike is conventionally distilled into shorthand devices like the use of nick-names in gangster films up to and including the 'Mr' men of *Reservoir Dogs*. A more evocative example is the genre's recurrent use of silhouettes, shadows or outlines as signifiers of the stereotype. Silhouettes and shadows are used traditionally as *doppelgängers*, as in the German Expressionist films of the 1920s and 1930s. Although visually reminiscent of *Nosferatu* and *M*, for example, a film such as *Scarface* uses the shadow or silhouette as a complex metaphor symbolising not just the gangster's repressed side, but the abstraction of the myth or ideal he both constructed and strives to live up to. In a minor crime movie such as *Bullets or Ballots*, in which chiaroscuro lighting accompanies Humphrey Bogart wherever he goes, the shadow (even creeping up Murnau-esque stairs) is a straightforward suspense device to signal the imminent arrival of the gangster. The symbolic function of the silhouette is, like much else, emphasised and stylised to excess by the French films of the 1950s and 1960s. Through the wet windscreen of his stolen car at the beginning of *Le Samouraï*, Alain Delon's etched outline (the felt hat, trenchcoat and cigarette) instantly proclaims his identity. Melville's play on the irony of the shadow (that it is both iconic and empty, to be feared and a trick of the light) is carried to almost self-parodying extremes in *Le Doulos*, as, in the semi-darkness, one gangster's silhouette is mistaken for another, and the wrong man is shot. The shadow crucially elides the abstract and the corporeal. The overriding tension of the genre, as it constructs and upholds the mythic gangster, is between the unresolv-able desires of each character to assert individuality, whilst paradoxically seeking to conform to the idealised silhouette. This collision is exemplified by the heist movie (*Rififi*, *The Asphalt Jungle*, *Reservoir Dogs*) in which the bringing together of disparate (and often desperate) individuals and the imposition of an uneasy uniformity ultimately prove fatal.

This tension between conformity and difference is similarly prevalent, particularly in the Prohibition films of the early 1930s, in the traditional gangster's mode of dress, which is both derivative of and distinguishable from the dress styles of the contemporary gentleman. In his chapter on underworld fashion, the French fashion historian Farid Chenoune notes that the elegance of the legitimate businessman and that of the 1930s and 1940s gangster (in both America and France) were never comparable, because 'dark ties on light shirts are as different from light ties on dark shirts as day from night' (Chenoune 1993: 196). Gangsters, therefore, are expensively dressed but can nevertheless be told apart, so Jean Gabin in *Pépé le Moko* is proclaiming his status through his black shirt and cravat, just as Richard Widmark is through his dark shirts and light ties in the 1950s. The underworld developed its own exaggerated style, patronising certain tailors who produced exclusive mobster clothes, like the Marseilles shirt-maker Séverin who specialised in silk shirts with the customers' initials embroidered on the breast. Such attention to detail, which Chenoune rather censoriously observes, 'betrayed a certain coarseness' (Chenoune 1993: 196), is something which many of the costume-orientated films utilise, inserting shots which are, in narrative terms, irrelevant. In *Miller's Crossing*, for example, there is a leisurely close-up of Leo's embroidered slippers before he goes downstairs to blast his potential ambushers. The clothes-fetishist gangster is identified instantly by such details, as in *Some Like it Hot* when all that is required to denote the arrival of an important mobster is an unblemished pair of spats. Another affectation of the real gangster that is mimicked in the films is his penchant for excessive colour coordination, every accessory matching the suit and coat. The use of white or off-white ensembles to denote extreme brutality probably derives directly from Al Capone. Both the real and the fictionalised gangster, therefore, occupy a paradoxical position in relation to fashion: whilst they appropriate the styles of high fashion, they do not ultimately want to blend in or be lost in it, so they cultivate 'an identifiable school of stylishness that, far from operating as camouflage, ultimately functioned like warrior dress' (Chenoune 1993: 196). It should not be forgotten, though, that however vulgar mob fashions were deemed to be, in the 1920s and 1930s the styles were, like many others in America, hugely influenced by the sartorial experimentations of the iconic Prince of Wales, whose trips to America in those years were reported daily in the fashion pages. The future Edward VIII was particularly fond of combining loud, dissonant colours and mixing patterns, checks and stripes, so the ensemble Tony Camonte is sporting in *Scarface* when Poppy exclaims 'that outfit's enough to give anybody the yips' would not have been untypical of him.

3.1 Paul Muni as Tony Camonte in *Scarface*
Courtesy of BFI Stills, Posters and Designs

The archetypal screen gangster was born in the 1930–33 period in Hollywood with such films as *Little Caesar*, *Public Enemy* and *Scarface*; in the years, therefore, immediately prior to the Volstead ('Prohibition') Act being repealed in 1933 and the tightening in 1934 of the Hays Code guidelines concerned with the representation of violence. The ubiquitous impeccably dressed and violent narcissist created in these films also symbolised a response to the erosion of masculinity that

73

occurred in the Depression years. In a parody of the American dream, the films characteristically chart the rise and fall of the immigrant, underprivileged small-time crook who climbs the 'queer ladder of social mobility' (Bell D. 1960: 115) to become a successful gangster, only to die the ambiguous tragic hero. This social ascent is again clearly signalled through costume. As 'the most reliably consistent trait of movie gangsters was their sartorial progression from dark and wrinkled nondescript clothing to flashy, double-breasted, custom-tailored striped suits with silk ties and suitable jewellery' (Rosow 1978: 185), the transition point from petty hoodlum to successful mobster is often the acquisition of a new wardrobe. The gangster's new-found power is put on display, crudely shown off, often in a scene that shows him getting fitted for a suit, as in *Public Enemy* when Tom (James Cagney) visits a tailor after executing his first big alcohol raid. In the subsequent scene he and Matt arrive transformed at a club, wearing their full finery of Homburg, belted coat, suit and breast-pocket silk handkerchief. Although this grand entrance echoes the traditionally feminine Cinderella scenario, the spectator is emphatically reminded that the gangsters' exquisite clothes signify desirable (rather than dubious) masculinity when Tom and Matt immediately prove able to pull two girls away from 'the couple of lightweights' they are with. The most outrageous of the peacock gangsters is Tony Camonte in *Scarface*, who is so impressed by Johnnie Lovo's dressing gown ('Hey, that's pretty hot. . . . Expensive, huh?') that the first thing he shows off when *he* gets rich is his own very similar one. Tony's rapid rise, like Tom's, is signposted by his transformed wardrobe. He buys loud suits, jewellery and tissue-wrapped shirts in bulk, bragging to Poppy, for instance, that he intends to wear each of his new shirts only once. The 1930s gangster's continuing rise is further marked by ever more refined accessories and details, and often he is shown (as is the case with Tony) in full evening dress when he is at the height of his powers.

The gangster's increased power being signalled by his expanding wardrobe problematises many of the conventional assumptions about men and fashion this chapter initially identified, not least the belief that the more narcissistic, the less butch the man. In his discussion of Annie Leibovitz's portrait of Clint Eastwood (in casual clothes and bound in rope) Paul Smith includes 'the careless ordinariness of his J.C. Penney clothing' among the features that 'contribute to Eastwood's presence within this culture as one of the more legitimated bearers of its masculinity, "real" or otherwise' (Smith 1995: 78). To be inferred from Eastwood's T-shirt, cords and trainers, is that he is a man of action with no time for vanity, and that fashion is for the idle. A refreshing alternative view was offered in the 1920s by Gerald Heard in *Narcissus: An Anatomy of Clothes* in which he begins by casting suspicion on those men who, when they visit the tailor, give the impression that they do not care about clothes, accusing such men of 'practising a sustained deceit'. Heard continues by disputing the antithesis between decoration and use (arguing, quaintly, that a tiger is no less efficient than a non-stripy cat) and asking, 'When did people begin to think a splendid and striking appearance betrayed a poor and vulgar mind?' (Heard 1924: 10–11). Heard later comments, however, that 'the study of clothes . . . suggests the rise of a complete self-consciousness' (21), suggesting, therefore, that an obsession with clothes parallels a growing absorption with the self rather than others.

Freud, in his essay 'On narcissism', refers to an antithesis between ego-libido and object-libido, that 'The more of the one is employed, the more the other becomes depleted' (Freud 1914: 68), and thus how, in the narcissist, the attraction to the self takes over from the attraction to others. This transferral of sexual energy away from the expected attraction to others (in this context the 'right woman') is already implied by the traditional gangster's sexual dysfunctionalism: for example, Tony Camonte's incestuous attraction for his sister Cesca, Rico's latent homosexuality in *Little Caesar*, and the tragic love triangle between Eddie, Panama and Jean in *The Roaring Twenties*. Sexual energy is similarly displaced onto clothes, the mutual admiration between gangsters frequently being expressed through an excessive attraction for each other's sumptuous garments (witness the scene in *Scarface* in which Tony feels Johnnie Lovo's dressing gown). This over-identification with appearance and the open display of fetishistic interest in each other's clothes has obvious homoerotic undertones, signifying a dual attraction for a man who the gangster both desires and wants to become. Further into his essay Freud lists what, according to the narcissistic type, a person may love as: 'what he himself is, what he himself was, what he himself would like to be, someone who was part of himself' (Freud 1914: 84). This simultaneous refraction and condensation of the image in the construction of an 'ideal ego' offers a productive way of extending the instabilities of the gangster beyond the American model, where competition and emulation are clearly foregrounded, towards the French gangster who is caught obsessively measuring his actual ego by the ego ideal he himself has created from past cinematic images.

In Godard's first film *A bout de souffle*, the protagonist Michel Poiccard (Jean-Paul Belmondo) is obsessed with American crime films. In one of its defining moments, Michel looks up at Humphrey Bogart's image on the poster for *The Harder They Fall* and murmurs 'Bogie' to his idol. He then becomes mesmerised by a publicity still of Bogart, stares back at it and imitates Bogie's gesture of running his thumb across his lips. Whereas the American criminals of the 1930s to 1950s were straightforwardly narcissistic, the comparable gangsters in the French films of the 1950s and 1960s are overtly reflective, taking the earlier Hollywood films as their common reference points and engaging in a mannered, self-conscious way with a specifically cinematic history. Michel, accumulating layers of Lacanian bric-a-brac, exemplifies this self-consciousness as he creates for himself a composite gangster ideal, appropriating the 'ideal' by collapsing the boundaries between his icon (the cinematic stereotype) and himself. From the moment Michel kills the cop at the beginning of *A bout de souffle* with an ostentatiously old-fashioned Colt revolver, he has constructed his own American B-movie around him; he embodies 'Bogie'. As with Freud's narcissist, Michel is in love with himself, what he (as an abstraction of a cinema gangster) was and what he would like to be (a perfection of the type). He similarly both references and modifies the conventional attire of the gangster, wearing a felt snap-brim hat (albeit a Trilby at a very jaunty, un-Bogart-esque angle), a loud check jacket and shades. The gangster has retreated into his own image and become a statement, his character has become distilled into a series of citations and gestures that, without the (fictional) original, would not exist.

Costumes in this context do not support but rather substitute characterisation. These men become gangsters when they look like gangsters, when their outline fits the mythical silhouette. As Heard suggests when saying, 'changes take place first in the outer and so pass to the inner' (Heard 1924: 40), appearance in some instances affects character or personality, not vice versa. The French film gangsters offer a meta-commentary on their American prototypes' dependency on appearance for an identity, both mimicking and critiquing their vanity and obsession with the right clothes. This is frequently achieved comically, as in the sequence in *A bout de souffle* when, on seeing Michel in the street, the first thing a friend does is to reprimand him for putting silk socks and a tweed jacket together, forcing Michel to defend his dress sense. Truffaut once commented that, having started shooting *Tirez sur le Pianiste*, he realised he disliked the gangster genre and so began treating it ironically, a reaction that clearly impinges on the car scene towards the end of the film in which Fido's kidnappers brag about the mythical luxury gadgets they can now afford: an air-conditioned hat, a London suit made from Australian wool, Egyptian leather-ventilated shoes and a tie that feels like silk but is made out of metal.

The gangster has been reduced to a silhouette, a series of metonyms that, as shorthand, signify and substitute for the whole. In his armoury the most consistent of the overdetermined accessories is the essential sharp felt hat. Taking his prompt from Freud's 'A hat is a symbol of a man (or of male genitals)' (Freud 1911: 478–80), James Laver, in one of his wilder speculative moments, develops the idea that the hat is a 'symbol of potent masculinity', maintaining that it is possible to gauge the curve of women's emancipation 'from the height of men's hats'. Laver's argument posits that, in the 1850s when male domination was at its height, so were men's hats, hence the popularity of the top hat. Towards the end of the nineteenth century, however, 'men began to wear, so to speak, the very symbol of their bashed-in authority: the Trilby hat'. Laver concludes his discussion by further suggesting that women wearing hats (as opposed to bonnets, which he saw as a sign of 'submission to male authority') was a defiant gesture by which they were symbolically saying 'votes for women' (Laver 1969: 121–3). As if they too have read the same pages of *The Interpretation of Dreams*, several screen gangsters form disproportionate attachments to their hats, although some of them unfortunately have to make do with a literally bashed-in Trilby like Sterling Hayden in *The Asphalt Jungle*. In *Scarface* Tony Camonte's secretary (a sort of parody of a parody Italian) adjusts his Homburg in front of the mirror before answering the telephone; he then removes his hat, lifts up the receiver and promptly proceeds to talk into the wrong end. Without his hat he's nothing.

In the 1930s 'doulos' or 'bitos' became French gangster slang for 'hat', and, as Melville's *Le Doulos* states at the beginning, 'doulos' also came to mean 'police informer'. Melville's criminals are frequently shown checking their reflections and adjusting their clothes, Bob in *Bob le Flambeur*, for example, or Jef in *Le Samouraï*, but nowhere is the hat as much of an overdetermined object as in *Le Doulos*. Although the attachment is never spelt out, there is a clear symbolic affiliation between Silien (Belmondo) and his flat-crowned Trilby. Two moments in the film are particularly significant in this respect. On arriving at the Americanised jazz bar The Cotton Club Silien deposits his trenchcoat and hat at the cloakroom. This seemingly insignificant action is made significant by the manner in which it is filmed. Belmondo takes his hat off and places it on the counter, holding it very precisely at the peak of the crown, a gesture that the cloakroom attendant copies directly as she takes up the hat and puts it on the shelf behind her, finally tucking a number 13 ticket into its ribbon. Melville stresses the opaque importance of this moment by following the movement of Silien's hat in close-up and resting on it (rather than the characters) at the end of the shot. The other loaded hat moment occurs in the last scene of the film as the fatally wounded Silien staggers over to a telephone, calls his girlfriend to tell her he will not be going round that night, checks his reflection in the mirror then dies. Again, Melville's degree of stylisation adds an alternative dimension to this otherwise traditional denouement. Belmondo's face and hat are perfectly enclosed by the small mirror at the centre of a heavy gilt frame, and the camera rests on this image as he scrutinises his reflection, raises his hat to smooth his hair, replaces it then slumps out of frame. The ironic theatricality of this end, the needless fetishisation of detail, is Silien's final recognition of the importance of appearance; he wants to go down looking like a perfect gangster. This vain ritual, however, is undercut by the final shot of the film: the upturned (useless, empty) hat resting on the floor.

In *A bout de souffle* Melville plays a writer who declares, at a press conference, that his ambition is to become immortal and then die. This honour is in danger of being bequeathed to the gangsters' hats not the gangsters. The Coen brothers' *Miller's Crossing* is another self-reflective film (this time referring back to the American films of the 1930s) that dwells on the gangster's over-identification with his hat. Hat imagery runs through *Miller's Crossing*, as an elusive chain of coded

3.2 Jean-Paul Belmondo as Silien in *Le Doulos*
Courtesy of BFI Stills, Posters and Designs

references to egos and alter egos. In the title sequence an immaculate Fedora, carried by gusts of wind, wafts through an autumnal wood and comes to rest, in close-up, amongst the leaves. The Fedora, associated throughout *Miller's Crossing* with Tom (Gabriel Byrne), becomes an insistent symbol of his masculinity and integrity, thus his only moments of vulnerability are when he is temporarily separated from his headwear. In absurd, nightmarish 'fort-da' fashion, Tom loses and regains his hat many times in the course of the film. He gambles it away, has it knocked off his head in several fights and even has a dream (echoing the title sequence) in which a gust of wind seizes it; and yet it always comes back. In his last gesture of the film, after saying goodbye to the Irish gang leader Leo, he pulls his (unscathed) Fedora particularly low over his forehead, obscuring most of his face. In this small, ostensibly meaningless gesture Tom indicates the desperation of the gangster whose identity is so caught up in his hat that losing it, having it wrested from his head, would mean losing himself.

In Melville's *Le Samouraï* the hit man Jef Costello performs a ritual each time he leaves his flat: he looks at himself in the mirror and runs his finger and thumb along the brim of his Trilby. *Le Samouraï* is a film constructed around gestures rather than words. For the first ten minutes there is no dialogue (which is why, reputedly, Delon immediately accepted the part of Jef [Nogueira 1971: 129]), and Jef, who eschews verbal and emotional communication, exists as an icon comprising a limited range of perfect clothes and precise actions. This cold, analytical film charts the inevitable disintegration of a mythic masculinity, an implosion directly signalled through his clothes. Referring to *Bob le Flambeur* Melville comments:

> There is a moment of truth in all my films. A man before a mirror means a stock-taking. When he walks up the rue Pigalle at the beginning of the film, it's in front of a rusty mirror that Bob mutters to himself: 'A fine hoodlum face!' With that phrase he sums up his entire life.
>
> (Nogueira 1971: 54–5)

Jef's routine scrutiny of his own reflection is a security measure. His image is his identity, and at the start of *Le Samouraï* it is refined and complete. Every subsequent moment of crisis in the film is marked by the fragmentation of Jef's self-possessed image – the repeated removal, either by others or by himself out of necessity, of crucial identifying garments such as his black Italian-style suit, Trilby and trenchcoat. The first potential crisis occurs during the line-ups in a Paris police station, Jef having been called in after a local night-club owner has been killed. At the first line-up Jef, looking rather ostentatiously like the only potential hit man, is positioned between an absurdly dissimilar group of both women and men, and, despite having been clearly seen after the shooting, is not identified. In the second line-up he and this time similar men swap garments in order to confuse the witnesses. This time, however, another witness is immediately able to put together the correct 'composite image' of Jef's face, hat and trenchcoat, Costello's rebus clues for 'gangster'.

Jef Costello's fallibility is rooted in his over-reliance on his image. He not only, as Freud outlines in *The Ego and the Id*, identifies with and introjects the attributes he sees in others (namely past gangster icons), transforming them through his unconscious to create his ego's 'ideals', he lacks any sense of an identity beyond those appropriated 'ideals'. Like Lacan's uncoordinated infant for whom 'the mirror-image would seem to be the threshold of the visible world' (Lacan 1949: 3) and who generates a unified sense of selfhood by making an imaginary identification with the whole reflection, Jef imposes and constantly identifies with the superficially self-sufficient image he has constructed for himself. As Lacan suggests, however, the unity projected by this mirror-image is an illusory consoling device that only appears to offer an emboldening correlation between the subject and the imagined ideal. The infant, like Jef, *mis*-recognises him/herself in that total form, the mirror stage being described by Lacan as a drama 'which manufactures for the subject, caught up in the lure of spatial identification, the succession of phantasies that extends from a fragmented body image to a form of its totality. . . . and lastly, to the assumption of the armour of an alienating identity' (4). Jef Costello serves as the epigrammatic distillation of the cinema gangster myth, a figure whose identity is signalled only by his superficial adherence to an imaginary, fictional and ultimately destructive ideal. As Lacan comments in 'Aggressivity in psychoanalysis', the 'human individual fixes himself upon an image that alienates himself from himself' (Lacan 1948: 19).

Jef wanders aloof through *Le Samouraï* as if defying his inevitable entry into the Symbolic where the falsity and fragmentation of the Imaginary ego is confirmed, defiantly denying speech and social communication in the knowledge, presumably, that such interaction will defeat him. The use of space and physical barriers are important in this respect, paralleling in part the significance of the archetypal clothes, as Jef is only secure when inside his apartment shut off from the outside world. When that space is invaded by the bugs planted by the cops, although he finds the devices easily, Jef's vulnerability is exposed. These spatial intrusions mirror the critical dissolution of Jef's sartorial image, moments of crisis in *Le Samouraï* being marked by the gradual, painful fragmentation of the initial Trilby, suit and trenchcoat 'ideal'. The crisis moment that graphically embodies Jef's inevitable disintegration occurs after he has been shot going to collect his money for the hit job at the beginning of the film. For the only time, Jef is forced to remove his 'suit of armour' in order to dress the bullet wound. In terms of clothes iconography this is a complex sequence. Fashion or clothes often seem to substitute an ideal body for the real body, and the sight of Delon's real body in a white T-shirt doubly signals Jef's vulnerability and the loss of his ideal, as he has become both the incomplete gangster and the object of the erotic gaze (the white

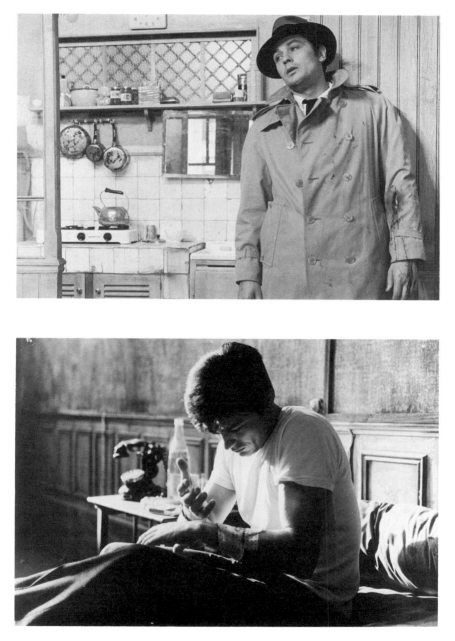

3.3 Alain Delon as Jef Costello, shot through his trenchcoat in *Le Samouraï* and Alain
Delon nursing his wound in *Le Samouraï*
Courtesy of BFI Stills, Posters and Designs

T-shirt conventionalised within cinema as an article of clothing that legitimately sexualises the male form).

From this scene on, Jef is no longer impregnable (he is, after all, forced to exchange his trenchcoat for another coat after being shot), and, as he becomes increasingly more desperate, so even his restabilised appearance signals his frailty. This new discrepancy between ego and ideal is emphasised during the protracted chase sequence through the Metro. At a time when it would be sensible, one would think, to travel incognito, Jef defiantly asserts his old gangster image by never even removing his give-away hat, as if it is this that still renders him whole. The elements that have fatally collided for Jef are his imagined and his actual identities; as Graham Dawson comments (in an essay about Lawrence of Arabia and British masculinity), 'Masculine identities are lived out in the flesh, but fashioned in the imagination' (Dawson, G. 1991: 118). Jef has made up, imagined an identity that is only impregnable *in* that imagination, as his suicidal reassembly and elaboration of his gangster image at the end of *Le Samouraï* emphasises. Clad in full battle gear of black coat, felt hat and pristine white gloves,[2] and carrying an unloaded gun to indicate that he has no intention of carrying out his final job, Jef arrives at the American bar ostensibly to shoot the pianist. Looking so much the part of the quintessential hit man he is inevitably, target practice-like, shot dead.

The self-conscious posturing of the excessively cool Michel Poiccard and Jef Costello exemplify an ambivalent attitude to the mythic gangster, both ironic and reverential. There is something precariously pathetic about Jef's earnestness, that Delon, with his 'harsh and pitiless' face (McArthur 1972: 170), is the ultimate French hard man with real underworld friends, whose only sustained relationship in *Le Samouraï* is with his caged, female bullfinch.[3] Jef's fragility is his solitude. Referring to comic book heroes, Peter Middleton comments that, 'Men who become self-sufficient cease to be men' (Middleton 1992: 25); in films such as *A bout de souffle*, *Le Doulos* and *Le Samouraï* the 'heroes' even stage their own reflective deaths. At the end of *A bout de souffle* the wounded Belmondo staggers to precisely the end of the street, takes a last drag of his cigarette and utters 'It really makes you sick' before closing his own eyes. Belmondo and Delon have the last call, because the subject wants to possess the wholeness offered by the mirror image; the motivation of the 'I' is to attempt to halt the process of fragmentation. In reality trying to freeze a developmental, subjective process that cannot be frozen is futile, in fiction it is not. As Melville cryptically utters in *A bout de souffle*, perfection is to attain immortality then die. This is the apotheosis of the gangster, deified by the fictional narrative, not troubled by the realm beyond the myth and still cool in death. It cannot last.

There are two ways in which the 1980s and 1990s French and American films have articulated the disintegration of the mythic gangster: one is by emphasising the tackiness of the *nouveau riche* mob lifestyle and milieux, as *Married to the Mob*,

Goodfellas and *Casino* do; the other is by continuing the French films' self-conscious dismantling of the icon, as occurs in *Reservoir Dogs*, *Pulp Fiction* and *Leon*. Too many problems now crowd in to permit the gangster to 'become immortal and then die', which is still arguably the romantic endeavour of Coppola's *Godfather* trilogy, which is as regressive in its views on organised crime and masculinity as it is in its tuxedo and waistcoat-centred costumes (which, in passing, are so inaccurate that dating the action is not always easy). *Goodfellas* relates ambiguously to its generic predecessors; it feeds into the myth, as perceived through Henry Hill's wide-eyed awe at the beginning, and it shows the flip-side reality of the Mafia's organised crime and increasingly flamboyant sleaze. The central correlative of *Goodfellas* is between violence and wealth, a fusion epitomised in the loud glamour of the mob's clothes. Scorsese himself has confessed to the attraction of this: 'When you're a kid you look and see these guys and they're very interesting people. To a kid they are beautifully and elegantly dressed, and they command a great deal of respect in your small world' (Scorsese 1990: 21). This fascination and awe is transposed to Henry's opening voice-over in *Goodfellas*:

> As far back as I can remember, I always wanted to be a gangster. To me, being a gangster was better than being President of the United States. Even before I wandered into the cab stand for an after-school job, I knew I wanted to be a part of them. It was there that I knew that I belonged, and to me it meant being somebody in a neighbourhood that was full of nobodies.

Henry imagines and craves the immortality; the trajectory of *Goodfellas*, however, progresses towards an end where Henry, far from being immortalised in death, enters the Witness Protection Programme and becomes an 'average nobody' wearing a towelling robe and collecting a paper off his suburban lawn. Although the real Henry Hill maintains he is now 'glad to be a shnook' (Hill 1990: 149), in mythic terms the fictionalised character is worse than dead, he's anonymous.

Scorsese has frequently said that *Goodfellas* is a film about lifestyle. His representation of the American 1960s and 1970s Mafia underworld emphasises realism and superficiality, sidelining the huge event (in *Goodfellas*, the Lufthansa robbery) in favour of the details of the Mafia's quotidian existence. This is a clear echo of the *nouveau riche* values displayed by the 1930s Mafia gangsters such as Tony Camonte, whose first impulse when he makes it big is to indulge in the trappings of instant wealth: silk dressing gowns, loud suits and gaudy furnishings. Unlike the French hit man Jef Costello who kills for money he never seems to spend, Henry Hill and the others in *Goodfellas* (or the equally vulgar families in Jonathan Demme's contemporaneous *Married to the Mob*) want their wealth to be seen and envied. In evoking the allure of wealth Scorsese, as he did with his adaptation of *The Age of Innocence*, fuses film style and narrative detail in *Goodfellas* and its virtual sequel *Casino*[4] to create the spectacle of conspicuous consumption. The stylistic excesses enforce an identification between the spectators and the characters who find themselves irresistibly drawn to the trappings of Mafia wealth. In *Goodfellas*, for example, when Karen, accompanied by the grandiose banality of 'Then He Kissed Me' on the soundtrack, is swept into the Copacabana on her first date with Henry, her enchantment is mirrored by the heady, uncut steadicam shot following her entrance through the club's back rooms to Henry's specially arranged front-row table. There are similarly dynamic, empowering sequences that integrate style and narrative in *Casino* (Ginger throwing the gambling chips in the air, the low-angle shots of de Niro standing over the casino), the purpose of which is captured by Jonathan Romney's review when he refers to this as 'the flashiest, most superficial film Martin Scorsese has ever made – which is to say, it serves its theme brilliantly' (Romney 1996: 40).

Conspicuous consumption has, since Thorstein Veblen's moralistic dissection of the economics of style in *The Theory of the Leisure Class*, been identified as a crucial attribute of fashion. Veblen's thesis is founded on the premise that esteem is granted only if wealth and power are not merely possessed, but flaunted and wasted, and that 'the principle of conspicuous waste requires an obviously futile expenditure; and the resulting conspicuous expensiveness of dress is therefore intrinsically ugly' (Veblen 1925: 124). After noting, with some exasperation, the incompatibility between 'expensiveness' and 'artistic apparel' (by which is meant aesthetically pleasing dress sense), Veblen is forced to conclude that 'restless change' is an end unto itself, and that the instabilities of fashion owe much to being representative proof that the wearer can afford newer (and uglier) clothes.[5] Excess, newness and ugliness are what dominate the Mafia lifestyle and the aesthetic of the films that represent it. The proud display to others of newly acquired wealth and possessions is a ritualistic moment in both *Goodfellas* and *Casino*, as when Karen, now Henry's wife, shows off her false York stone wall or Ginger talks her bemused baby daughter through her jewellery collection. The characters fall in love with wealth. A comparably sensual though vacuous routine is the pan or track along rows of clothes, mesmerising because of their sheer bulk. Veblen emphasises that the woman is the man's functionary or 'chattel', a display cabinet whose consumption is not for her own sustenance but 'contributes to the comfort or the good repute of her master' (Veblen 1925: 62–3). Although in *Casino* this is very much the role Ginger is allotted by both the production (for whom she is the quintessential 'clothes horse') and her husband Ace, who presents her with a fully stocked walk-in wardrobe after their wedding, in general, Scorsese's Mafia men are those who show off their wealth, not just those who generate it. As Karen in *Goodfellas* notices about the Mafia wives at her first hostess party, they 'had bad skin and too much make-up. And the stuff they wore was thrown together and cheap, a lot of pantsuits and double-knits'. The money goes into dressing the men.

In keeping with generic tradition if not with established perceptions of masculinity, it is Scorsese's male characters who are the primary objects of spectacle and fetishisation. Narcissism mixed with consumerism is traditionally a feminine trait, and the man who mixes the two (as Julian does in *American Gigolo*) is necessarily viewed as deviant. To counter the potential passivity of this reduction to pure spectacle, men in cinema often adopt aggressive postures or ostentatious display mechanisms; thus resuming the active role by seizing the initiative and showing themselves off, as Henry Hill does when he appears in his first flash suit and, with a big smile and his arms outstretched, asks his mother, 'What do you think?'. Henry therefore deflects femininity by embracing narcissism. The pan from Henry's shoes to his face as his mother tells him he looks like a gangster intentionally echoes the same camera move that a few minutes previously had picked out the patent toes, turn-ups, double-breasted jacket and pinkie ring of a mob leader. *Goodfellas* signals Henry has conclusively made it when Ray Liotta

3.4 Ray Liotta as Henry Hill (with Joe Pesci) in *Goodfellas*
Courtesy of BFI Stills, Posters and Designs

(as the adult Hill) is introduced in 1963 with the same lazy, fetishistic pan up his body, taking in his tasselled grey loafers, the stirrupped trousers of his grey sheen suit and his trademark Gabicci-style striped shirt over white vest.

Conspicuous consumption and restless change tends to prevail in Scorsese gangster films amongst the gangsters on the make. Whilst the older, established gangsters in *Goodfellas* such as Paulie Cicero have an equally established and consistent image built around short-sleeved silk shirts over slacks, a character such as Henry is forever manically tinkering with his style; his clothes are showy, and get more extreme as he gets more important. The recurrent features of Liotta's wardrobe are his light wool shirts or cardigans and the narrow, pointed collars of his evening shirts which, at the height of Henry's powers, are outrageously long. In *Casino* Ace is given fifty-two costume changes in all, an extravagant display of excessive consumption transferred to the level of production. Scorsese refers, for example, to the elaborate ritual he and costume designer Rita Ryack went through every morning choosing 'which shirt, then which tie, then which jewellery' down to the matching watch-faces, even for the opening explosion sequence (Christie 1996: 10). The wealth for wealth's sake aspect of Ace's particular brand of conspicuous consumption is illustrated by this daily routine being applied to the selection of outfits that are not markedly different one from the other except in colour. Virtually every suit Ace wears has the same leitmotif: a single colour or matching tone that coordinates suit, shirt and tie. In his visual consistency Ace thus refers back to the older Mafiosi like Paulie Cicero (and in a sense de Niro in *Casino* has become a Scorsese elder statesman), and to Al Capone's quirk of wearing ensembles based on one colour.

The fetishising of the male clothes in *Goodfellas* and *Casino* preserves the childish awe experienced by both Scorsese and Henry when they first see the neighbourhood gangsters wearing and parading their affluence. Because the clothes are what makes a gangster a gangster, it seems appropriate that the demise of both Henry and Ace is symbolised through costume. Henry emerges from his suburban home at the end of *Goodfellas* in a towelling robe; the uniform of a loser, a nobody, a garment that is not just ordinary, but one that frequently signifies a character who cannot be bothered to get dressed. Ace's image disintegrates to a similar level of sartorial banality, as at the end of *Casino* he winds up wearing a conspicuously ordinary and large pair of reading glasses. His hysterical, obsessional fixation with his appearance is, however, used prior to this demise as a metaphor for Ace's hubristic instability. When, for example, a call comes through to his office to say that one of the city officials has come to see him, Ace gets up from his desk and is revealed to be wearing, beneath his classically immaculate shirt and tie, only boxer shorts, shoes and fine, almost sheer socks. He walks over to his wardrobe to select the trousers that will match. This moment is a comic reflection on the Mafia's total absorption with the superficial and ephemeral; it also marks the beginning of Ace's decline. Although Scorsese's gangster costumes are tastelessly showy rather than understatedly chic, there is a parallel to be drawn between Ace's downfall and Jef Costello's in *Le Samouraï*, in that both are represented through the gradual (at first insignificant) disrobing of the narcissistic hero, emphasising the vulnerability of the men through the brief exposure of their bodies. Appearance is all to the wise guys of *Goodfellas* and *Casino*; as one shouts to the cops arresting Paulie, 'Whoever sold you those suits had a wonderful sense of humour'; worse than death is the anonymity they have to endure if they survive.

Scorsese's focus is on Mafia reality, on tackiness, greed and instant wealth, and in this he most clearly recalls the Hollywood films of the 1930s. In the last films to be considered, *Reservoir Dogs*, *Pulp Fiction* and *Leon*, there are stronger visual and costume links with the self-conscious films of the French tradition. The films of Tarantino and Besson are also preoccupied with citing and acknowledging the representation of the fictional gangster over the real. Tarantino's two features as director have been attacked for being pieces of cinema about cinema. *Reservoir Dogs*, for instance, was wearily labelled 'a film about film, about fiction' (Taubin 1992: 4), and 'unmistakably cinematic' (Rich 1992: 4), and Tarantino's rather self-inflating retort to the criticisms of his films as cheating pastiches is 'Great artists *steal*, they don't do *homages*' (Dawson J. 1995: 91). Perhaps there is a point to reinstating the positiveness of the homage, which, as has been suggested throughout this discussion, has been the impetus behind much of the gangster genre since the 1930s. Gangster films are about looks, they are about making the spectator desire what the gangsters possess (if only, as in the moralistic Hollywood films of the post-1934 era, to set up materialistic, violent demons just in order to shoot them down). Tarantino understands this, commenting about costume, 'I've always said that the mark of any good action movie is that when you get through seeing it, you want to dress like the character' (Dargis 1994: 17). These are the dual mechanics of desire and identification that function in the successful gangster film. As the gangster's own narcissism fused and confused love of the self with love of the Other, so the spectator's response to his image incorporates recognition and idealised envy. Tarantino's comment in the same interview about how, for Jean-Pierre Melville, it was important to give his characters 'a suit of armour', is echoed visually in both *Reservoir Dogs* and *Pulp Fiction*, in which the hit men wear similar Italianate suits to Jef Costello, but have dispensed with the hats and coats. As with Melville's protagonists, the disintegration or fragmentation of the care-fully constructed look marks significant junctures in each character's narrative. There is, though, an ironic understanding from the start of Tarantino movies that these suits are covering up for a lack of identity and represent his characters' dysfunctionalism.

The black suits worn for the heist at the beginning of *Reservoir Dogs* were all designed by Betsy Heimann to be similar but slightly different. They are reminiscent in part of the costumes in several earlier films, such as John Woo's *The Killer*, and conform to the early 1990s retro-chic (of French designer Agnès B., for example) which was heavily influenced by the Italian-cut suits of the late 1950s and 1960s as worn by Alain Delon in *Le Samouraï*. The sharp *linea Italiana*, which over those decades dominated men's fashions in Europe and America, comprised tapered, cuffless trousers and a slim-fitting single-breasted jacket which had to be short, so 'even in a sitting position [on a Vespa] it would not touch the seat' (Chenoune 1993: 244). Although far from overtly sexual, the lack of pleats and excess material meant that the 'continental look' followed the contours of the man's body much more closely than previous styles had. The versions in *Reservoir Dogs* remain intact symbols of virile, active masculinity until

3.5 Harvey Keitel as Mr White in *Reservoir Dogs*
Courtesy of BFI Stills, Posters and Designs

precisely the end of the title sequence, when the 'dogs', having dissected the lyrics of Madonna's *Like A Virgin* over breakfast, swagger '*Wild Bunch* style' and with 'a sort of unnatural slowness', as Andrej Sekula, the cameraperson on the film, puts it (Dawson J. 1995: 62), to their jewellery heist. Tarantino has said, 'You can't put a guy in a black suit without him looking a little cooler than he already looks' (Tarantino 1993: 53). Whether or not this is the case, the focus of *Reservoir Dogs* is the dismantling of this faith in image as armoury – whilst, paradoxically, retaining the allure that the spectator would like to emulate. From the titles on, the film charts the crumbling of this coolness, already furtively undermined by the presence among the suited men of Nice Guy Eddie in his fluorescent shell suit.

Reservoir Dogs is a film about disguise and the ability to sustain a disguise, a feature that is represented by the persistent use of juxtapositions between character and dress, the most blatant example of which is Mr Orange, an undercover cop who over several scenes is shown laboriously assembling his persona as a gangster. There are several stages to this construction of a false identity. First Tim Roth goes through his lines to himself, he then progresses to acting them out from a makeshift stage to a colleague, before finally recounting his learnt history to the 'dogs' in a bar. Mr Orange's transformation is symbolised through his changes in costume from a check shirt to a white T-shirt and leather jacket, which is the outfit he wears when leaving for the job. That this is a parody of the self-identifying, self-validating manoeuvres of Melville-esque gangster heroes is illustrated by Mr Orange, immediately prior to leaving, turning to a reflection of himself in the mirror and reassuring himself, 'you're super cool'. So Mr Orange learns the codes of the gangster, and demonstrates the performative value of masculinity itself which, like the ubiquitous suit, can be put on and taken off. The uniform suits are an elision mechanism whereby any subtext that might disrupt that image's integrity remains masked. *Reservoir Dogs* is full of reminders of the fragility of this 'cool' image and the hopeless dysfunctionality of a group which, superficially, looks cohesive. There are, for example, the homoerotic implications that fleetingly surface, first as Mantegna's *St Sebastian* is glimpsed on Joe's wall just prior to the boisterous homosocial fight between Mr Blonde and Eddie, and secondly as the physical tenderness between Mr Orange and Mr White develops, culminating in a *pietà*-like pose at the end. The defining contradiction is between the symbolic signification of the sharp suits (conventionalised masculinity) and the frailty they expose, as for most of the film they are roughed up and drenched in blood.

Tarantino uses the symbolism of the dark suit to similar effect in *Pulp Fiction*. In this second film, however, the assured masculinity embodied at the outset by Jules and Vincent in their black Agnès B. suits is more gradually and pathetically eroded, as over the course of the action their studied suaveness is slowly dismantled and finally ridiculed. When talking about the film, Tarantino has referred to the tension between getting 'these genre characters in these genre situations' and then plunging them 'into real-life rules' (Smith, G. 1994: 34). The same could be said of how *Pulp Fiction* puts together and then fractures a masculine ideal. In its focus on the anxieties of traditional cinematic action heroes on which the male characters are substantially based, *Pulp Fiction* charts, through its fragmented narrative structure, a series of struggles to challenge but, some would argue, to ultimately reassert those archetypes (Fried 1995: 6–7). Although the issue of proving masculinity is also what drives the representation of subsidiary characters such as Christopher Walken's war veteran and Butch (Bruce Willis), the boxer who refuses to take the fall, the fragile composition of the ideal is more overtly critiqued in the Jules and Vincent sequences.

In the first section, 'Vincent Vega and Marsellus Wallace's wife', the two hired hit men are in control of their dialogue, their image and the situation. As with *Reservoir Dogs* the collapse of the image is signalled by the use of excessive amounts of blood that, on a prosaic level, simply ruin their outfits. This is elaborated in part three, 'The Bonnie situation', which begins with two accidents: the 'miracle' of Jules not being touched by bullets shot at point-blank range, and Vincent killing the hostage in the back of the car. The desire to preserve their image at all costs is represented through the symbolic acts of washing themselves and the car's off-white interior, to regain the wholeness they thought they possessed at the beginning. After scrubbing down, 'the Wolf' (Harvey Keitel), despite being in a hurry, indulges in a piece of ritualistic humiliation of Jules and Vincent. He orders the two blood-drenched gangsters to strip as he, and the would-be macho Jimmie, hose them down. This scene of mockery relegates the sight of debilitated, depleted masculinity to the level of indulgent spectacle. As was also the case in *Le Samouraï*, the point at which we are shown the gangster's real body under the idealised 'suit of armour' is also the point at which the myth is lost. This realisation is underlined after the hosing down in *Pulp Fiction* by a cut from black to Jules and Vincent in bright T-shirts and shorts; a disastrous image that even the towelling-robed no-hoper Jimmie feels superior to as he mocks, 'you look like dorks'.

In both *Reservoir Dogs* and *Pulp Fiction* the image of masculinity is destroyed in the most spectacularly obvious way possible, negating the view that what we are really witnessing here (as has been suggested) is paranoid masculinity's flight from the return of its silent Other. The discrepancy between man and myth is under-lined in *Pulp Fiction*'s final sequence. After an attempted robbery, Jules and Vincent leave the café they have ended up in. They try to swagger out of the diner as if nothing had happened, tucking their guns into their waistbands and synchronising their movements, just as they had done at the beginning; but whereas earlier they were still dressed in their designer suits, now they are in bright and cheery nerd colours. Jules and Vincent want only to put their suits on and face the world, instead they find themselves condemned to the perpetual ridicule of the Emperor in his new clothes. As Tarantino comments, 'What's interesting is how they (Vincent and Jules) get reconstructed . . . their suits get more and more fucked up until they're stripped off and the two are dressed in the exact antithesis' (Dargis 1994: 17). The immaculate attire spied only briefly at the beginning of Tarantino films fulfils a similar function to Lacan's elusive phallus, persuading the characters to go in search of an ideal that they think they once embodied, but which was never theirs for the taking.

George Simmel in his chapter on fashion concludes that, 'the peculiarly piquant and suggestive attraction of fashion lies in the contrast between its extensive, all-embracing distribution and its rapid and complete disintegration' (Simmel 1904: 322). No sooner is a dominant look established, therefore, (and in film terms becomes generic), than it crumbles. In *Reservoir Dogs* and *Pulp Fiction* the emphasis is on the transition from integrity to fragmentation. In Luc Besson's *Léon*, the wholeness is absent from the start, as the unidentified Other of gangsters past hangs over its shambolic 'I', a dishevelled French-Italian-American New York hit man. Peter Middleton begins *The Inward Gaze* with the question 'What happens when a man reflects on his gender?', to which he answers, predictably perhaps, that the 'real man' is a fantasy (Middleton 1992: 3). It could be mooted, therefore, that men who reflect on themselves necessarily find themselves wanting. Echoing Lacan's idea of an ego resembling the superimposition of various coats borrowed from its props department, Middleton also speculates that 'the fantasy of manhood seems to be created out of a bricolage of fragments from the masculine public world' (20), thus suggesting (despite the desire to hold onto a fixed notion of manhood that permeates much of the book) that masculinity is necessarily a performative act. When discussing sexual difference Stephen Frosh asserts, '"Masculinity" might be a constructed category, but it is one which has been taken to have content' (Frosh 1994: 90). If one takes the multiple redefinitions of the screen gangster as examples of a male-dominated genre perpetually deconstructing ideals of masculinity, then it could be proposed that, by the films positing the very possibility that construction *is* content, the act of construction not only reveals but creates this lack. *Leon* focuses the issues of performative masculinity, of an identity constituted only at the moment of performance and construction, within the specific confines of a cinematic genre.

Leon's look is gangster anti-fashion, although as Simmel, for one, comments, 'the man who consciously pays no heed to fashion accepts its forms just as much as the dude does' (Simmel 1904: 307). This notion of denial as affirmation can be transferred to how Leon fits into the gangster genre, as his *démodé* and eccentric counter-image suggests that he simultaneously acknowledges and discards the tradition he belongs to. The costumes Leon wears comprise all the correct components, but are unconventional versions of each of them. In fact, the

3.6 Jean Reno as Leon in *Leon*
Courtesy of BFI Stills, Posters and Designs

conventional gangster image belongs to the corrupt DEA official, Stansfield (Gary Oldman), and it is he who worries that a bullet fired at him has ruined his beige suit. Leon has a hat, but it is a woollen skull-cap, not a Fedora; he has braces (like Vito Corleone, for example) but they are over T-shirts and buttoned vests; he has pleated trousers, but they are threadbare and short; and he has a coat, but it is, tramp-like, several sizes too large. Sartorially, therefore, Leon offers a commentary on the gangster's generic evolution and definition, something which is also carried through into his character traits and affectations.

Leon is the inverse of the Tarantino films in the way it juxtaposes conventional reality and ideality. Both *Reservoir Dogs* and *Pulp Fiction* put the gangster ideal on display in order to demonstrate its unobtainability, so each man is measured against an oppressively uniform and masculinised look that, from the outset, is bound to decompose. As a gangster Leon always looks wrong, so the anachronism functions in reverse. His outward scruffiness, therefore, (usually taken, as in Smith's discussion of Clint Eastwood, to symbolise 'butch') jars with his role as the fit, trained, masculine action hero stereotype when doing his job. He also fore-fronts, very self-consciously, the notion that men are constructions just as much as women, by selecting a particularly haphazard and eclectic array of signs, as if any masculine model will do, just so long as he's male. In one scene we see Leon open-mouthed at a Gene Kelly roller-skates routine, whilst in another, during a version of charades, he (very badly) impersonates John Wayne. Leon is the comic, posturing reflection of the self-taught loner trying to construct himself too consciously according to archetypes, not knowing which to follow or which attributes to appropriate.

The performative aspect of this wayward masculinity is clearly expressed in his relationship with his under-age moll Matilda. Leon, unlike most gangsters who have preceded him, resembles a child. At the beginning of the film he cannot read, his money is minded by a boss who gives him instalments of pocket money, and he seemingly lives off milk. As Leon and Matilda establish their nomadic relationship, it is Matilda who appears the more adult and street-wise of the two and who teaches Leon how to read. In return, he reluctantly instructs her in the art of 'cleaning' (being a hit man/woman), getting her fit and giving her sniping practice. As the film progresses, Matilda gradually takes on Leon's attributes, so, for example, when she goes into the DEA building intending to kill Stansfield, she has acquired a skull-cap and dark glasses similar to his. Although Leon had been impressed by her ability to hit a jogger in Central Park during shooting practice, he is also slightly disconcerted. Besson's film, considering Matilda's age, is tinged with a dubious romanticism, but it also represents the collapse of the gangster's image and identity. It is more than Leon's image which is emptied here. Through the transferral of himself and his ideal to Matilda, Leon reveals his essential lack. Gangsterism, if it can be so quickly learnt by Matilda, is no longer related to 'essence' or 'content' or even to masculinity, because masculinity itself is a collection of mementoes to be discarded or assumed by whoever chooses to pick them up. By the time we arrive at *Leon*, the screen gangster's image comprises a set or arbitrary but immediately intelligible signs, garments and accessories that distinguish the gangster and define his identity, but that are no longer a safe haven for the man's fragile ego.

Like most male-centred genres, the cycle of gangster films is about the man's acquisition of attributes that prove his masculinity and differentiation from the feminine. It also problematises this genderisation by making one of the key signs of the protagonist's success a concern with appearance and self-display. The complexity of the gangster figure is that much of the time his masculinity is directly measured by his narcissism: the smarter the clothes, the more dangerous the man, and the more damaged the clothes, the more vulnerable the man. One of the intentions of this chapter, therefore, has been to examine narcissism as a component rather than opponent of masculinity, which is more in keeping with how style, fashion and spectacle are currently viewed positively in relation to men. But there is simultaneously a tension here. Just as male fashions reputedly demonstrate conformity and a dislike of change, so the development of the gangster genre, with its extreme reflectivity and introspection, has proved not only adaptable but retrogressive. Melville continued, well into the 1960s, to nod back to 1940s *noirs*, Godard re-evaluated American popular cinema and culture,

Scorsese consistently cites Truffaut as an influence, and Tarantino references Melville, Godard and several other past film-makers. Throughout the genre's innovative scavenging, there has lurked the uncomfortable undercurrent that, perhaps, however conventional, the assumed gangster image cannot offer power or control or define identity. Clothes only make the illusion of the man.

4

THE SCREEN'S FASHIONING OF BLACKNESS

Shaft, New Jack City, Boyz N the Hood, Waiting to Exhale

Robert Townsend's 1987 film *Hollywood Shuffle*, about Hollywood's first black acting school, is a satire on the roles traditionally available to black actors in white mainstream cinema. An advertisement for the school runs:

> Learn to play TV pimps, movie muggers, street punks. Classes include Jive Talk 101. Shuffling 200. Epic Slaves 400. Dial 1–800–555-COON. Don't try to be cool. Call Hollywood's first black acting school.

Townsend's argument is with the enforced stereotyping of blacks by a white industry, that if a black actor wants to work, s/he has to be prepared to portray the heirs of Mammy and Stepin' Fetchit. An additional dilemma is that even many mainstream black films, despite being made by black film-makers and frequently funded by black backers, deal in a similar currency of clichés. The critical issue, from Blaxploitation to Samuel L. Jackson parading in pristine 'pimp gear' through *The Long Kiss Goodnight*, is stereotyping. A reason for the current revival of interest in Blaxploitation is perhaps a recognition of the films' irony and kitsch value, that *Shaft*, *Superfly* or *Cleopatra Jones* offer knowing reconfigurations of traditional images of blackness, at least to a postmodern audience familiar with the complexities of quotation and recontextualisation. This discussion of black cinema, like the accompanying discussions of gangster films and *femmes fatales*, has as its focus characters who are defined and read via their clothes, but whereas the gangster or the *femmes fatales* exploit and play on notions of gender, stereotypes and the masquerade, the black characters in black films from *Shaft* to *Waiting To Exhale* enact a more complex, ambiguous tension existing at the juncture between gender, dress and race.

Three major factors led to the emergence of a mainstream black cinema in the early 1970s: a substantial drop in American cinema audiences, a drop in the average age of that audience, of whom, between 1969 and 1971, 74 per cent were under the age of 30 (Reid 1988: 29), and an increasingly vociferous and militant black contingent which, following on from the last decade's civil rights action, was demanding greater recognition and visibility in mainstream culture for African-Americans. Hollywood, therefore, needed a formula for cheaply made films that would make some quick money and could be relied upon to attract a mixed-race youth market. The wave of black action films which came to be dubbed 'Blaxploitation' (low-budget Hollywood products using black stars and directors) began with the almost simultaneous release in 1971 of Melvin Van Peebles' *Sweet Sweetback's Baadasssss Song* and Gordon Parks' *Shaft*. Both films were immensely (and unexpectedly) successful; *Shaft*, for example, grossing $12m in its first year in North America alone, having cost a fraction of that to produce, and thus saving MGM from bankruptcy (Bogle 1994: 238). These two films established the prototypes for subsequent black action characters: Sweetback the hustler brought up in a brothel, John Shaft the cool private detective who averts a black/Mafia New York gang war. A year after *Sweetback* and *Shaft*, *Superfly* made $11m within two months, and 'outgrossed every movie on the market' (Bogle 1994: 239).

Prior to Blaxploitation, the presence of blacks in film had been minimal, and largely confined to insignificant (usually servile) characters who hung around the peripheries of white narratives. African-Americans in mainstream cinema were too often depicted as brutal primitives (*Birth of a Nation*), dippy servants (*Gone with the Wind*, *Duel in the Sun*) and, if they acquired any prominence at all, unthreatening, largely asexual bourgeois sophisticates usually played by Sidney Poitier (*To Sir with Love*, *Guess Who's Coming to Dinner*). An interestingly ambivalent role that conflates many of the racist stereotypes whilst part of an ostensibly liberal, anti-racist film, is that of Tom in *To Kill a Mockingbird*. Tom, who has lost the use of one arm, exemplifies one racist stereotype (the symbolically castrated, emasculated servant) whilst finding himself wrongly accused of fulfilling another (the raper of white women). He is either construed as vulnerable and in need of help from the articulate, sympathetic white man, or as a bestial outcast. Both stereotypes repress any sense of Tom's blackness other than how it pertains to the white characters. He is their hidden Other, whether this is the defendant's repressed sexuality or the lawyer Atticus' fear of the vengeful oppressed. On the whole, however, blacks were absented from cinema and television screens, a denial which bell hooks describes as constructing an 'oppositional gaze':

> Watching television was one way to develop critical spectatorship. . . . Black looks, as they were constituted in the context of social movements for racial uplift, were interrogating gazes. . . . Before racial integration, black viewers of movies and television experienced visual pleasure in a context where looking was also about contestation and confrontation.
>
> (hooks 1992: 117)

hooks describes the melodrama *Imitation of Life* (in which one character, though born to a black mother, is so pale she can pass as white) as being a crucial juncture in her development as a critical black spectator of mainstream film. The film's denial of the daughter's black identity leads hooks to literally stop looking and to turn away from Hollywood, 'to protest, to reject negation' (121).

The alternative to turning away, epitomised by Blaxploitation, is to increase African-American visibility within the mainstream structures already in place. By the early 1970s the presence of black artists in white cultural contexts was increasing; Otis Redding at Monterey in 1967 and Sly Stone at Woodstock in 1969 performing to huge, primarily white audiences were no longer isolated exceptions. Entry into the dominant culture was critical. As Van Peebles has commented about *Sweetback*, he elected to make the film for a mass, 'unpoliticised' black spectatorship because

> the film simply couldn't be a didactic discourse which would end up playing (if I could find a distributor) to an empty theatre except for ten or twenty aware brothers who would pat me on the back and say 'it tells it like it is'.
>
> (Reid 1988: 26)

Although Van Peebles wanted 'a victorious film. A film where niggers could walk out standing tall' (26), the argument against the kind of exposure granted by the Blaxploitation movies has always rested on the assumption that the films, predominantly produced by whites, were necessarily compromised from the outset. Both *Sweetback* and *Shaft* were directed by African-Americans and used blacks in other capacities besides acting (on *Shaft*, for example, the soundtrack is by Isaac Hayes and the editor is Hugh A. Robertson); but both were also produced and distributed by whites.

There has been much debate in the black community surrounding Blaxploitation, much of the negative criticism tending to emphasise the lack of creative and financial control granted to the films' directors and the representation of the male protagonists as macho sex machines. The films were quickly deemed exploitative by black activists, and certain civil rights groups sought to have Blaxploitation films banned. In his analysis of the films Reid concludes, 'so, they did not create mythic black heroes. Instead, like doll-makers who painted Barbie's face brown, they merely created black-skinned replicas of the white heroes of action films' (32), whilst a more vituperative attack is launched by Tom Brown, then editor of *Black Journal*, when he labels the Blaxploitation films 'a phenomenon of self-hate' (Singleton 1988: 20). Conversely, the views among black audiences was that Blaxploitation films gave them what they wanted, namely 'blacks who won' (Silk and Silk 1990: 164). There is a particular conflation of signs and characteristics that render black action films more pleasurable and spectacular to a black audience than the criticisms imply, a dynamism based on the fusion of music, sexuality, success and flashy clothes that signals the arrival of a strong identifying model for a black audience. Why these films have recently been revived is that they achieved iconic status, symbolising a significant, transitional moment in the history of black involvement in popular cinema. As novelist Mike Philips remembers:

> I nearly hadn't gone to see *Shaft*. Up to that time I tended to avoid Hollywood movies with black people in them, because – with exceptions, such as *In the Heat of the Night*, – the experience was usually irritating or embarrassing, if not downright offensive. *Shaft* was different. If my reaction to it had changed a few years on, at the time, along with most of the black people I knew, *Shaft* made me feel good.
>
> (Philips 1996: 25)

Blaxploitation films are distinctive for their extreme fetishisation of clothes, and the significance of appearance to the heroes' identities. In *Shaft*, *Superfly* and *Cleopatra Jones*, costumes function as important signifiers that transfer to the spectacular the success and desirability of the protagonists who wear them. John Shaft is the most measured of the three, and most overtly aspirational in terms

4.1 Richard Rowntree as Shaft in *Shaft*
Courtesy of BFI Stills, Posters and Designs

of his appearance. His wardrobe is streamlined and consistent, comprising a selection of brown tweed suits, beige, polo necks and two long leather coats. As the action progresses, his clothes get increasingly black and cool, until the final ensemble (in which he saves a kidnap victim and averts a gangland war virtually single-handed) is a long black leather coat, matching leather trousers and black polo neck. The image Shaft exudes is one of control, the clothes functioning metonymically to draw together the disparate facets of his character: his competence as a private detective, the ease with which he operates in the inner city, and his sexual irresistibility. Shaft's wardrobe represents his equivocal social position, simultaneously comfortable in the white-dominated establishment (see, for instance, his sharp tweed suits) and the black-dominated urban street. It is, however, significant that John Shaft is also symbolically independent of the film's oppositional social forces, differentiated from Androzzi whose clothes are worn and scruffy, and from the black community which falls into three dominant stereotypes: classic gangsters (felt hat, old-fashioned suits), street-wise hustlers and informers (large cap and shades as worn by the Antonio Fargas character), urban terrorists (Afro hair, hippie shirts). Shaft's last look is significantly black, and an obvious allusion to the all-black chic of the Black Panthers. The change in dress also coincides with the overt strengthening of Shaft's alliance with the black sections in the film (the urban terrorists and the kidnap victim) at a time when the divisions within the narrative (notably the imminent gang war) are along racial lines. Above all, John Shaft's image was credible to a black audience, the first realistic portrayal of black masculinity on the screen. As Mike Philips says, 'The funny thing was that I knew dozens of guys who looked and sounded like him, but I'd never seen a black man who was anything like them up on the screen' (Philips 1996: 25).

Youngblood Priest in *Superfly* is a more exotic and more problematic Blaxploitation hero. Although as a film *Superfly* recalls the social commentary aspect of *Shaft* (as in the opening high-angle shot of a rough urban street revealing the desperate trying to hustle a bit of money), Priest is also an excessive 'clothes horse' whose costumes to an extent precede and define him, thus establishing a discursive link between clothing and spectator not unlike that discerned in couture-led films such as *Trop Belle Pour Toi!*. The clothes in the later black action movies function independently of character and narrative, and the changes are frequently unmotivated by either. The extreme example of this prioritisation of dress style is Cleopatra in *Cleopatra Jones*, whose whole look alters with every sequence, and whose wardrobe is made up of a shambolically eclectic variety of turbans, floaty skirts, fur coats, platform footwear and jewellery. Despite the serious intent behind *Superfly* (which has largely been overlooked), it shares with *Cleopatra Jones* the compulsion to read the characters through the costumes. Priest's successful pusherman look of long, relaxed hair, wide brimmed hat, flared

4.2 Tamara Dobson as Cleopatra Jones in *Cleopatra Jones*
Courtesy of BFI Stills, Posters and Designs

coat and stacked heels was widely imitated on the street in the early 1970s, and known simply as 'fly' (Singleton 1988: 20). Priest classically embodies the funk styles of the early/mid-1970s, a loud, radical reaction to the suavity an icon such as Poitier embodied, or the attitude that bred Motown Records' 'charm school' for teaching black singers how to be more white in their dress, choreography and deportment. These were images that would appease rather than threaten the white community. The funk look of Blaxploitation and the musicians George Clinton and Bootsy Collins, on the other hand, is preoccupied with difference not assimilation. In terms of dress, 'funkiness' came to be expressed by the 'Pimp Look', an eclectic amalgam of clashing styles most often seen on pimps, hustlers and other ghetto figures who had got rich by dubious means. Ivan (Jimmy Cliff) in *The Harder They Come* is a classic incarnation of the Pimp Look, posing for photographs in a garish combination of white cap, leopard-skin shirt open at the chest, long chain, leather waistcoat and snakeskin shoes. The Pimp Look is blatantly sexual, tight around the hips and crotch and low cut over the chest; the funksters are 'dressed to slay' (Wolfe 1977: 184).

Superfly, like the funk scene, is memorable for its clothes, predominantly the gaudiness and the detail of Youngblood Priest's hustler costumes: the oversize white stitching on his black suit, the swishing maxi coat, the pale snap-brim hat. Unlike Shaft's homogenous look that denotes stability, Priest's wayward wardrobe interferes with the film's more depressing, less macho message that drugs run the black ghettos and Priest will probably never escape that environment. The sheer number of costume changes given to Ron O'Neal in *Superfly*, like Robert de Niro in *Casino*, are part of a pattern of conspicuous consumption, exemplifying the attitudes of both his character (the successful cocaine dealer) and the clothes fetishism that intrudes on the film as a whole. *Superfly* is a clothes movie where the costumes also get in the way of narrative comprehension; as a subsidiary character walks into frame wearing a striking red 'stingy-brim' (pork-pie) hat, one inevitably forgets to listen to the dialogue. Like *Cleopatra Jones* after it, *Superfly*'s fixation on clothes means that the film regularly contravenes continuity logic by adding

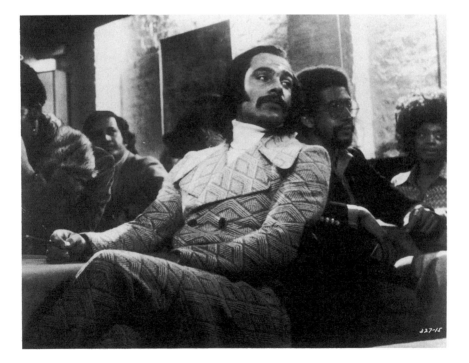

4.3 Ron O'Neal as Priest in *Superfly*
Courtesy of BFI Stills, Posters and Designs

accessories or changing outfits altogether mid-sequence. In one particularly frenetic sequence towards the end of the film (when the use of the same music track suggests continuous action) Priest leaves his apartment in a beige jacket and hat, gets out of his car having acquired a long brown suede coat and finally arrives at his friend Eddie's in a different leather and suede Cavalier-style suit. The clothes are thus on show more than the man. Through his costumes, Priest, unlike Shaft, does not show off his social aspirations (for all their glamour, these are recognisably street clothes) but rather his instant wealth. These are *nouveau riche* clothes, the Harlem equivalent of Ray Liotta's shiny suits and pointed collars in *Goodfellas*. Priest, like the white gangsters, defies the supposed rule that the strong, virile male cannot also be eroticised, vain and glamorous; but 1970s funk and black fashions often undermined that kind of conservatism.

What Kobena Mercer has termed a 'defiant "dandyism"' has historically been the underpinning feature of black subcultural styles, 'where 'flashy' clothes are used in the art of impression management to defy the assumption that to be poor one necessarily has to 'show' it' (Mercer 1994: 120). Ted Polhemus makes a simple yet useful distinction when commenting, 'There are two basic moves in streetstyle: Dressing Up and Dressing Down' (Polhemus 1994: 17). Whilst many white groups express the latter tendency, the majority of black fashions illustrate the former. The most influential black male street style was probably the 1940s zoot suit, which combined extrovert glamour with the aggressive assertion of black identity. The 'zootie' look worn by African-Americans and Mexican 'Pachucos' (later mimicked and modified by the zazous in Paris) comprised a large, exaggeratedly long jacket, padding to the shoulders and hips, heavily pleated trousers that tapered sharply to show detailed, often two-tone leather shoes, a wide-brimmed and perhaps feathered felt hat and long gold chains that drooped from the belt line to shin level. The fascination of the zoot suit is summarised by Malcolm X's detailed description of acquiring his first zoot suit:

> I was measured, and the young salesman picked off the rack a zoot suit that was just wild: sky-blue pants thirty inches in the knee and angle-narrowed down to twelve inches at the bottom, and a long coat that pinched my waist and flared out below my knees. As a gift, the salesman said, the store would give men a narrow leather belt with my initial 'L' on it. Then he said I ought to also buy a hat, and I did – blue, with a feather in the four-inch brim. Then the store gave me another present: a long, thick-lined, gold-plated chain that swung down lower than my coat hem.
>
> (Malcolm X 1968: 135)

Malcolm X walked through crowded public places just to turn heads, a habit eulogised in the opening sequences of Spike Lee's biopic *Malcolm X*, during which Malcolm and his partner swagger ostentatiously through crowded Boston streets in bright zoot suits, feathered hats and gold accessories, looking to be looked at. Wearing a zoot suit was not just about style, as Lee's portrayal implies, but about increasing visibility. The zoot suit took on political connotations during the 1940s by deliberately violating wartime rationing laws which, in 1942, advocated a 26 per cent cut-back in the use of cloth for a man's suit, effectively outlawing the manufacture of anything as extravagant as the zoot suit. As the number of 'zooties' did not decline, however, the wearing of the zoot suit came to be regarded as unpatriotic, leading to the 1943 riots across America between zooties and the army and police. Like many black street styles since, the suit became, as Stuart Cosgrove argues, 'an emblem of ethnicity and a way of negotiating an identity. The zoot suit was a refusal: a subcultural gesture that refused to concede to the manners of subservience' (Cosgrove 1989: 4). As Elizabeth Wilson comments:

> In the early days of the Harlem expansion, ghetto fashions seem to have expressed the desire of a particularly oppressed urban multitude for some joy and glamour in their lives, and counter-cultural dressing is usually most distinctive when it expressed hedonism and rebellion simultaneously.
>
> (Wilson 1985: 200)

Black identity has always been more emphatically expressed through clothes and appearance than white identity has, and the zoot suit was an aggressive assertion of both difference and sexuality. Blaxploitation costumes, likewise exaggerated and parodic, could also be viewed as complex signifiers, symptomatic of a desire to make a political statement through the extreme visibility of a physical, confident, narcissistic look. The black 'macho goddesses' (Bogle 1994: 251) emerged as a stereotype in the 1970s with Tamara Dobson and Pam Grier's Blaxploitation roles, later echoed and mimicked by Grace Jones. Dobson in *Cleopatra Jones* constructs an image of blackness as exotic, non-specific 'otherness' which flits between African, Middle Eastern, Indian and hippie influences, apparently indiscriminately. Cleopatra is introduced wearing a multi-headed fur coat, and an assortment of bright turbans, a feathered hat, long tunics, chains and high heels; her extreme appearance is incoherent and excessive, and hardly suited to her role as government agent. Yet the disparity adds to the exoticism. Cleopatra's obsessive costume changes can (like those in *Superfly*) be viewed as fissures which (consciously or not) undermine the narrative by preventing identification with and absorption into the action. Gone, with Cleopatra Jones, is any semblance of the realism or social awareness of *Shaft* or even sporadically *Superfly*, and as a result her clothes exist as pure spectacle beyond the boundaries of the dominant narrative trajectory. This potentially liberating intrusion which interferes with a traditional identification between spectator and female image is, though, compromised during the final chase sequences, as Cleopatra detaches her skirt to facilitate her karate kicks. Moments such as this problematically fetishise the

103

representation of female power (Tasker 1993: 21), and reduce the woman to the level of gratuitous spectacle.

The films' commodification of blackness is a consistent feature of Blaxploitation. As John Shaft, Youngblood Priest and Cleopatra emphasise sexuality and aggression so, the detractors argue, they do not articulate new models but instead perpetuate old, demeaning stereotypes. A reassessment of these limiting opinions is dependent largely on how the protagonist's appearance is to be read in relation to such historical stereotypes. As Tasker comments whilst grappling with the unresolved ambiguities of black action movies, 'As with the production of the action heroine as phallic woman, the construction of the black action hero as a stud both acknowledges, makes visible, and also retains elements of that history of representations' (Tasker 1993: 38–9). Blaxploitation films could, therefore, be interpreted as arguing against the prescriptive white mythologisation of the black hero/heroine as a figure defined by his/her sexuality and corporeality through ironic distancation. Underlying Tasker's analysis is a probing into the reasons why initial critical reactions to black action movies were so vehement. Arguing for a positive reconsideration, Tasker concludes, 'The black action films may well prove to be so unsettling precisely because they seem to be so acutely aware of the issues of representation that are at stake in their construction of the black hero' (Tasker 1993: 39). An interpretation which allows for knowingness as opposed to naiveté on the part of those involved in Blaxploitation films goes some way towards explaining the continued references to the genre (such as Samuel L. Jackson's jherri-curl wig and sideburns in *Pulp Fiction* and his immaculate pimp gear in *The Long Kiss Goodnight*) and the current re-releases of the original films.

The next resurgence of black cinema came in the late 1980s, the catalyst for which was Spike Lee's hugely influential first feature, *She's Gotta Have It*. This new wave of films was more realistic, analytical and politically self-critical than the Blaxploitation movies had been, less celebratory of black machismo and more aware of the tensions within the communities. A 1990s film that clearly recalls the style emphasis of Blaxploitation is Mario Van Peebles' *New Jack City*. The stylisation of the costume and production designs for *New Jack City* consciously goes against the gritty realism of contemporaneous 'Home-Boy' films such as *Boyz N the Hood* or *Straight Out of Brooklyn*. *New Jack City* blends realism with mythic exaggeration and symbolism. The crack baron Nino Brown, for instance, as he acquires more power and gets more ruthless, wears an increasingly caricatured set of clothes. The action takes place in 'The City', a representative location that strongly resembles New York and its pattern of cocaine consumption in the 1980s, and spans the years 1986 to 1989 (a period of maximum expansion in the real North American crack trade). In these three years Nino Brown, in a cynical reworking of the American dream, goes from being a standard successful dealer to commandeering an entire apartment block (The Carter Building) which becomes his hyper-efficient mass-production crack factory decked out in chrome and plastic. The Carter, with its elaborate security system, production line, dispatch chute and smoking room, is a department store version of the tightly run *oficina* Terry Williams describes in *The Cocaine Kids*, and like '*la oficina*', The Carter mimics the structures of legitimate business. By the late 1980s, Williams notes, around 80 per cent of New York's cocaine users are buying rocks not powder, and that, with lower prices, faster service and better quality, cocaine distribution 'increasingly resembled a fast food chain' (Williams 1990: 52), leading to several large, run-down properties being taken over by dealers to cope with increased demand.

Nino, like The Carter, is both plausible and mythic, a duality illustrated by the parodic hyperbole of his street-influenced clothes. Nino embodies the 'stereo-typical chain-wearing, elaborately coiffured, sex and violence crazed black drug dealer' (Merelman 1995: 108), but not in the most stereotypical way, as his costumes juxtapose a variety of black and white reference points which, visually, transport him out of the narrow confines of the 1980s cocaine scene. Though sartorially confusing, Nino's look remains symbolically coherent. The most expected design touchstones for Nino's costumes are the B-boy/hip-hop styles of the mid to late 1980s; his 'Dukie Ropes' and medallions, though, are bigger and gaudier than anyone else's, and his earrings and rings heavier. But, as with the Blaxploitation heroes his styles recall, Nino's clothes possess an additional imaginative eclecticism. Other specifically black fashions are alluded to, such as the urban terrorist chic of the Panthers' all-black uniform, scarf and beret and the ubiquitous tight polo neck of the Blaxploitation era. The image is then complicated by a number of symbolic references to other fashions and styles. Nino's gold braid and buttons recall the traditional styles of military uniforms (and, ironically, those of the Salvation Army), as do the high collars and flat-fronted shirts he wears throughout the latter part of the film. Conversely, his fedoras are a clear citation of the Hollywood gangster style of the 1930s, an old fashioned affectation that is consistent with *New Jack City*'s persistent references to the grandiose romanticism of Mafia movies such as *The Godfather*: the emphasis on the crime 'family', the obsessional loyalty and the violent betrayal. Within Nino's look there are also more idiosyncratic citations, such as the range of side-buttoned shirts which echo John Wayne's ubiquitous Cavalry shirts.

If one is seeking an overall influence on Nino's costumes, the designer whose work they most readily resemble is the Parisian couturier Coco Chanel, however inappropriate this seems to the narrative context of *New Jack City*. The features that echo Chanel are the clean silhouettes, the use of single bold colours and the presence of excessive gold accessories. Chanel, in creating her revolutionary 'classic chic', espoused a definitive ethos that was entirely compatible with black

4.4 *New Jack City*
Courtesy of BFI Stills, Posters and Designs

street fashion's notion of 'dressing up' and of using clothes as a means of displaying identity. Chanel's perspective on the relationship her fashions had with street styles was very different from that found in the later work of some of the 'street cred' designers such as Jean-Paul Gaultier and Gianni Versace, who sought inspiration from styles evolving beyond the restrictive confines of haute couture and the upper classes. Perhaps because she came from a country which, like Italy, the other important centre of European haute couture, lacks an extensive street style tradition, Chanel preserved a distance between her styles and the street, commenting once, 'I like fashion to go down into the street, but I can't accept that it should originate there' (Mackrell 1992: 73).

Chanel's relevance to much black fashion stems both from her actual styles (in particular her costume jewellery) and her prioritisation of clothes for the street and work over clothes for the drawing room. From 1924 when she opened her accessories workshop and launched her 'fake jewellery that looks real' range, costume jewellery became an integral part of Chanel's 'classic chic'. Chanel's square-cut box suits (which were sold, in barely altered form, from the 1950s onwards) and her use of ostentatious fake jewellery became her most recognisable trademarks. Her use of fake gold and gems is a feature strongly echoed by the black hip-hop styles of the 1980s/1990s, most notably her chunky gold-look chains which were used as belts or handbag straps, the matching buckles and buttons which adorned her tweed suits and patent shoes, and the huge Byzantine crosses studded with brightly coloured glass. Chanel created a new chic out of what had previously been discarded by couturiers for being fake and cheap. This glamorisation of the ordinary proved, in fashion terms, to be a radical innovation, prompting Christian Dior (whose excessively feminine styles Chanel loathed) to remark, 'with a black sweater and ten rows of pearls she revolutionised the world of fashion' (Mackrell 1992: 33). Putting on fake finery for work, and thus collapsing the boundaries between leisure and functional wear, is precisely what characterises the opulence displayed by the 'classic black chic' in *New Jack City*. The exaggeratedness of Chanel's accessories (accentuated the more by being contrasted with the understatedness of her actual garments) is a parody of the inherent exclusivity of couture. In a similar vein Nino's costumes are an ironic synthesis and self-conscious allusion to the ways in which blacks have traditionally been equated with excess.

The dominant leitmotifs of both Nino's costumes and Chanel's designs raise questions about the construction of a subcultural style. Both denote, in different ways, an oppositional attitude to a culture or structure which has been established as normative; in Chanel's case the expensiveness and glamour of haute couture, in Nino's whiteness. As with zoot suits and Blaxploitation clothes, Nino's flamboyance is recognisably black. The use of bold colours, generous tailoring and expressive accessories (recalling the zoot suit) construct and define his racial identity rather than merely reflect it. Black dress has traditionally become defined as symbolic of opposition because it offers a visual challenge to the dominant white codes of dress and openly defies, through its studied opulence, the social position a racist society has allocated its black community. In this sense the complexities of black street clothes signal a social fissure and a desire to affirm and rearticulate racial identity. What is most interesting about Nino's appearance is the ostensibly arbitrary appropriation of fashions and designs from elsewhere, and their subsequent recontextualisation within a new, cohesive symbolic framework. In *Subculture and the Meaning of Style* Dick Hebdige refers to the manner in which subcultures articulate and define their difference and Otherness through the recycling of objects (such as the punk's safety pin) which can, when newly appropriated, 'take on a symbolic dimension' they previously lacked (Hebdige 1979: 2). In this way the 'stolen' subcultural sign is 'open to a double inflection: to "illegitimate" as well as "legitimate" uses' and is 'made to carry "secret" meanings: meanings which express, in code, a form of resistance to the order which guarantees their continued subordination' (18). Thus the reappropriation of the standard insignia of socially dominant groups can be divested of their original meaning by being placed within a different, unfamiliar context. There is, however, a coherence inherent in this selection procedure and a cogency about many of the black signs which complicates Hebdige's belief in the arbitrariness of the objects chosen.

107

A quintessential example of the fetishisation of the ostensibly insignificant object occurs in Spike Lee's *Do the Right Thing* when one of Buggin' Out's Air Jordan Nike trainers is soiled when a white neighbour accidentally runs over it with his bicycle. At over $80 a pair, these Nikes are not purely arbitrary signs randomly appropriated, but are status symbols because of their economic value. The significance of this confrontation is established in advance by Buggin' Out being the most overtly political figure in *Do the Right Thing*, who tries, for example, to effect a boycott of 'Sal's Famous' Pizzeria over an argument about the Pizzeria's exclusively Italian-American 'Hall of Fame' photographs. Following the chaos theory that imbues much of the film (that a seemingly insignificant action can precipitate a major confrontation), the dirtying of the pristine trainers proves the catalyst for an argument with the yuppie about white attitudes and ownership of brownstones in a black neighbourhood like Bed-Stuy. At the centre of this argument is an overdetermined object (the Nike) which becomes loaded with a signification it initially did not possess, a discrepancy which is in turn underlined by the discrepancy between the alternative attitudes to it expressed by Buggin' Out and the neighbour. By locating the Nike within a different context, Buggin' Out constitutes a new, exclusive black signifier. Later in the film, as if consolidating his integrity and victory (over a character we never see again and who is, significantly, the scruffiest individual on the block), Buggin' Out's Air Jordans are shot in extreme, reverential close-up as he repairs the damage with some whitener.

Do the Right Thing reduces several of the racial identities to a series of such overdetermined objects or garments, the most personal being Mookie's baseball shirt which had belonged to Jackie Robinson (the first black Major Leaguer) and had been given to Lee by a friend. More stereotypical are the cartoon Italians (Sal and his two sons) who run the Pizzeria, straightjacketed into the tired, macho cliché of white vests and medallions. Costumes are similarly used as simplifying signifiers where the black characters are concerned, for example in the portrayal of the trio of older African-American 'corner men' who sit all day on the sidewalk in their white caps, Panamas, tight shirts and trousers, the epitome of the old racist image of the work-shy Negro. Lee is adopting a very old-fashioned form of cinematic typage in this film, symbolising a character through a single gesture, garment or accessory; a reductive technique that loses the celebration of eclecticism found in either Blaxploitation movies or *New Jack City*. Thus Radio Raheem's political anger is conveyed via his oversized boogie box blasting out Public Enemy, his (brass) 'Love' and 'Hate' knuckle rings and his sharply cut flat-top; whilst the bumbling, simple Smiley, clutching his photographs of Malcolm X and Martin Luther King and wearing smart button-down shirts and peg tops, signifies a gross oversimplification of the choice facing African-Americans in the 1960s.

Indeed, very few of the objects appropriated by recent black subcultures are arbitrary. Although the stealing of Volkswagen insignia might be construed as such, the stealing of Mercedes signs cannot, because again the prohibitive price of the car it is attached to is a significant factor in its appeal. Similarly the fetishisation of the designer label within black street styles (the progression, for example, from Adidas to Vuitton and Gucci) is not the result of random selection, but a coherent socio-political statement which is proof that street kids can afford luxury items. It is also significant that the hip-hop styles of the 1980s caricatured functionalist clothing (the crotch on jeans hung near the knee, sports jackets drooped off shoulders, and trainers left unlaced); they were ironic, subversive gestures that implicitly criticised the styles they were citing. As the argument returns to the designer, it now appears that films such as *Do the Right Thing* and *New Jack City* pose a further problem with regard to the construction of a black subcultural style. Hebdige's theorisation of subcultures centres on difference and the signposting of opposition to the dominant, normative culture. As Hebdige articulates it, the process put in motion by the evolution of a subculture 'begins with a crime against the natural order' and ends with the formation of a recognisable style that is 'a gesture of defiance or contempt [and] signals a Refusal' (Hebdige 1979: 3). But what occurs when this 'Refusal' becomes assimilated, through exposure in the mainstream media or commercialisation, into the normative culture? Hebdige makes reference to Stuart Hall's argument that the resistant otherness of a subculture is perpetually being returned to the 'dominant framework of meaning' by being mass-produced and commercialised. This has occurred at a very obvious level with the reappropriation (and thus sanitisation) of black, music-based subcultures of the 1980s and 1990s, as white adolescents (as demonstrated by *Kids*) affect and reclaim the styles of their black counterparts (baggy jeans, unlaced trainers, baseball caps). This movement is the inverse of Nino's adoption of a style which refers (however ironically or unconsciously) to the exclusivity of haute couture, but is nevertheless part of the same cycle of homogenisation. Nino's look is the correlative of his capitalist aspirations, and he is at least partly motivated by a desire to be understood and found symbolically compatible with those he emulates. What gives the representation of Nino a dynamic ambivalence is that the continuous struggle between assimilation and segregation is enacted through the eclecticism of his appearance. A subcultural style, therefore, can be both confrontational and conventional.

The pursuit of fashionability has, primarily by those who despise it, been characterised as a repetitive tussle between exclusion and inclusion. The guiding paradox of many black street styles is that, whilst their distinctiveness proclaims the wearers' difference from the normative, white hegemonic model, the effectiveness of such looks is dependent on being instantly recognised as a member of a group, gang or subculture by those both in and outside it. One of the more significant aspects of how black street styles particularly embody the duality of radicalism and conservatism is through their interaction with more mainstream culture. In the early 1900s George Simmel offers an explanation for the evolution of fashion, later referred to as the 'trickle down' theory, which perceives trends to be started by the rich, upper classes and copied by those on the street. Once the styles are being copied and have thus become *passé*, however, the style innovators progress to different fashions which, in turn, become appropriated by the less wealthy in an attempt to remain *à la mode* (Simmel 1904: 297–9).[1] The cycle is thus perpetuated over and over. Simmel's understanding of fashion as a general psychological tendency towards imitation is appropriate to the fluctuating interaction between white and black fashions, where the imitation increasingly goes both ways, as current haute couture is influenced by street styles, and not just vice versa. The significance for this argument of the social tendencies outlined by Simmel lies in the realisation that, contrary to expectation, style (and even a subcultural style) is necessarily preoccupied with sameness and homogeneity as much as it is with segregation and difference.

The film which most clearly exemplifies this conflict between integration and segregation, and the concomitant expressions of these differing attitudes via dress, is John Singleton's *Boyz N the Hood*. This is an excessively schematic 'home-boy' movie narrativising the difference/sameness duality as options facing the black male kids in South Central Los Angeles. It is both more hopeful and more problematic than its contemporaries *Straight Out of Brooklyn* and *Menace II Society*. *Boyz* is a 'rite of passage' film, charting the maturity and development of Tre from his childhood, when his mother (Reva) sends him to live with his father (Furious), through to his adolescence. The costumes, though realistic, have a representative function, symbolising the fundamental choice facing the adolescent Tre between the paths of 'good' and 'bad' manhood, represented by his father (Furious) and his best friend (Doughboy). Although the differences between these two contrasting figures are clearly delineated, the film also indicates how subcultural signs, like clothes, can be misinterpreted. A third of a way through the film there is a party to welcome Doughboy home after his most recent stint in detention, a sequence which crystallises the dilemmas facing Tre and the signifying of those dilemmas through costume. Tre is dressed in an expensive ensemble of black peg tops and a black and orange shirt, to which the classically attired home-boy Doughboy responds ambivalently, first taunting Tre for being 'GQ smooth', and then exclaiming, 'you look like you been selling rocks'.

The cliché is that in urban black communities (and in films that take place in them) there is an inevitable correlation between crime and affluence, so smartness on the streets of late 1980s LA is instantly equated with crack dealing. Clean-cut Tre laughs Doughboy's insinuation off, but the brief exchange succinctly identifies a problematic area in terms of black clothes, identity and self-identification. The sartorial links Tre is striving to make are with his respectable, working, articulate father Furious, who, rather than signifying a 'hood affinity, represents a conformity which is less threatening to the white-dominated community beyond. Flash street styles are also (once again) representative of socio-economic aspiration and desire; to look and be as rich as white kids, and gradually to become indistinguishable from them. As Mike Davis comments:

> But the Crips and Bloods – decked out in Gucci T-shirts and expensive Nike airshoes, ogling rock dealers driving by in BMWs – are also authentic creatures of the age of Reagan. Their world view, above all, is formed of an acute awareness of what is going down on the Westside, where gilded youth practice the insolent indifference and avarice that are also forms of street violence.
>
> (Davis, M. 1990: 315)

The signs, however, are not always clear. As is the case with uniforms, culturally symbolic clothes usually collapse the difference between identity (how the wearer conceives of his/her clothes) and identification (how society understands them). This uniformity is particularly prevalent in inner-city gang and drug cultures, as exemplified by the colour-coded differentiation of the 'Bloods' and the 'Crips' in Dennis Hopper's *Colors*, which is set in a similar South Central location. Terry Williams describes how the members of the drug ring followed in *The Cocaine Kids* all wear the 'obligatory' gold ropes and half-laced sneakers which signify their membership of a particular gang (Williams 1990: 56). Remaining recognisable is as mandatory for the gangs and drug rings as looking cool and well dressed; it is a declaration of group affiliation. Reading identity into a black male's outward appearance can also lead to dangerous social stereotyping, as occurred during the Operation Hammer raids carried out by the LAPD in the late 1980s around South Central. Their Chief of Police, Daryl Gates, gave the officers involved in the anti-gang manoeuvres license to arrest anyone whose clothes and hand signals suggested that they might be gang members; so red shoe laces and giving high-fives became tantamount to a proof of guilt (Davis, M. 1990: 272–3).

These exaggerated and exhibitionistic 1980s/1990s hip-hop styles are worn in the film by Doughboy (Ice Cube) and the other adolescents except Tre. The characters mimic the real fetishisation and display of designer labels, the upmarket sportswear and the jewellery, first made into a universally recognised street uniform after the success of Run DMC's 1986 hit 'My Adidas'. This iconography then becomes the basis for conventional rap images of aggressive, posturing masculinity, exemplified by the controversial video for Ice T's *OG – Original Gangster*. For all its verisimilitude, *Boyz N the Hood* has also been widely interpreted as a parable of an adolescent's progression to manhood (Diawara 1993, Dyson 1993). The exclusive, confrontational styles worn by the kids are counterbalanced

4.5 Ice Cube as Doughboy in *Boyz N the Hood*
Courtesy of BFI Stills, Posters and Designs

by Tre's overtly symbolic father Furious, who stands for the alternative option to a rap life on the street. At a time when there are more single mothers in the African-American community than any other in North America, the issue of masculinity, and in particular the progression from adolescence to manhood, has been addressed and readdressed from several perspectives. One writer on the current state of African-American masculinity makes a comment pertinent to *Boyz N the Hood* when saying, 'The socialisation of black males without conscious and caring black men around is, more often than not, replaced with gangs or other negative groups' (Madhubuti 1990: 73). The overriding source of tension in 1980s urban black households is identified as the men's sense of inadequacy when confronted with the effects of a racism which prevents them from carrying out 'their expected traditional sex roles' (Spencer 1995: 34). The problems and questions that face all adolescent men in America, Spencer and others argue, are exacerbated in the specific case of African-Americans, who find it harder to form a solid self-identity because the role models they should have (fathers or significant others) are often absent. The defining relationship in black homes is reputed to be between a dominant woman and an emasculated man, a discrepancy that is 'of major importance in fostering an exaggerated masculine style' (Spencer 1995: 37). Adopting similarly exonerating language, Haki Madhubuti talks of African-Americans who have been 'destroyed' and 'neutralised' in their homes and communities, and so 'have ceased to have a major influence on the development of their children' (Madhubuti 1990:

112

72). In this context of worrying about growing up to be good men, there is a tacit condoning of the need for male aggression to be somehow displayed, and an over-whelming belief (as visualised in *Boyz N the Hood*) that single mothers have 'serious difficulty raising sons' (Madhubuti 1990: 73).

This background explains the emphasis on the importance of available role models in films such *as Boyz N the Hood*, *Juice* and *Straight Out of Brooklyn*, whether the model is Dennis' violent, alcoholic, downtrodden father in *Brooklyn*, or the articulate Furious in *Boyz*. The choices in *Boyz N the Hood* are stark and the only governing factors male: either emulate the staid Furious or slide into the red polo necks and 'Dukie Ropes' of the gang members who kill Ricky. Unlike Doughboy's

4.6 Cuba Gooding Jnr (Tre) and Larry Fishburne (Furious) in *Boyz N the Hood*
Courtesy of BFI Stills, Posters and Designs

crowd, Furious embodies, in his chinos, check shirts, knitted wool tops and glasses, the utopian vision of the politicised but moderate black adult male. Although he is an active member of the depressed South Central community, Furious's repertoire of sartorial signifiers make him into a latter-day Sidney Poitier, a positive black figure who both appeases whites and pleases blacks and wears the ubiquitous style of the colourless middle classes. Furious, like his clothes, is reasonable and moderate; his look is safe rather than oppositional.

The relationship, however, between black styles and the clothes of the white American middle classes is not straightforward, for instance the so-called Preppie look allegedly originated in Harlem (Lurie 1981: 99). What is being offered as a 'good' role model to the adolescent males in *Boyz N the Hood* is a universal, unthreatening image all sectors of the audience would be able to identify with. Ricky, Tre's friend from across the street who wants to go to college on a football scholarship, dresses much like Furious in shirt, tie and dark peg tops when trying to impress the university representative. This is the image of respectability. Furious remains the film's mouthpiece for black community consciousness, who gives Tre and Ricky a lecture about keeping the neighbourhood black and resisting white 'gentrification', but his costumes counter-productively indicate that in order to achieve stability or respectability the black male must renounce such 'bad' demonstrations of racially specific excess and flamboyance as the hip-hop/rap looks. Furious's look and demeanour tacitly affirms that such styles are inevitably allied to violence. In Chapter 2 of this book, J. C. Flügel's notion of the 'Great Masculine Renunciation' is discussed in relation to the anti-exhibitionistic uniformity of men's fashions from the 1850s onwards (Flügel 1930: 110–19). The motivation for the move away from spectacular and individualistic clothes as idenitified by Flügel was the growth in middle-class jobs and hence the increase in male professional employment; a development which led to clothes becoming recognisably work-related and functional. Furious, who works as a real-estate agent (for which he wears a mundane suit and tie), is, significantly, the only major male character in *Boyz N the Hood* to have a steady job. As he represents the 'good' role model and the street kids the 'bad', the blandness of Furious's look is, as Flügel suggests, symbolic of sophistication and a progression away from that baser model.

Correlatives of this transition away from self-display are seen by Flügel to be the man's renunciation of the passive eroticised position and the displacement of his eroticism onto the increasingly fetishised female body. The underlying suggestion that (heterosexual) men are not narcissistic was challenged at length in the previous chapter discussing American gangsters. What is of more concern here is the idea that men are no longer overtly sexual in their dress and social appearance, and that they perceive such a 'loss' to be a necessary precondition of their successful ascent into adulthood. There is an interesting comparison to be made between Furious in *Boyz N the Hood* and Nino in *New Jack City* on this issue. Furious not only recalls Poitier's functional, suave and unspectacular dress style, he also echoes Poitier's seriousness and lack of overt eroticism. Despite a series of discussions about sex in which he issues Tre with fatherly advice ('any fool with a dick can make a baby, but only a real man can raise his children'), part of Furious's mature persona is that he, not unlike the Poitier role model, has been desexualised. To be taken seriously, does a black man have to renounce sex? Certainly Tre implies this by holding back on sleeping with his girlfriend (until their college places and 'escape routes' from South Central are assured), whilst his fellow teenagers are getting their partners pregnant.

Nino, on the other hand, recalls the sexualised, spectacular black male body of the Blaxploitation films. He, like Shaft or Priest, is a 'sex machine' (to quote from the title track of *Shaft* and James Brown's 1970 funk hit, 'Sex Machine') who alternates between business and sex with a racial cross-section of women. An over-attention to Nino's physique, his 'absolutely corrupt male body' (Fuchs 1993: 207), runs through *New Jack City*, and in particular the fetishisation of his well-developed chest. In one scene with his partner Gee Money and their girlfriends, Nino is wearing an electric blue silk suit and gold chain, but with no shirt – the black trimming on the jacket and the bright rope around his neck thus drawing attention to his muscular torso. Nino's chest is similarly focused on in a self-conscious, fetishistic way later in the film when, playing basketball with members of his gang, it glistens with sweat (whereas the other bare chests do not).

4.7 Wesley Snipes as Nino Brown in *New Jack City*
Courtesy of BFI Stills, Posters and Designs

Nino is a fantasy figure, reduced, at moments like this, to the purely spectacular. It is also apparent that it is the women who are attracted to and pursue Nino, implying that his desirability (like that of the Blaxploitation prototypes) is more important than his own desires. The black buck stereotype (the black man in popular iconography becomes over-identified with his sexuality and genitalia) is obviously hugely problematic. This reduction and objectification of the black male (as in Robert Mapplethorpe's *Man in a Polyester Suit*) has been the most insistent criticism of 1970s Blaxploitation characters, who are frequently judged to be a 'string of witless, brutal black heroes' who kill white villains and satisfy their 'sexually unsatisfied white women' (Cripps 1978: 130). Nino is dangerous because he is attractive. He also conforms to the phobic, neurotic image of the black man who is defined by his sexuality, who is his penis. The sexual commodification of the black hero has, paradoxically, become a means of sustaining his difference and independence; Nino Brown, after all, would not find himself invited into the bourgeois white drawing rooms of *Six Degrees of Separation*, successfully passing as Sidney Poitier's son and smoothly integrating himself into white society. Conversely, Furious has constructed an identity around the visual disappearance of Otherness and the repression of overt, aggressive sexuality. In this he has made himself accessible and unthreatening to a multiracial audience.

Access to the dominant culture and the middle class has been a recurring and important feature of black cinema, as has the necessary desire to increase the visibility of blacks on the screen. These issue are interestingly complicated in the recent adaptation of Terry MacMillan's *Waiting to Exhale*, a narrative centred on the interconnecting lives of four significantly differentiated women (Savannah, Bernadine, Gloria and Robin). *Waiting to Exhale* is a well-intentioned 'feel good' movie which focuses on the importance of all-female friendship regarding relationships with a succession of men who are represented crudely as either drop-outs, sexual inadequates or conformist Poitier clones. The strength of the film is that it unquestioningly positions the black, affluent, successful woman as the norm against which the other characters are to be compared and judged. Blackness is no longer deviant, exotic and Other: this is an unchallenging, mainstream, middle-class film. In fact *Waiting to Exhale* radically reverses the traditional pattern of racial identification that conditions the black spectator to view most Hollywood films with bell hooks' critical, oppositional gaze. Here it is the *white* spectator who, finding her/himself marginalised on the level of representation, is compelled to access the narrative through identifying with the dominant *black* characters. This is a simple inversion, but one that radically challenges the traditional imaging of normativity as (in terms of race) white.

The costumes and appearance of the four protagonists issue a challenge to the preconceptions of the white audience expecting Otherness and at least an implicit sense of their own stable identity. The argument, being undertaken at the level of

4.8 *Waiting to Exhale*
Courtesy of Ronald Grant Archive

design, is with the assumption (held by blacks as well as whites) that the less contrived a black individual's style, the more in touch with her/his racial identity s/he is. Kobena Mercer, for example, (with reference to Michael Jackson) questions the suggestion that 'hairstyles which avoid artifice and look natural, such as the Afro or Dreadlocks, are the more authentically black hairstyles and thus more ideologically right-on' (Mercer 1994: 98–9). A conventionalised example would be Nino Brown in *New Jack City*, whose excessively sculpted hair reflects his 'bad' character. As if tempting its audience to think along these lines, *Waiting to Exhale* fetishises hairstyles and the endless potential of 'relaxing', (largely via Gloria who works in a hair salon), and only has one overtly symbolic haircut, which is Bernadine's radical crop after her husband leaves her. None of the women look 'natural', instead, they suggest serious investment in hair creativity, manufacturing a range of curls, flicks and waves. Mercer continues his chapter on hair by requesting the depsychologisation of hair-straightening, asking us instead to 'recognise hairstyling itself for what it is, a specifically cultural activity and practice' (99). Hair the raw material has no innate significance, it becomes invested with 'meaning and value' by such cultural practices (101). Mercer's argument asks for the relaxation of Hebdige's prescriptiveness when interpreting oppositional looks as necessarily reflective of identity, suggesting instead that the variety of black hair shapes and styles 'may be seen as both individual expressions of the self and as embodiments of society's norms, conventions and expectations'

(100). Whereas the politicised Malcolm X condemned his conk and zoot suit years, Mercer argues that now, with the range of cremes, gels, dyes on the market, experimentation with hair-straightening does not mean the same as it did before the era of the Afro and Dreadlocks (124); that the conk and other forms of 'syncretic practices of black stylisation . . . recognise themselves self-consciously as products of a New World culture; that is, they incorporate an awareness of the contradictory conditions of interculturation' (121).

Waiting to Exhale likewise confronts the notion that a strong black identity is only symbolised through clothing which conventionally emphasises difference. With few exceptions, the four protagonists of *Waiting to Exhale* wear safe, anti-exhibitionistic, generically middle-class clothes that are not ostensible statements of a specifically black identity. Gloria, an older single mother, is the only character who expresses a consistent racial identity through the afrocentricity of her clothes (loud prints, bright colours); the other women by and large dress in unexceptional but expensive business wear, although Robin's white dress knotted at the waist to reveal her midriff is a notable exception. Style and identity, the film implies, is about appropriating diverse elements from anywhere and giving them a new, fluid, relaxed intonation; it is not confined to the construction of a stable, identifiable image. The costumes further suggest, along with the emphasis of the narrative itself, that this is a film that prioritises gender over race, which means that they should not be interpreted exclusively as referents to a racial identity. As *Waiting to Exhale* redefines the relationship between white and black that constitutes the former as the norm and the latter as Other, so it also inverts and subverts the conventional dynamic between men and women. The subjects of the film are the four women, and it is the men who are objectified, caricatured, marginalised.

bell hooks concludes her essay 'The oppositional gaze' by making reference to Stuart Hall's contention that identity is constituted 'not outside but within representation' (hooks 1992: 131). Subjectivity, therefore, is constructed through visibility. The importance of being able to look at blackness on the screen is what links all the films examined in the process of this discussion. *Waiting to Exhale*, to which the notion of visibility is of particular importance, highlights the need to rethink the conflation of style and racial 'identity', to acknowledge that black subcultural discursive strategies are less restrictive than they once needed to be. Racial politics are here only implied, in that omnipresent blackness is the film's given, and it is whiteness (as, for instance, in the case of Bernie's husband's new partner) which is abnormal and has to be explained. Although films such as *Boyz N the Hood* similarly focus on exclusively black environments, the spectre of Otherness, the knowledge that what is being depicted is a ghettoised community, hangs over them. 'Home-boy' movies are all about what it means to be black. In *Waiting to Exhale*, the factor which links the women is not race but gender, to the extent that (with little respite) the action and dialogue revolve around their ruminations on sex with and desertion of men. In the street films of the 1980s, the analysis of racial identity was 'a man's thing', and women remained peripheral to or, in extreme cases, excluded from the dominant narrative. Sometimes this bias is formalised, as occurs in *Boyz N the Hood* in which Tre is symbolically handed over to Furious with Reva's words, 'I can't teach him how to be a man; that's your job'; at other times it is not even acknowledged. *Waiting to Exhale* is a riposte to such unthinking sexism, that in the process demarginalises blackness by establishing it as normative.

5

CLOTHES, POWER AND THE MODERN *FEMME FATALE*
The Last Seduction, Disclosure, Single White Female

The assumption that the *femme fatale* is a figure of male fantasy has always seemed dubious. A classical *femme fatale*, the dead Rebecca who lingers over Hitchcock's film with the pungency of an expensive scent, is symbolised in death by her renowned beauty and the clothes Mrs Danvers has obsessively preserved. Rebecca, however, despised and mocked the men she ensnared with these trappings of femininity; seducing the male in order to destroy him. In 'Fragments of a fashionable discourse' Kaja Silverman furnishes a reason for this resistance and unease when she comments (after Flügel):

> The endless transformations within female clothing construct female sexuality and subjectivity in ways that are at least potentially disruptive, both of gender and of the symbolic order, which is predicated upon continuity and coherence. However, by freezing the male body into phallic rigidity, the uniform of orthodox male dress makes it a rock against which the waves of female fashion crash in vain.
>
> (Silverman 1986: 148)

Expressed here is a traditional conflation: that, whilst remaining 'potentially disruptive', the vicissitudes of female dress ultimately undermine the woman and render her subservient to (and the victim of) the man who retains his iconographic stability. The justification for this sacrificial offering of the desirable, feminine woman has been sought in her appearance: the conscious eroticisation of her look through seductive clothing and make-up, and the use of this look to manipulate men. But why presume that a tempting female image is necessarily conditioned by either the narrative of the films she inhabits or the framework of male fantasy? This discussion of the modern *femme fatale* (who can be dated from *Body Heat*) sets out to challenge some of the established arguments surrounding feminine appearance and dress, and to develop the theorisation of women's clothes as an alternative or disruptive filmic discourse begun in the opening chapter on haute couture. Women, both on and off the screen, have been over-identified with their image, and the self-conscious irony of a film like *The Last Seduction*, for example, begins to suggest that women are capable of using this enforced identification for their own ends. The rejection of the belief that the way a woman looks is conditioned by men is consolidated in the discussion of *Single White Female*, a film that sheds doubt on the conventional idea that women dress for the benefit of men at all.

Historically, feminist reactions to fashion have been negative. In her vituperative attack on women and dress in *The Second Sex*, Simone de Beauvoir detects a direct correlation between a woman's eroticisation through dress and her lack of power and freedom:

> Woman [unlike man], is even required by society to make herself an erotic object. The purpose of the fashions to which she is enslaved is not to reveal her as an independent individual, but rather to offer her as prey to male desires; thus society is not seeking to further her projects but to thwart them.
>
> (de Beauvoir 1949: 543)

De Beauvoir's argument rests on the opposition between adornment or display and 'natural' womanhood, condemning with particular vehemence those details of fashionable styles (from high heels to fragile hats) that are both constricting and non-functional. A dangerous extrapolation made in these pages is that the accentuation of femininity is a natural correlative of male rather than female fantasy. Fashion is used, in de Beauvoir's estimation, to absent woman and reduce her to an idealised sign, so that 'once she is "dressed", [she] does not present *herself* to observation' but rather 'the character she represents but is not' (547). Women are so conditioned to resemble and identify with 'something unreal, fixed, perfect' (547). In a particularly sharp passage de Beauvoir concludes, 'In her evening dress the wife is disguised as a woman, to serve the pleasure of all the males and gratify the pride of her proprietor' (546–7); she is a commodity with no intrinsic value, reduced to an over-identification with the ephemeral superficialities of appearance. The pursuit of elegance and beauty, therefore, is oppressive, trivialising and demeaning.

Later feminist rejections of feminine clothes have perhaps been most succinctly expressed by Susan Brownmiller in her book *Femininity*, published in 1984 and clearly much influenced by *The Second Sex*. Brownmiller, quite comically at times, dwells on clothes as polarising agents: between feminine and feminist women; between the real and the artificial; between women and men. By consistently emphasising difference (men's clothes are functional, women's are not; skirts are signs of oppression, so trousers become a feminist statement) Brownmiller inevitably condemns any attire that is not trousered anonymity as 'bad', 'frivolous' and 'indulgent' because 'the nature of feminine dressing is superficial in essence' (Brownmiller 1984: 56). Brownmiller writes as if skirts themselves are morally reprehensible, and adopts a tone of resigned superiority when commenting, for example, that 'Serious women have a difficult time with clothes, not necessarily because they lack a developed sense of style, but because feminine clothes are not designed to project a serious demeanour' (74). Such puritanism is not only self-defeating but disingenuous, as Brownmiller obviously misses the excessive frivolities she deems inappropriate to a feminist demeanour, and persists in only attributing stylishness to a fashionable but rejected femininity. At one point, Brownmiller rounds on the 'backsliders' who apologetically but relentlessly began reincorporating feminine details (namely the reviled 'skirts and dresses') into their wardrobes, accusing them of weakly missing 'some whimsical indulgence in the feminine aesthetic' (55). She does, however, rather endearingly, appear to be transferring her own loss onto the condemned 'backsliders' as the protesting tone of this passage attests:

> They missed the frivolous gaiety of personal adornment, they missed the public display of vulnerability and sexual flirtation. . . . Some of them longed to show off their legs again, and some of them, I know, missed shopping.
>
> (55)

Of course it is the barely disguised Brownmiller who misses flirting and shopping. What is significant about this passage is that it implies, as did de Beauvoir's analysis, that there is an inevitable and universally accepted correspondence between the feminine aesthetic and political weakness. Nevertheless, for all her disavowal of femininity, Brownmiller in trousers is as much a slave to patriarchal oppression as her be-skirted sisters; she simply sees herself as rejecting rather than pandering to an omniscient, omnipresent male gaze:

> At this particular moment in history when the ratios of sexual preference seem to have gone awry and vast numbers of homosexual men and straight single women are roaming the range in search of love, sex and meaningful relations, it is obvious that these two groups dress up to enhance their sexual attraction while lesbian women or heterosexual men dress more carelessly or conceal their bodies, having no urgent need to attract the judgmental male eye.
>
> (70)

In later paragraphs it becomes abundantly clear that the category 'women' does not encompass lesbians: so only men pay attention to outward appearance and women lack scopophilic discernment? If they achieve nothing else, the implicitly lesbian clothes-obsessed scenarios of films such as *Black Widow*, *Basic Instinct* and *Single White Female* emphatically restore the erotic social gaze to women.

Clothes, power and the modern *femme fatale*

De Beauvoir and Brownmiller are in accordance with many male fashion historians and commentators in their belief that women's emancipation could only occur with the rejection of feminine clothing. James Laver, for one, assumes that the first thing an emancipated woman does is to try and look like a man by cutting her hair and disguising her waist, whilst George Simmel sees in the would-be liberated woman not just the desire to emulate men but to stress 'her indifference to fashion' (Simmel 1904: 310). A dissenting view which could be transposed to 1990s stilettoed feminism is proffered by David Kunzle in *Fashion and Fetishism*. The majority of this study concerns tight-lacing, as discussed in Chapter 2 of this book, but Kunzle expands his arguments to include other garments and looks. He comments, for instance, that feminist fashion writers too easily conflate the social application of the term 'freedom' with its use when talking about clothes, suggesting that, far from being looser and more 'liberating', women's fashions (the 1870s corset or the Edwardian 'hobble skirt') were tighter and ostensibly more restrictive during periods of greatest political gain (Kunzle 1982: 40–2). Kunzle's response to fetishism could be extended to imply the existence of an interrelationship between provocative and erotic clothes and women feeling and being in possession of power. The presumed incompatibility between wearing sexually alluring clothes and being a feminist, however, prevails into the 1990s. In her sceptical response to the 1980s vogue for feminine parody and pastiche exemplified by Madonna's constant metamorphosis, Rosalind Coward in *Our Treacherous Hearts* states:

> These ideas seem attractive . . . but they have failed to dislodge a fundamental unevenness between men's and women's relationship to sexual display and adornment. Women are still unshakeably concerned with rendering themselves sexually desirable and conforming to prevailing ideals, even if on first glimpse these ideals are many and various.
>
> (Coward 1993: 154)

Although the male gaze is never explicitly mentioned by Coward, a perception of sexual difference and fixed gender disparity underpins this well-worn argument based on the notion that 'It is still women, not men, who are the aesthetic sex' (154). Perhaps women who acknowledge the ideas of play and pastiche in the way they dress are in large measure reacting against the monolithic fatalism of Coward's brand of feminism: that the 'prevailing ideals' will always be male, that women will always be looked at, and that the gender dynamic is never going to change.[1]

The logical extension of these feminist arguments against fashion is that women who 'dress up' are the 'treacherous' collaborators; as ridiculous an assertion as Edmund Bergler's that fashion is essentially created by homosexual men who impose deliberately 'punitive' and 'caricaturing' styles on women because of their 'hidden enmity against the female customer' (Bergler 1953: 4–8). In a letter to the feminist magazine *Spare Rib* written in 1983, a woman enquired, 'Do you criticise your sisters because they don't wear dungarees and Kickers? Is a woman any less emancipated because she "chooses" to wear make-up and stilettos?' (Coward 1993: 153, Wilson 1985: 236). The divergent responses of Elizabeth Wilson and Rosalind Coward to this same letter exemplify the opposing feminist views on fashion. Coward's discussion is permeated with a not so closeted puritanism which, after acknowledging the growing belief 'outside feminist circles' that 1970s feminism 'got it wrong', goes on to insinuate that there is 'harm in women's cultivation of their sexual appeal' (Coward 1993: 153). Wilson, instead, detects a crucial ambivalence in the traditional feminist approaches to fashion, that, with a puritan voice, they condemn the 'consumerist poison of fashion', whilst with a pro-free choice voice they 'praise the individualism made possible by dress' (Wilson 1985: 237). Wilson goes on to suggest that the pervasive 'feminist uniform' of the 1970s was as prescriptive as the New Look appeared to Simone de Beauvoir, and makes the essential observation, 'If liberated dress meant doing your own thing, no one ever commented on how strange it was that everyone wanted to do the *same* thing' (Wilson 1985: 240).

Femininity, from Freud onwards, has conventionally denoted passivity, weakness and vulnerability, all qualities that individuals of both genders should, it could reasonably be assumed, wish to reject. The supposedly paradoxical notion of 'powerful femininity' has, as it was in discussions of fashion, been the premise for many feminist and other analyses of female representation in *film noir*. *Noir* has traditionally been approached in terms of difference, both within the narrative and in terms of the spectator/text relationship, a concern with genderised binary oppositions which ultimately concludes that these women-dominated films are pieces of 'men's cinema' after all. Of the classic *femme fatale* Janey Place, writing in the late 1970s, states, '*Film noir* is a male fantasy, as is most of our art. The woman here as elsewhere is defined by her sexuality . . . women are defined *in relation to* men, and the centrality of sexuality in this definition is a key to understanding the position of women in our culture' (Place 1992: 35). There are very similar assumptions being made here as were being made in the feminist discussions of feminine fashion, most significantly that a woman defined by her sexuality is necessarily oppressed because she is defined for and in relation to men. Despite her ability to manipulate and seduce the men around her, therefore, the *femme fatale* is somehow impotent and harmless. Mary Ann Doane, for example, tries to define the constitution of the *femme fatale*'s deadliness:

> Her power is of a peculiar sort insofar as it is usually not subject to her conscious will, hence appearing to blur the opposition between passivity

and activity. She is an ambivalent figure because she is not the subject of power but its *carrier*. . . . In a sense, she has power *despite herself*.

(Doane 1991: 2)

Doane's argument comprehensively disempowers the *femme fatale*, who she defines as only unconsciously and vicariously powerful, the construct and embodiment of a dominant male fantasy.[2] The opaqueness of this description of the *femme fatale* pertains to a tradition which defines women as needlessly mysterious. Geoffrey Nowell-Smith, for instance, says in 'Minnelli and melodrama', '"Masculinity", although rarely attainable, is at least known as an ideal. "Femininity", within the terms of the argument, is not only unknown but unknowable' (Nowell-Smith 1987: 72), a distinction repeated virtually verbatim by Steve Neale in 'Masculinity as spectacle' when he comments, 'Masculinity, as an ideal, at least, is implicitly known. Femininity is, by contrast, a mystery' (Neale 1983: 19). The problem with such a delineation is that the woman, by being relegated permanently to the realm of the 'unknown', is also rendered invisible except in the imagination. Femininity thus becomes an empty surface on which male fantasies can be incessantly imposed and enacted, which is how the *femme fatale* has been widely treated. A component of such a hierarchical structure of fantasy is that the *femme fatale* is destroyed at the end, so cancelling out her potential danger.

Film noir dwells self-consciously on the manipulation and exaggeration of femininity, the extreme artificiality of the *femme fatale*'s look and the equally excessive innocence of her on-screen counterpart. In *Out of the Past*, for example, Kathie's duplicity is emphasised by the 'naturalness' exuded by the 'good', small town, outdoor Ann. Both *Double Indemnity* and *The Postman Always Rings Twice* begin with Phyllis and Cora looking in mirrors and applying lipstick, whilst they in turn are being looked at by the men they are about to seduce. Similarly the 1980s *noir* *Black Widow* opens with Catherine/Renée making up her face. The eroticisation of the *femme fatale*'s body is signalled as important for establishing the subjective look as male, a scopophilic containment of the female image that is often crudely indicated, as in *The Postman* when Frank's lust is mirrored by a titillating pan from the lipstick Cora has dropped, along the floor, past her pristine peep-toe sandals and up her long bare legs. As Kathie tells Jeff at the end of *Out of the Past*, though, he has chosen to imagine her as someone she never said she was. The knowingness displayed by both Phyllis and Cora, the recognition that they are intentionally adopting a physical image compatible with the most stereotypical male fantasies is elided by commentators such as Place and Doane, and is picked out by a radical later *noir* like *The Last Seduction*. Many of even the 1940s *femmes fatales* use their sexuality consciously and so obviously (like Cora closing the door on Frank as he ogles her) that they are belittled by being seen as powerful 'despite themselves'. As Elizabeth Cowie points out in an essay which challenges the tendency to characterise *noir* as a consistently masculine form,[3] 'these films afforded women roles which are active, adventurous and driven by sexual desire', and such a strong image of women cannot simply be cancelled out by a conventionalised ending (Cowie 1993: 135–6).

Contained within the traditional interpretations of both feminine fashions and the visual representation of the *femme fatale* is the belief that a strange sublimation process occurs when women dress which does not allow for dissonance; that there is a necessary correspondence or identification between body, mind and clothes. A woman (and a female film character) is more likely to be 'read' through the way she looks than her male equivalent. As Jane Gaines posits in her analysis of the narrative function of female dress in classical Hollywood, 'a woman's dress and demeanour, much more than a man's, indexes psychology; if costume represents interiority, it is she who is turned inside out on the screen' (Gaines 1990: 181). The symbolic iconography of the classic *femme fatale* is a limited, clearly demarcated register of clothes, based on the contrast of light and dark (in keeping with the chiaroscuro *mise-en-scène* but also indicative of duplicity), frequent wardrobe changes (not necessarily motivated by action) and the insertion of distinctive, often anachronistic garments or accessories. The most insistent anachronism is the use of pale clothes (for example the white dress and hat Kathie is wearing in *Out of the Past* when she first meets Jeff in Acapulco), a clear example of inverse symbolism. More interesting is the occasional use of intrusive, significant detail

5.1 Jane Greer as Kathie Moffatt (with Robert Mitchum) in *Out of the Past*
Courtesy of BFI Stills, Posters and Designs

such as the nun-like headwear added to the already stylised costumes for the final, fatal appearances of Cora at the end of *Postman* and Kathie in *Out of the Past*. Jane Gaines discusses how one of the 'rules' of classic Hollywood was that 'costume must be justified or motivated by characterisation', and if, as George Cukor says, it 'knocked your eye out', then it had failed to do its job (Gaines 1990: 192–5). Although not notably decorative, Cora's folded white towel (which frames her face like a Madonna's) and Kathie's exaggeratedly demure travelling outfit are not discreet complementary costumes, but jarring narrative interjections that question, as well as underline, the *femmes fatales'* duplicity. Is not the gaze of the hapless men in *film noir* at least in part mocked because they never understand the complexity of what they are looking at?

This question is more conclusively answered by looking at the later *noir*-inspired films, notably *The Last Seduction*. Whatever 'backlash' counter-strategies are put into play in these 1980s/1990s films, and there are many, subjectivity resides more with the woman than the man. In these modern *noirs*, the castrating potential of the *femme fatale* is not always nullified by the conventional narrative closure pattern of the 1940s; in both *Body Heat* and *The Last Seduction*, for instance, the cool, phlegmatic heroines out-smart all the men and get away with it. The narratives fail to contain their threat. *The Last Seduction* is John Dahl's third *noir*-esque film after *Kill Me Again* and *Red Rock West*. It centres on Bridget, a quintessential contemporary *femme fatale* who, in addition to being more intelligent, scheming and alluring than any of the men in the film, is also professionally successful. This final attribute is what differentiates most modern *femmes fatales* from their 1940s predecessors. Not only is the entry into the job market important for signalling the *femme fatale's* ability and intention to usurp the traditional social male role, but it is also an indication that she is no longer defined by her appearance alone. One of the most desperate scenes among the classic *films noirs* is the bored Cora listlessly cleaning her sandals of an evening.

Bridget is the embodiment of the self-conscious *femme fatale* who successfully uses a conventionalised, overtly sexual image of femininity which acknowledges its cinematic antecedents and suggests a full awareness of how that image affects men. The ambiguity, therefore, no longer rests with the image (whether such a stereotyped femininity can be perceived as feminist) but with the possession of the image. *The Last Seduction* confronts (even more clearly than Bridget's classic predecessors) the issue of excessive femininity being compatible with feminism, as it is Bridget who controls the effect of an image (based on short, tight black skirts and stilettos) that no doubt Brownmiller and Coward, for example, would term 'oppressed'. The fashion designer Jean-Paul Gaultier describes his ideal woman as 'the daughter of the one who made women's lib. She knows her power, but she uses it in a determined way, with a jerk and a twist. I hate the image of servility. . . . Codes are changing' (Kaplan, L. 1993: 267). One scene in *The Last*

127

Seduction exemplifies the change that has occurred in the dress codes traditionally deemed to define and confine within a patriarchal discourse. By this point in the film, Bridget has run off with her husband's money, decamped from New York to Beston, Buffalo, changed her name to Wendy Kroy and started dating Mike. One morning, Bridget and Mike are talking in bed, and he starts a sentence which Bridget completes: 'I'm beginning to feel like some sort of . . . sex object? Live it up.' Dressed only in black knickers, stocking and high heels, Bridget then strides away from the bed, dominatrix style. The importance of this obvious fetishisation of the female form is that it presents an argument against a possible conventional reading of the scene which would emphasise how Bridget's legs are exposed and framed with the tireless male gaze in mind. Feminist film criticism based in psychoanalysis has wrongly prioritised modes of representation and the scopophilic, fetishistic engagement of the spectator with the classical film image over every other factor, including narrative contextualisation. *The Last Seduction* is one of the most challenging examples of modern cinema in this respect, a film that does not shrink from using and confronting the eroticisation of the female body, but re-contextualises that eroticisation within a narrative constructed around a dynamic female subject. A knowing walking stereotype, Bridget dares Mike and the spectator to desire.

Bridget, like other *femmes fatales*, conforms to a positive feminist appropriation of Joan Riviere's theory of 'womanliness as masquerade', when 'women who wish for masculinity may put on a mask of womanliness to avert anxiety and the retribution feared from men' (Riviere 1929: 35). Riviere's notion of the powerful woman who alleviates male anxiety by disguising her 'masculine' strength behind a mask of feminine sexuality, flirting with men rather than challenging them, offers a model for how Bridget operates in relation to the lovers she seduces. The manipulation of femininity outlined by Riviere in her analysis of her client does not readily conform to the view of womanliness as passive, because the active agent in the relationship remains the woman performing the masquerade. As Mary Ann Doane suggests, the masquerade possesses destabilising effects that confront the masculine structure of the look and defamiliarise female iconography (Doane 1991: 26). This form of distanciation is emphasised in Bridget's relationship to her own seductive social image. From her first meeting with Mike when she perversely turns him on by telling him to 'fuck off', *The Last Seduction* offers a categorical denial that Bridget's overt sexuality (not only her clothes, but her sharp, dismissive repertoire of gestures) signifies a submissive desire to be desired by men. Instead, her hard-edged image is an emphatic denial of male presumption, a mark of aggression, not covert compliance, in keeping with the equivocations displayed by Riviere's patient who also feels intense hostility towards men. *The Last Seduction* rejects, therefore, the notion that womanliness as masquerade is simply a placatory gesture which, rather than challenge masculine supremacy, merely affirms it.

Clothes, power and the modern *femme fatale*

The most radical aspect of Riviere's analysis is her argument against 'genuine' womanliness. Instead, she proposes that there is no difference between womanliness and the masquerade: 'whether radical or superficial, they are the same thing' (Riviere 1929: 38). The strength, from a feminist perspective, of this position cannot be understated; for in rejecting essentialism, Riviere paves the way for a rejection of femininity as a construct of male fantasy, dependent as that fantasy is on a notion of 'woman' as fixed and immutable. It is the radicalism of the assertion that womanliness and masquerade are the same thing which greatly preoccupies Stephen Heath in his response to Riviere. In 'Joan Riviere and the masquerade' Heath maintains that by 'Collapsing genuine womanliness and the masquerade together, Riviere undermines the integrity of the former with the artifice of the latter' (Heath 1986: 50). Heath is adamant that the masquerade is undertaken for the benefit of the to-be-pleased man, that, 'the masquerade is the woman's thing, hers, but it is also exactly *for* the man, a male presentation, as he would have her' (50). This slippage is crucial, and exposes an intensely male fear of the very concept of masquerade: why is the performance of excessive womanliness a presentation for the man '*as he would have her*'? Heath's panic presumably stems in part from the realisation that, if there is no such thing as 'genuine' womanliness, then there is no such thing as 'genuine' manliness or a stable subjective male position.

The Last Seduction realises a male nightmare by granting the stable, subjective position to its female protagonist, thus running counter to the formal insistence of most classic *noirs* upon the subjectivity of the male, usually granted through control of the voice-over narration. First, Bridget's control of her masquerade is indicated by the uncharacteristic consistency of her appearance. The *femme fatale*'s duplicity is traditionally manifested through the persistent alteration of her look, her changeable wardrobe becoming a straightforward metonym for her untrustworthiness. The need always to present a different image, however, is also a mark of psychological and emotional instability, and thus an undermining mechanism that, from the perspective of potentially threatened men, nullifies the *femme fatale*'s potential danger. A pattern seems to be emerging suggesting the more costume changes, the more deranged the *femme fatale*, that her pathology is somehow inscribed on her clothes. This tendency is consistent, for example, with the restless representation of the pathological Laurie in *Gun Crazy*, whose sartorial instability is echoed by later examples such as Dolly in *The Hot Spot*, Catherine/ Renée in *Black Widow*, Jude in *Mother's Boys* or Hedy in *Single White Female*, all of whom undergo multiple costume changes and alterations of appearance. Their more dangerous counterparts are those, like Bridget in *The Last Seduction* or Matty in *Body Heat* and Catherine in *Basic Instinct*, who either wear the same outfits twice (usually at key narrative junctures) or present a heavily consistent image. The control these characters exert over the action and characters around them is straightforwardly reflected in their controlled appearances.

As the women in these films acquire greater stability and strength, so the traditionally male subjective privilege is denied the film's men. These 'designated fucks' (as Bridget labels Mike) are marginalised, ignored, beaten, without having recourse to even a narrational voice. Physically, these men are shown to embody lack, and so function as symbolic opposites to the films' images of feminine sophistication. This lack is likewise expressed iconographically through how these characters are dressed. The male lovers in *films noirs* are normally portrayed as inadequate where clothes are concerned, compared with the sharply dressed *femmes fatales*. *The Last Seduction* relishes this imbalance in scenes such as the one in which Mike runs out into the street, blithely parading his loss of power dressed only in crumpled boxer shorts. Tom's stained tie at the beginning of *Disclosure*, or Nick's middle-aged V-neck jumper for the night-club scene in *Basic Instinct* similarly function as symbols of emasculation, of not belonging, of not under- standing the rules of the game. In most instances, these men are also verbally declared to be stupid, the most direct put-down being Matty's during her first conversation with Ned in *Body Heat*: 'You're not too smart. I like that in a man'. The men vainly attempt to retaliate against being categorised as inadequate with lumbering assertions of their masculinity. Nick in *Basic Instinct* repeats, for example, with evident pride, that he considers sex with Catherine to have been 'the fuck of the century', and the rebuffed Mike tries to ingratiate himself once more with Bridget during the first bar scene in *The Last Seduction* by telling her he is 'hung like a horse'. Bridget counters this counter-measure by unzipping Mike's trousers and going in search of that 'certain horse-like quality'. This bumbling need to crudely state their masculinity is evidence, if any were needed, that the penis is nothing like the phallus. It is significant, therefore, that both Mike and Tom are only sexually aggressive when the *femmes fatales*, Bridget and Meredith, force them to be. This manliness as masquerade is phallic panic, a desperate, embarrassing, hysterical reaction to encroaching insignificance.

In *The Last Seduction* this insignificance is signalled by Bridget's successful deployment of masquerade in her relationship with Mike. Mike, as Stephen Heath would advocate, goes vainly in search of the 'genuine' womanliness behind what he perceives to be the 'facade' of Bridget/Wendy Kroy, but Bridget defies this fixity, and presents instead a recurrent reminder of femininity's performative value. Mike, during the 'dominatrix' scene described above, probes Bridget for an explanation for her hardness, and asks her softly what she is so scared of. In response, Bridget plays along, putting on an act of vulnerability and explaining 'I've been hurt before'. Mike, eager to be restored to the position of masculine protector, willingly falls for this, but is jolted from his feeling of superiority when Bridget truculently comes out of character asking, 'Will that do?'. She performs and breaks one masquerade to reveal that there is no outer skin, and no 'inner' womanliness. What is interesting about *The Last Seduction* is that Bridget's masquerade-within-a-masquerade (when she is feigning the sweet or vulnerable woman) is bad and unconvincing. To the spectator, it seems implausible that anyone could be gulled by this superficial performance of an insubstantial stereotype. Whenever Bridget performs helpless femininity it is deliberately and ironically transparent. It is as if she has no need to try, because Mike and the others will believe what they want to believe. Bridget's successful manipulation of others hinges on this received notion that men (there are no other major female characters in *The Last Seduction*) see in women a reflection of their own desires. She thus aggressively presents her body and her repertoire of clothing clichés as the site of male inadequacy, which rather than comfort Mike confront him (and any men who may identify with him) with the unobtainability of his fantasy. The spectator, therefore, compelled to witness this performance, is also compelled to identify with Bridget, a direct reversal of what occurs in most 1940s *films noirs*.

Bridget's masquerade is characterised by its reflectiveness; she does not mirror Mike's desires but throws them back at him. Her most brutal performance is saved for the end as Mike, who has been persuaded to kill her husband Clay, is in her New York apartment. Having chickened out of murder, it is left to Bridget to dispatch Clay, who now lies dead on the sofa. Bridget has arrived for this scene in

5.2 Linda Fiorentino as Bridget in *The Last Seduction*
Courtesy of BFI Stills, Posters and Designs

131

an uncharacteristic masculine trouser suit, complemented by white vest, braces and two-tone brogues. Dressed, therefore, like a man, Bridget subsequently reveals to Mike she has discovered the secret of his unsuccessful marriage, namely that his wife Trish is a transvestite. She laughs and drops her trousers to reveal a pair of male underpants, goading Mike into raping her with taunts of 'I'm Trish, rape me'. Bridget's final, most elaborate and cruel masquerade reflects back at Mike not her excessive femininity, but Mike's terror of his own repressed homosexuality. In another reversal of convention, the male becomes dependent on the female for self-definition; the masquerade, therefore, far from reinforcing the stability of the masculine position, effects its destabilisation.

The most conclusive masculine renunciation of them all occurs in *Disclosure*, a film imbued with a weary resignation, which is nevertheless intent on converting castration into triumph. *Disclosure*, which, like *The Last Seduction*, has at its core a similar preoccupation with gender relationships between a successful and aggressive woman and a more submissive man, fails to convert this radical potential, and instead opts for a 1940s narrative conservatism by closing with the recuperation of masculine integrity, however debilitated and compromised. Tom is a loser. Overlooked for promotion in favour of an old flame, Meredith, he then manages to be manipulated into starting to have sex with her. Although he breaks this off and subsequently wins a ludicrous sexual harassment case against her, he is not restored to a position of superiority by the end, but rather overlooked at work again in favour of another woman. Most regressive is the film's representation of Meredith, the phallic woman who possesses both professional and sexual power but is conventionally defeated by being humiliated and sacked. *Disclosure* remains a man's film, but an apologetic one constructed around the persistently emphasised weakness of Tom.

As with Mike's in *The Last Seduction*, the fragility of Tom's masculine ego is represented through the rise of the homosexual repressed. Returning home after the aborted sex with Meredith, Tom has a nightmare in which Bob, his boss, makes a pass at him in the lift. It is not immediately apparent that this scene is a dream (it cuts from Tom sitting up in bed talking to his wife to a pan down from black to the office building entrance), and for a while is intended, bizarre as this seems within such a regressive framework, to string the spectators along. The two men have a detailed discussion about Tom's uncharacteristically suave suit. Bob starts by admiring it and asking Tom if he can feel it, after which he becomes intrigued by the fabric ('Is it tropical wool?'). Tom replies matter of factly that it is a wool/viscose mix which is 'what makes the pants drape so well'. Bob's advances become more overtly sexual as he touches Tom and compliments him on his physique, then echoing Meredith's words from earlier that evening: 'Now you have the power Tom, you have something I want'. Finally Bob lunges towards Tom to kiss him, and with this distorted, close-up point-of-view shot Tom wakes up screaming.

5.3 Michael Douglas as Tom (with Donald Sutherland) in *Disclosure*
Courtesy of the Ronald Grant Archive

The overriding connotation of the nightmare in *Disclosure* is that, as in cinema's pathologisation of the gangster's vanity, male fascination with dress and appearance is a perversion, and representative of disintegrating heterosexual masculinity. Following on from Nietzsche's assertion that 'woman would not have the genius for finery if she did not have the genius for the secondary role' (quoted in Heath 1986: 50), or de Beauvoir's remark that, 'A man's clothes, like his body, should indicate his transcendence and not attract attention' (de Beauvoir 1949: 543), Tom's scream is a response to having transgressed the stereotyped rules and having imagined himself in the feminine role. Furthermore, Tom does not reluctantly inhabit this role, but is content to be in it, for the more revealing aspects of this sequence are Tom's ease during the conversation with Bob and the narcissistic idealisation of himself as an expensively dressed man. Masculine functionalism, however, is restored in the subsequent scene when Tom enters in crumpled trousers. The lift scene is a moment of disruption and unease, when the camouflaged danger of subversive sexuality is fleetingly permitted to surface. Many *noirs* (most famously *Double Indemnity*'s representation of the relationship between Neff and Keyes) show the male fear of the feminine as a denial or deflection of a fear of homosexuality. The source of the male terror is expressed in *The Last Seduction* and *Disclosure*: there is only one thing more frightening and emasculating than being seduced by a phallic woman and that is being seduced by a man.

133

As consolidated by his 'victory' in the sexual harassment hearings against Meredith, Tom's masculine self-assertion is presented through the submission of the feminine. Unlike Bridget's similarly aggressive, ultra-feminine image in *The Last Seduction*, Meredith's blurring of the boundaries between sexuality and work (in terms of her sex life and work) is ultimately what, within a far more traditional film, defeats her. Until this defeat, however, Meredith is another masculine woman who masquerades, a very 1990s *femme fatale* with a history of seducing subordinate male colleagues she has then sacked rather than killed. One pervasive attitude towards women's clothes established in the 1980s is that erotic femininity and professionalism are incompatible, a view most elaborately expressed in John T. Molloy's influential book *Women: Dress for Success*. According to Molloy, his exhaustive studies of women's office clothes 'prove that to succeed in business and dressing to be sexually attractive are almost mutually exclusive' (Molloy 1980: 21). In this highly prescriptive book, Molloy draws up guidelines for the successful woman's 'business uniform' which include the de-emphasising of the bust by a blazer which 'should cover, not accentuate the contours of your body' (70), the below-the-knee skirt suit and low-heeled, plain pumps. Molloy's discussions of gender distinctions as they pertain to clothes are contradictory, and imply an unresolved relationship between sexuality and social appearance. Molloy denounces any style that emphasises femininity, whether this is the 'secretarial' sweater or bras that fail to completely obscure the nipples, but he also argues that the 'imitation look' (a woman directly emulating a man by wearing masculine clothes or fabrics) makes her look 'winsome not authoritative' (28). Either extreme, whether feminine or masculine, is ultimately bad in Molloy's estimation because they both, whether through proximity or distance between gender and image, emphasise femininity. The resulting paradox is that women in business should be identifiably female but asexual; sexed but not sexed.

Molloy's dogmatic guidelines have been substantially modified in the late 1980s and 1990s. The 'power dressing' of the more modern executive woman conforms to a different, more directly sexual dress code that includes the stilettos and tight, short skirts worn by both Meredith and Bridget. *Disclosure*, though, betrays a similarly regressive attitude towards the cross-over between sex and work to Molloy's book. Meredith embodies everything Molloy advises against: she wears a skirt inches above the knee, high-heeled shoes, a close-cut waistcoat, she sports bare legs and keeps her hair long. Like Tess in Mike Nichols's *Working Girl*, she has 'a mind for business and a bod for sin'. The ambivalence of this image, its potential for radical masquerade is inevitably dissipated in *Disclosure*. During the harassment hearings Meredith, the businesswoman, is punished for violating the unspoken code which forbids the fusion of professionalism and sex when she admits, 'I am a sexually aggressive woman, I like it.' This is signalled as the beginning of her demise by the horrified, condemnatory silence of those present. It is hardly surprising, therefore, that in a film which denigrates female independence as keenly as it disavows male dominance, the person who replaces Meredith in her job should be a safe and unthreatening Molloy archetype: a middle-aged mother in 'serious' rather than 'frivolous' clothes (to use Brownmiller's juxtaposition), the sort of woman any man would entrust a job to. One of the reasons a *femme fatale* such as Meredith is disliked and destroyed is surely that, for all her femininity (and the suggestion of passivity and weakness that reputedly brings) her image remains representative of power.

5.4 Demi Moore as Meredith in *Disclosure*
Courtesy of BFI Stills, Posters and Designs

Both in terms of fashion and film iconography, the clearest illustration of this ambivalence lies in the *femme fatale*'s quintessential attribute, her legs. Women's legs, because of their contradictory connotations, have been the site of much debate among feminists and others. The exposure of women's legs, after centuries of concealment, has been both welcomed and criticised because, although women have become more mobile, their bodies have also been put more prominently on display. Historically, the relationship between women's legs, sexual politics and eroticism has been complex. As legs inevitably facilitate movement, in times of greatest oppression, fashion historians such as James Laver have argued, they have been hidden and restricted. The most extreme examples in western fashion have been the 1860s crinoline, which gave the woman the appearance of floating rather than walking, and the 1910s Hobble-skirt, which, with the accompanying fetter worn underneath to prevent the ripping of the narrow skirts, made it impossible for women to take steps of more than two or three inches (Laver 1969: 224–5). In China the enforced binding of women's feet performed much the same incapacitating function.[4] It is because the shrouding or binding of legs became indicative of women's thwarted power that dress reformers such as Amelia Bloomer in the 1850s and Viscountess Hambledon in the 1880s rebelled against the imposition of cumbersome skirts and tried to pioneer the wearing of trouser-like garments instead. As Anne Hollander notes, 'naked legs were active' (Hollander 1975: 214), an observation that the more liberated women's fashions to emerge after the First World War such as the Flapper dress would seem to confirm. Similarly, Flügel celebrates the emergence of women's legs when, in 1930, he writes, 'legs have emerged after centuries of shrouding, and adult woman at last frankly admits herself to be a biped' (Flügel 1930: 161).

In addition, however, Flügel also notes that legs, after skirts were raised in the 1920s, became the woman's 'chief erotic weapon' (162), a link with sexuality which has only occasionally been broken.[5] The sexual importance of legs (and particularly women's legs because of their forbiddenness) is to do with their proximity to the sex organs; the seventeenth century poet John Donne, as he travels around his mistress in *Love's Progress*, discovers that the vulva can be arrived at more swiftly from the feet and legs, and Hollander remarks that, 'Legs appear in art when the theme is overtly dirty-minded' (Hollander 1975: 218). When discussing 'bifurcation' (literally splitting in two, but in the nineteenth century a euphemism for a pair of women's legs hidden from view) Brownmiller first applauds the advent of shorter skirts in the 1920s as 'an important advance in the history of women's rights' (Brownmiller 1984: 58), but then feels compelled to condemn the 1960s mini (the extreme result of this advance) for its eroticisation of the female form. Feminist writers on clothes have not found an adequate response to the liberated exposure of women's flesh, keen to damn the crinoline but equally uneasy when considering the hotpants, minis and other skimpy garments. As Elizabeth Wilson comments, Brownmiller is abiding by a false logic that, if her argument is to be sustained, must necessarily position the erotically appealing and the functional as opposites. The rationale for such an opposition is ideological, not practical.

The *femme fatale* is 'characterised by her long, lovely legs' (Place 1978: 45), and the male character's desire is often signalled by a directed glance at them (as in *The Postman Always Rings Twice*). Both *The Postman* and *Disclosure* also introduce Cora and Meredith directly through close-ups of their shoes and legs. Similarly there is a frequent over-identification of the *femme fatale* with accessories that adorn her legs, the accessories functioning as coded messages between her and the man who desires her. At the first meeting between Phyllis and Walter, *Double Indemnity* labours the metonymic use of Phyllis's anklet (engraved with her name) and her pom-pom sling-backs, a link between the man's desire and the woman's shoes even more blatantly underlined in an early scene in Dennis Hopper's 1990

5.5 Barbara Stanwyck as Phyllis Dietrichson (with Fred MacMurray) in *Double Indemnity*
Courtesy of BFI Stills, Posters and Designs

neo-*noir The Hot Spot*. Harry's attraction to Gloria is here shown through a subjective pan up her legs and a lingering close-up on her ostentatious, fruit-laden sandals. Dolly (who is also interested in Harry) notices the attention he pays Gloria's shoes and interjects, 'I have a pair of shoes like those, I'll wear them more often; they seem more effective than I remembered'. In the sex scene in *Disclosure*, Tom's comparable look at Meredith's exposed legs is not a simple a case of lust, it also registers their potential danger. Meredith's threat is represented by the small gesture of shifting the position of her legs from being almost demurely together to being assertively and invitingly apart, a movement which suggests both the assumption of a more masculine pose and her sexual availability.

The significance of the *femme fatale*'s 'long, lovely legs', therefore, is that, as symbols for femininity, they represent two things: power and sexuality. The two attributes are brought together in the consistent emphasis placed on high-heeled shoes, particularly the ubiquitous black stiletto worn by the majority of the modern *femmes fatales*, an ambivalence discussed by Kunzle in relation to fetishism and sado-masochism:

There are those whose locomotion in high heels is an aggressive appropriation of space and time (which is why high heels are no enemy to feminism),
the contrary and complementary associations are with precariousness and
imbalance. . . . The higher and more unstable-looking the heel, the more
clearly these contradictions are expressed, and the more clearly is the
duality exposed between woman immobilised, viewed as passive sex-object,
and woman elusive, (literally) *impeding* sexual fulfilment.

(Kunzle 1982: 18)

The established feminist response to sado-masochism is again offered by Coward
when talking about fantasies: 'After all, it is invariably women who are represented
in the masochistic position, usually in the most clichéd ways, and that remains
a problem when women are still subject to real sexual assault and real sexual
victimisation' (Coward 1993: 182). Coward, who is obviously unfamiliar with the
more common sado-masochistic scenarios, dismisses as 'myth' the possibility that
women could explore sexual extremes without 'harmful consequences'. This is
not the only way in which feminists have approached sado-masochism; Gamman
and Makinen, for example, in their discussion of female fetishism and the leather-
clad Emma Peel from *The Avengers* write that 'this sort of active image is rarely
discussed by critics as pleasurable at all', and that feminist debates too frequently
'dismiss all images of strong women as enacting "phallic replacement"' (Gamman
and Makinen 1994: 205–6). Coward's blinkered analysis misses the point that
women can appropriate the pleasures of sado-masochism, and that most accounts
of sado-masochistic relationships stress the ritual of male not female masochism.
Krafft-Ebing, for example, recounts several turn-of-the-century cases of men
known to prostitutes as 'boot lovers' because they enjoyed nothing better than to
be trodden on in high-heeled boots or shoes (Krafft-Ebing 1899: 160–78), and
Clavel Brand, writing in 1970, similarly tells the stories of various men who
like being trampled on by women in stilettos, one of whom enjoys having his
erect penis trodden on (Brand 1970: 69–89). Shoe fetishism scenarios (alluded
to iconographically in *film noirs*) are strongly sado-masochistic, and almost always
structured around the woman as the strong, dominating partner who is wor-
shipped by the weaker man, as Krafft-Ebing comments, 'It is highly probable that
the majority – and perhaps all – of the cases of shoe fetishism [sic], rest upon a basis
of more or less conscious masochistic desire for self-humiliation (Krafft-Ebing
1899: 159). Such scenarios are also commonly structured around ornate, feminine
and high-heeled footwear, not unlike the shoes worn by the *femmes fatales*.

For all the superficial compatabilities in the representations of Meredith and
Bridget, there remains a fundamental difference with regard to the current
debates about gender power dynamics. *The Last Seduction* explores the male desire
for humiliation, that Mike is aroused by being hated, treated like a sex object and

manipulated by Bridget. *Disclosure* alludes to a past sexual relationship between Tom and Meredith likewise based on violence and power, but when Meredith assumes the dominating role, she is perceived as predatory and deviant. The conventional gender dynamic of the *film noir* (and the recent derivative films) is that of the submissive male/dominant female, but most of the films deny and defy this, in favour of a last-gasp reassertion of male subjectivity. *The Last Seduction* does not collude in this unerring belief in the fixity and endurance of the dominant masculine position, rather it poses the question of what happens if the woman is the film's only viable point of active spectator identification and beats them all. *Disclosure*, like the majority of films featuring a fatal woman, offers the sanitised alternative: the battered, bruised but morally victorious wimp.

In *Single White Female* the fetishistic shoe becomes a murder weapon as a man is stabbed through the eye with the silver heel of a black stiletto. A film such as *Single White Female* shifts the emphasis away from difference and the victory or otherwise of the emasculated 'hero' by following the other dominant trend of these current *noir*-esque films: the exploration of relationships between women. Within this convention, the female characters become defined against each other and not against a male opposite. The doubling or mirroring of female characters has emerged as a consistent feature of modern *noirs*, and pertains to the cinematic fascination with symbiotic relationships between markedly different women established in films such as *The Dark Mirror* and *All About Eve*. The mirroring patterns in the modern *noirs* is heavily schematic, and the symbolism of the costumes functions in the most obvious ways. The most consistently employed oppositional model juxtaposes good and bad women, subsequent films echoing the mirroring of Beth (the 'good' wife) and Alex (the 'bad' mistress) in *Fatal Attraction*. The significance of the opposition between the two women is made very clear in the final scene as it is the injured, weak Beth rather than her husband who eventually kills Alex, the Medusa-curled monster from the deep. This pattern, a development of the original *film noir* matrix of older husband, unhappily married *femme fatale* and male lover, is adopted in 1980s/1990s films such as *The Hand That Rocks the Cradle*, *Presumed Innocent* and *Mother's Boys*. Sometimes modifications are made (in *Presumed Innocent*, for instance, the 'good' woman turns out to be 'bad'), but the format remains the same. The opposition is usually enforced by the *femme fatale*, who early in these films creates a conflict with the other 'innocent' woman. Meredith in *Disclosure* requests to see Tom's family photographs and passes comment on his wife's homely appearance, whilst Jade in *Mother's Boys* goes to visit her estranged husband's girlfriend at her work. What then ensues is a territorial game in which the 'good' women strive to fend off the encroachment of their 'bad' rivals. These rivalries are further emphasised by the contrasting physical appearances of the two women and their symbolically differentiated costumes. A standardised set of signifiers have evolved for the *femme fatale*, such as bleached hair, boldly coloured, sexual clothes, heavy make-up and cigarettes. Conversely, their 'good' counterparts usually possess a more 'natural' look of brown hair, minimal make-up and more casual, looser and paler clothes.

This use of female opposites (which inevitably stereotypes women along Madonna/Magdalen lines) is developed into the more complex configuration of ego/ego-ideal set up in films such as *Body Heat* and *Basic Instinct*, in which the differences between paired female characters, in terms of looks, clothes and identities, become blurred rather than exacerbated. Matty in *Body Heat* is not only mistaken for her closest friend, Mary Ann, but has in the past exchanged identities with her. Likewise in *Basic Instinct*, Catherine Tramell looks significantly similar to her two confidantes and lovers, Roxy and Hazel, and at college was involved in an obsessional lesbian relationship with one of the other murder suspects, during which time the two students started to look increasingly alike. This play on fluid, unfixed identities is in some respects a simple problematisation of the instability of the *femme fatale*'s appearance; it is also, however, a narrative manoeuvre (particularly as the men in these films are at best dispensable) that engages with lesbian and 'homosocial' attraction. Alison Lurie comments that, 'To put on someone else's clothes is symbolically to take on their personality' (Lurie 1981: 24), an exchange that, from classic examples like *Rebecca* and *All About Eve*, has been a focal concern of obsessional woman/woman-based films. Jackie Stacey, when referring to issues of lesbian and female spectatorship, argues that a fascination between women is not necessarily propelled exclusively by identification or by erotic desire, but is rather 'a desire to see, to know and to become more like an idealised feminine other' (Stacey 1988: 115). In a later consolidation of this article, Stacey emphasises that her intention is not to de-eroticise desire by suggesting an overlap between desire and cinematic identification, but to eroticise identification between women (Stacey 1994: 29). In many of the obsessional new *noirs* this complex intersection between sexual and platonic recognition is played out within the narratives. In *Black Widow*, this complex process of identification operates throughout the relationship between Alex, a reporter, and Catherine/Renée, a woman who changes identity each time she kills a husband. Despite the ostensible heterosexual framework within which the deadly 'black widow' operates, the film's eroticism, its tensions of identification, are contained within the obsessional interaction between the two women. At the beginning of the film the physical disparity between the two women is accentuated: Alex is dishevelled and asexual, whilst Catherine/Renée wears bright, eroticising clothes and has a heavily made up face. As the film proceeds and Alex hunts Catherine/Renée down, the women become increasingly physically similar, and it is significantly the weaker Alex who alters to look like her double. This erosion of the two women's physical differences directly parallels the developing lesbian attraction-identification between them which culminates in two kisses, one during mouth-to-mouth resuscitation practice, the other on Renée's wedding day. Catherine/Renée is ultimately caught, therefore, by an elaborate process of self-identification with a mirror image of herself.

The melodramatic apotheosis of the ego/ego-ideal film arrives with *Single White Female*, the most overtly lesbian of the obsessional fatal women films, and one that offers a pathological example of this subtle fusion of desire and narcissistic identification. At the beginning of the film, Allie, who has recently split up from her boyfriend, and Hedy, the 'deviant' flatmate she mistakenly chooses to live with her, look very different: Allie dresses in smart New York suits of short skirts and belted jackets, whilst Hedy shuffles into the apartment in a shapeless pinafore and cloche hat. Despite looking safely gauche, she is, however, introduced through a close-up of her feet as she creeps up on Allie unawares, and so is generically defined as fatal from the outset. It is Allie who, at this stage, paradoxically resembles the clichéd image of the *femme fatale*, in tight, black clothes that focus the attention on her long, lovely legs. In an obsessional narrative the confusion and ego-weakness this ambivalence reflects is significant because it suggests Allie's vulnerability to the predatorial encroachment of a neurotically possessive character such as Hedy. Gradually Hedy (who, rather predictably, is still mourning the twin she wrongly feels responsible for killing) alters her look until she closely resembles Allie. It is at this point that Allie realises her flatmate is dangerous, and, although she only wants Hedy to leave, she ends up having to

5.6 Bridget Fonda (Allie) and Jennifer Jason Leigh (Hedy) in *Single White Female*
Courtesy of BFI Stills, Posters and Designs

kill her. Hedy's fatal pathology is the destructive desire to both acquire and assume the character of the other, to destroy Allie as she becomes her, to steal Allie's identity in order to create her own. The assumption that identity is synonymous with appearance is similarly treated as pathological. The recurrent symbolic moment repeated throughout *Single White Female* to denote the shifting relations between Hedy and Allie is the double reflection in the mirror. This preoccupation with checking and rechecking their image is both a sign of weakness (Allie and Hedy both seek validation of the self through the acknowledgement of the symbiotic Other) and a means of charting the gradual disintegration of the physical differences between them.

Countering the prevailing opinion that women who dress fashionably do so within an exclusively heterosexual framework and with the male erotic gaze in mind, Jennifer Craik notes, 'Despite the rhetoric that women dress to please men, other evidence suggests that women primarily dress to please other women' (Craik 1994: 56). The alternative exclusively female dynamic proposed here suggests a way in which the notion of an eroticised identification can be linked with the obsessive belief that clothes reflect an individual's identity: that swapping clothes is both a sexual and a social manoeuvre. The loss of identity and the appropriation of the Other that occurs throughout *Single White Female* is not simply the return of a repressed homoeroticism as has been proposed, it is a more confused (and confusing) smudging of the lines between appearance and personality, a searching for an ideal based on a recognition of the self in the superficial attributes of another. The standardised 'homosocialism' of these films is indicated in *Single White Female* through a series of bonding sequences just after Hedy has moved in: decorating the apartment together, taking a photograph of themselves cavorting on Allie's bed with their new puppy. Hedy has moved in because Allie has recently split up with her adulterous boyfriend Sam, and her jealousy escalates as Allie later renews this heterosexual relationship. This is familiar territory; the complexity resides, however, in the mutuality of the obsessive fascination between the two women, that it is Allie, for example, who instigates a shopping trip and admires Hedy as she tries on new clothes that happen to look just like her own, and who later sneaks around her flatmate's room dabbing on her perfume and trying on her earrings. As with many euphemistic film representations of homosexuality, it is Allie's unarticulated narcissism that provokes her intense preoccupation with Hedy. She becomes fascinated by someone who is fascinated with her, following much the same pattern as *Black Widow*. As *Single White Female* develops, the ostensible stability of sameness, of looking like someone else, becomes a nightmarish metonym for the instability of both Allie and Hedy.

Hedy has been borrowing and wearing her clothes for some time, but Allie's crisis point comes when she discovers that her flatmate has replicated, not merely scavenged or emulated, her entire wardrobe. This transitional moment is emphasised by Allie walking between the two cupboards and holding up the identical sets of clothes for scrutiny. Again there is a destabilising confusion between sameness and difference, and the horror lies not in the pathological pursuit of someone else's identity (which is a commonplace cinematic scenario), but in the ease with which one character can pass for another. Allie's shock, therefore, registers more the accuracy and success of Hedy's mimicry than the obsessional instability behind it, a response captured in her annoyed disbelief as Hedy descends the stairs in the hairdressing salon having been given the same red bob. Comparable scenarios in other films tend to preserve the differences between women who appear similar, so the two identities interconnect, but do not coalesce. Hedy's copying of Allie is not so obviously a performance or a falsification; she can even have sex with Sam without him immediately noticing she is not his sexual partner. Sam's error is to conflate appearance and identity, to presume that a silver coat, black stilettos and red hair signify the person (Allie) he recognises from that collection of signs. Whilst discussing the tacit segregationalism of Allie, a single white female, placing an advertisement specifying that she is 'seeking the same',[6] Lynda Hart comments how she also 'pays an exorbitant price for failing to recognise the terrors of sameness' (Hart 1994: 114). This is a slightly reductive appraisal of the complex mutations and elisions operating in *Single White Female*, and the parameters of this terror should be widened to encompass the notion of unfixed and performative identities the film touches on. To return to Riviere, who posited that there was no such thing as 'real' womanliness, only the masquerade, *Single White Female* suggests a similar lack of faith in essentialism. It is manifestly so easy to pass for someone else. This lack of self, rather than the duplication of the self, is what Allie needs to bury and destroy, a feat she accomplishes during the obligatory *Fatal Attraction*-like exorcism of the demon woman at the end. Despite this ritualistic cleansing, the final image is not a photograph of the happy, united family (as in *Fatal Attraction*), but a collage of Hedy and Allie's faces making up a single image. To extend Lurie's comment, clothes and superficialities are identity.

It is worth mentioning again the scene in *Single White Female* in which Hedy, dressed as Allie, goes to Sam's hotel room at night and performs oral sex on him. Sam fails, until it is too late, to realise his partner is not Allie because he believes in the correlation between appearance and identity, a 'blindness' which Hedy punishes by stabbing out his eye with that most equivocal of signs, the stiletto. Sam's credulity is representative of a distinctly male understanding of women and clothes, rooted in the assumption that women are readily decipherable through how they look, a misapprehension already being played upon in classic *noirs*, and complicated further in these more recent films. All three of the fatal women discussed in this chapter (Bridget, Meredith, Hedy) open up the potential for a radical strategy to counter this limiting interpretation of feminine imagery, as they all test, manipulate and discard the stereotypes on offer, and thus render these supposedly transparent signs unreadable. In the course of this chapter two further assumptions about femininity and clothing have been challenged, namely that power and sex in a woman is a destructive, mutually exclusive combination and that women who dress in anything other than a functional way do so with male eyes and a male audience in mind. Both *The Last Seduction* and *Single White Female* give space to women's erotic identification with the female form, the former through the narrative contextualisation of Bridget's aggressive sexuality, the latter by situating desire within an exclusively female framework. Both films also destabilise and weaken the male position. Not only do these strategies question the omniscience of the male gaze as a necessary concomitant of the mainstream representation of women, but they rearticulate the masquerade. If appearance is identity, as the scenario in *Single White Female* suggests, then an individual is the sum of their superficial, socially constructed parts. The films discussed here nevertheless adhere to the notion of fixed genders, and in the two subsequent chapters the radical, performative possibilities of clothes are examined with relation to films that, at their core, are problematising gender itself.

Part III
BEYOND GENDER

6

THE COMEDY OF CROSS-DRESSING

Glen or Glenda, Mrs Doubtfire, The Adventures of Priscilla, Queen of the Desert

The intention behind this final section of the book is to contrast the questioning and blurring of gender identities that occurs when characters do not wear the clothes deemed socially appropriate to their sex. These discussions suggest an important difference, too frequently elided, between the mechanisms and effects of 'cross-dressing' and 'androgyny' as they are used in film. Whereas in cinema cross-dressing is used to desexualise the transvestite and deflect the potential subversiveness of the image through comedy, androgyny sexualises the transvestite by increasing the eroticism of their ambiguous image. The former is about laughs, the latter about sex. A gag which runs through Howard Hawks and Cary Grant comedies, for example, is the number of times the narratives necessitate Grant to cross-dress. The device is most extensively used in *I Was a Male War Bride* in which Grant, as Henry Rochard, must masquerade as an Admiral's wife in order to leave Europe after the Second World War with his new American wife, but also appears in both *Bringing Up Baby* and *Monkey Business*, which both require him to don, *in extremis*, an item of women's clothing. The motivation for the cross-dressing in *Monkey Business* is particularly weak, as Grant/Barnie gets cold in an open-topped car, and the nearest garment to hand is his wife Ginger Rogers'/Edwina's fur jacket. In *Bringing Up Baby*, Susan (Katherine Hepburn) has dispatched the clothes of the man she is in love with to the cleaners in order to prevent him from leaving her house. After showering, the only garment David (Grant) can find to put on is a precariously diaphanous woman's dressing gown with fur trimming, the outfit he has on when he answers the door to Susan's aunt Elizabeth. The femininity of David's appearance is accentuated by being immediately juxtaposed with the image of one of Hollywood's rich, hearty, masculinised matriarchs in felt hat, loud check suit and sensible shoes.[1] Bypassing pleasantries, Elizabeth immediately draws attention to the anomaly of a tall man in a dainty woman's robe, telling David he looks 'perfectly idiotic' and enquiring why he is wearing those clothes anyway. Most accounts of this exchange focus on Grant's reply that he 'just went gay all of a sudden', taking this to be a teasing allusion to the actor's, now well-documented, bisexuality (for example, Garber 1993: 396). More interesting in terms of what the scene conveys about gender and mismatched clothes than this possible *double entendre* on the word 'gay', however, is the dog George's reaction to the vision of a cross-dressed man. From the moment he sees David slumped on the stairs, George remains transfixed, unable to avert his gaze and provoked into several minutes of incessant, close-range yapping. (If it is presumed that this is an incidental, insignificant detail, it should be noted how the barking interferes with the audibility of the simultaneous conversation between Susan and Elizabeth.) Clothes are not just clothes as the naive David thinks, they are how the social world 'reads' and contextualises the individual. The traumatised George thus functions in *Bringing Up Baby* as a comic verbalisation of a fearful, desperate anger at seeing gender identity boundaries transgressed rather than neatly defined.

One interpretation of the deployment of cross-dressing is that the donning of opposite sex clothes does not undermine but rather reinforces prescriptive gender codes, that a person's 'core gender identity', as Robert Stoller terms it, shines through despite and even because of the contradictory apparel (Stoller 1968: 29). Cary Grant's masculinity, therefore, is re-emphasised by being veiled. Neverthe-less, this does not explain the violence of George's reaction to David's unruly image, which pertains much more to the notion of drag as an abnormalising process than a normalising one. Peter Ackroyd recounts how historically transvestism has also been emblematic of danger, chaos and rituals of misrule, and outlines several cases of cross-dressing being adopted during riots and uprisings as a sign of rebellion. In 1631, for instance, peasants rebelling against the King's enclosure of forest land went under the name of 'Lady Skimmington', and in the 1830s and 1840s male rioters against Welsh turnpike tolls were led by 'Rebecca' and other transvestites. As Ackroyd comments, 'In such cases transvestism has a central, anarchic purpose in the destruction of the established social order', and cross-dressing becomes an act of defiance, not a signal of stable affirmation (Ackroyd 1979: 54). There is something in Grant's disconsolate and increasingly aggressive image during this brief exchange in *Bringing Up Baby* that continues in the tradition of the cross-dressing rioters, adding a tinge of nonconformity and perversity to this otherwise felicitously formulaic comedy.

The importance of George the dog is that he is not a participant in the cross-dressing scene but its spectator, and as such occupies much the same position in relation to the unfolding narrative as a cinema audience does when watching a film. As such, George's reactions to Grant's attire signal a fissure (in the instance of *Bringing Up Baby*, barely disguised) between the normalising intentions of the traditional cross-dressing scenario and the abnormalising subversion of that by the unconventional costume. If the normalising reaction to a male character in drag is along the lines of, 'he's really a man under those feminine clothes, so let's treat him as such', the abnormalising response might go something like, 'you're worrying me in those clothes, take them off and put on some proper ones'. The latter, like George's frenetic barking (and telling pursuit of Grant into the room where he is going to change into some men's clothes), is the response of the spectator who, whatever safety mechanisms are in place, nevertheless comprehends the potential deviancy of the masquerade. Besides examining the exclusively fictional uses of cross-dressing in films such as *Tootsie*, *Mrs Doubtfire* and *The Adventures of Priscilla, Queen of the Desert*. this chapter will also include a discussion of Ed Wood's semi-autobiographical *Glen or Glenda*, in which Wood and his alter ego 'Shirley' play a transvestite modelled on himself. Real cases of transvestism offer more disruptive images than the tempered and rationalised counterparts created by mainstream cinema. Glen/Ed Wood does not (intentionally) sanitise or commodify the potential deviancy of the cross-dresser through the mechanics of comedy.

Since Deuteronomy decreed, 'The woman shall not wear that which pertaineth unto a man, neither shall a man put on a woman's garment; for all that do so are abomination unto the Lord thy God' (Deut. 22:5), dress codes have been conditioned by a belief that clothes should solidify gender identity, not question it. In the genderised costumes examined in the last section of this book, clothes were indeed reflective of the dominant, established and unquestioned sex of the wearer. Cross-dressing severs this relationship between body and social appearance, signifying that the biological body is also culturally inscribed. For the purposes of this discussion of the cracks evidenced by the cross-dresser in mainstream narratives, the divergent theoretical standpoints of Robert Stoller and Marjorie Garber seem particularly useful. First, however, the terms 'cross-dressing', 'transvestism' and 'drag' should briefly be differentiated. Cross-dressing has become the generic term for the set of social and psychological conditions that necessitate the wearing of clothes of the opposite sex. Whilst Garber uses the terms 'cross-dressing' and 'transvestism' interchangeably, Stoller emphatically differentiates between the two, stipulating that transvestism should only refer to fetishistic cross-dressing, 'that is erotic excitement induced by garments of the opposite sex' (Stoller 1985: 176). This distinction between sexual and non-sexual cross-dressing is of particular relevance to the comic use of cross-dressing in mainstream film. Stoller also proffers the opinion that the female transvestite does not exist, that women only cross-dress to gain access to the greater social freedoms afforded men. His contention that, 'I have never seen or heard of a woman who is a biologically normal female and does not question that she was properly assigned as a female, who is an intermittent, fetishistic cross-dresser' (195) will be expanded upon in the following chapter's discussion of *The Ballad of Little Jo*. The final category, 'drag', is exclusively applied to cross-dressing as theatrical performance, primarily in a gay context as seen in *The Adventures of Priscilla, Queen of the Desert*.

Firmly imbued with an intensely Freudian phallocentricism, Stoller places a determined emphasis on the 'real' sex of the individual cross-dresser, rejecting the idea that transvestism or cross-dressing can alter the individual's 'core gender identity'. Thus the transvestite's relationship to his (sic) clothes is sustained by the desire to reinforce sexual difference, the femininity of his appearance paradoxically reinforcing the his essential masculinity:

> Transvestite men may try to be very feminine when dressed in women's clothes. Yet they do not truly feel that they are females. They *wish* they were (at least to the extent of being a woman with a penis) and their transvestism is an acting out of that wish, but *they know they are not*. Their core gender identity is male; that is, they know their bodies are male, that they have been assigned since birth to the male sex, that they were reared as males, and that all the world unequivocally considers them to be and always to have been males.
>
> (1985: 30)

This paradoxical overdetermination of the 'real' sex under the apparently subversive clothes (and in Stoller's rather hysterical tone there lurks the suggestion that he doubts himself on this point), is supposedly not far removed from the gangster in his suit and fedora or the *femme fatale* in her high heels and seductive skirts. Transvestites, in Stoller's estimation, have simply chosen a different outfit with which to demonstrate their essential sex. Marjorie Garber's understanding of cross-dressing is very different, proposing a radical rethinking of the subject and calling for the cross-dresser/transvestite to be seen as a 'third term' which exists outside traditional gender binaries. Garber's argument is that the tendency has been to 'erase' this third term, and that this appropriation of the cross-dresser 'as' one of the two sexes is emblematic of 'a fairly consistent desire to look away from the transvestite as transvestite, not to see cross-dressing except as male or female manqué' and thus to 'underestimate' the object (Garber 1993: 10). This theorisation of the transvestite precipitates a 'category crisis', not just by questioning firmly held notions of 'male' and 'female', but by eluding categorisation altogether and occupying instead 'a space of possibility structuring and confounding culture' (17). Cross-dressing, as Garber perceives it, therefore, is a state of perpetual mobility and mutability, which clearly runs counter to Stoller's firm belief that binary gender classifications cannot be transcended.

Garber's formulation of cross-dressing as a consistently radical act is only consistently evident in real cases. Mainstream cinema's limitation of its subversive potential occurs through the marginalisation of fetishistic transvestism, Ed Wood's persistent references in his films to his own angora fetish proving a rare counterbalance to this conservatism. The cross-dressing in films such as *First a Girl* and its remake *Victor/Victoria*, *Some Like it Hot* and the later Hollywood examples *Tootsie* and *Mrs Doubtfire* are what Garber terms 'progress narratives' (67) or plots in which the cross-dressing is forced upon characters reluctantly, usually for reasons of socio-economic necessity. Thus the two musicians in *Some Like it Hot* become Josephine and Daphne to flee the Mob, unemployed performers like Victoria in *Victor/Victoria* and Michael in *Tootsie* cross-dress in a last-ditch attempt to make money, and Daniel, the divorcee in *Mrs Doubtfire*, takes a job as his ex-wife's housekeeper so he can see more of his children. These are all clear strategies to generate comedy and to side-step the latent issue of perversion, similar to Stoller's (as derived from Freud) notion of transvestite disavowal which one could gloss, 'I am impersonating a woman but nevertheless you and I know that I am still a man'.

The fissure between the sexed body of the actor and the gender being performed is often crudely emphasised, as in two quintessential popular images of cross-dressing set against overtly macho military milieux: Henry Rochard (Cary Grant) as 'Florence' in *I Was a Male War Bride* and Sgt. Klinger in the television series *MASH*. Both these examples pursue 'progress narratives', as Rochard, caught up in military bureaucracy, has to disguise his sex to be allowed on an American ship, whilst Klinger dresses as a woman in a vain attempt to get sent home from Korea. The drawing together of uniforms and cross-dressing is particularly rich (and titillating) because of the military's innate conservatism. Ed Wood, for instance, had red panties and a bra under his uniform during the Second World War (and was most concerned about being injured lest someone should discover his feminine underwear); Klinger's draft dodging has historical antecedents. As Magnus Hirschfeld recounts in *Military Fitness and Transvestism*, there have always been cases of men presenting themselves before draft commit-tees in women's clothes, only some of whom were real transvestites. Far from ostracising either Rochard or Klinger from the macho arena, their cross-dressing appearances ensure that they are subsumed into it; in a manner reminiscent of Stoller, their outfits serve to accentuate not dissipate their masculinity.

Garber has noted a tendency on the part of critics 'to look through rather than at the cross-dresser, to turn away from the close encounter with the transvestite' (Garber 1993: 9). This is a crucial observation for characters such as Rochard and Klinger who, with every gesture, act through their women's clothes to deny and defy their relevance. A significant visual feature of both costumes is how makeshift they are. The intention is not to create, in either case, a credible illusion of femininity, but to reflectively allude back to masculinity via an ill-composed caricature created from a few thrown-together signifiers. The supreme detail of this distancing procedure is Henry's horse's tail wig, crudely tied in a knot under his cap. This functions as a costume version of the conventionalised gestural slip (the male cross-dresser tripping in high heels, hitching up stockings and adjusting girdles) which likewise serve as reminders that the performer is uneasy in women's clothes and ready to discard them.

6.1 Cary Grant as Florence in *I Was a Male War Bride*
Courtesy of BFI Stills, Posters and Designs

To look 'at' as opposed to 'through' the clothes would be to acknowledge what is perceived to be problematically deviant about cross-dressing, namely an attraction to the clothes themselves. (Krafft-Ebing in *Psychopathia Sexualis* brackets transvestites as 'clothes fetishists', so making this point; Krafft-Ebing 1899: 238). The attempted normalisation of the cross-dressing process within mainstream narratives is, however, a falsification of the actual experience of, and reasons for, transvestism. What characterises the majority of transvestite case histories (excepting the accounts of frustrated transsexuals) is an acute sense of the *pleasure* derived from dressing up. The catalyst for adult transvestism is often an incident

in childhood which has little to do with pleasure, such as the child being compelled by a parent to wear the clothes of the other sex, being told they cannot have
a certain item and so developing a fetish for it, or running out of a garment and
so borrowing their sibling's (Krafft-Ebing 1899, Stoller 1968); all scenarios
that ostensibly conform to Garber's 'progress narrative' pattern in which cross-
dressing is necessitated rather than desired. What subsequently predominates in
the real case histories, however, is a passion for the clothes themselves. One of
Hirschfeld's cases describes how it gives him erotic satisfaction to look at himself
in a mirror 'wearing a corset, dainty petticoat, charming clothes, a hat, a veil,
bracelets and necklaces' (Hirschfeld 1935: 197), whilst the seventeenth-century
nobleman François Timeléon de Choisy recounts entering a room dressed in
women's clothes and being 'gazed at to my heart's content: the novelty of my
robes, my diamonds and other finery all attracted attention' (Ackroyd 1979: 9).
Like Mark Simpson's definition of drag as 'an ecstasy of surfaces' (Simpson 1994:
188), these descriptions evoke a sensuous, detailed and affectionate enjoyment of
the clothes themselves.

Allied to the pleasure of being seen dressed up, is the cross-dressing narcissism
specific to the transvestite. Hirschfeld identified various categories of transvestism
(concisely listed in Docter 1988: 6–20) including the 'automonosexual' transvestites who, like the case study quoted above, direct all their desires towards the
contemplation of their own cross-dressed image in the mirror. This is the most
extreme form of transvestite narcissism, but there are diluted transmutations
which are far more common. Peter Ackroyd rather dogmatically assumes that the
transvestite's moment of self-contemplation in front of a mirror is a sad, lonely,
indulgent activity which leads to a 'fruitless *confrontation* with his new mirror
image' (my italics; Ackroyd 1979: 18). Most of the time transvestites do not
describe anything remotely resembling a 'confrontation' with their cross-dressed
image; as one man comments to Nancy Friday, upon seeing this other reflection
'it becomes an effort to avoid collapsing or fainting with ecstasy because now
I am quaking and trembling all over' (Friday 1980: 416). Another one of Friday's
male interviewees also describes enjoying dressing up as a girl saying, 'I look
in the mirror and usually have a hard-on from the soft panties and novelty of
looking so cute' (408–9). What characterises all of these cases and distinguishes
them from straightforward narcissism is the enforced segregation between actual
body image and the different gender-assigned body the transvestite routinely
eroticises. In this respect, therefore, the transvestite does not merely blur gender
as Garber, for one, suggests, but also embodies difference, as both genders
become somehow inscribed on the performative reflective image. This final
manoeuvre is exemplified by Julien Eltinge's series of trick photographs depicting
a wedding between his masculinised and feminised personae.

In *Glen or Glenda* Ed Wood upholds the theory that the transvestite is made up of two halves. *Glen or Glenda* is categorised as one of the worst films of all time, and is remembered for Ed Wood's signature incongruities: bizarre pieces of archive showing buffalo stampedes, cars cruising on the freeway and steel works inserted at grossly inopportune moments; Bela Lugosi as a baffling omniscient puppet master; incomprehensible dialogue. It is probably not remembered as one of cinema's very few attempts to offer a serious analysis of transvestism. After a preface asking society to 'judge not' what they are about to see, *Glen or Glenda* opens with a dramatisation of the real suicide of a transvestite and the subsequent discussion between the police officer assigned to the case and a sex therapist. The doctor then recounts the parallel stories of Glen and Alan, the former a transvestite, the latter a transsexual, to indicate to the policeman that not all cross-dressing cases are alike. Glen (played by Ed Wood) is the focus of the film, and his story contains most of its autobiographical references, although Alan's cross-dressing during active service in the 1940s alludes to Wood's own wartime experiences. *Glen or Glenda* has a thesis which it pursues in earnest (namely that transvestites and transsexuals are not criminals despite their social stigmatisation) which is interwoven with the representative narrative of Glen and his engagement and eventual marriage to Barbara. The film is a confused and confusing patchwork of documentary-esque explanations of transvestism, idiosyncratic psycho-babble, unrelated library footage that Wood just happened to possess, and expressionistic dramatisation. Due to Ed Wood's lack of time, budget and talent it is impossible to offer a theoretical analysis of *Glen or Glenda* that can be in any way meaningful. Instead, it stands as a unique alternative to the cross-dressing comedies, a personal testimony which in turn emphasises all the 'perverse' details such sanitised views omit.

Glen or Glenda significantly reinstates the fetishistic element of cross-dressing and thus the importance of women's clothing to both the character's arousal and his identity. There is, for example, the repeated pacing (as both Glen and Glenda) past the window displays of lingerie stores, the sensual attachment to Barbara's angora sweater and the lingering perusal of a diaphanous night-gown. In its unintentionally comic, earnest way, *Glen or Glenda* stresses the pervasiveness and normality of the transvestite's arousal from women's clothes, asking the spectator to imagine the 'soft, pink panties' a rough, tough labourer might be sporting under his overalls and making the crucial distinction between transvestism and homosexuality. Substantiating this there is a sequence showing a 'deviant' homosexual trying to pick up Glen dressed as Glenda and a ponderous piece of voice-over stating matter-of-factly that the transvestite's sex life 'in all instances remains quite normal'. Ed Wood is here responding to a common misconception, frequently worked into cross-dressing comedies, that the sexuality as well as the gender of those in the wrong trousers is ambiguous and perverse. Both Victor/Victoria in *Victor/Victoria* and Michael/Dorothy in *Tootsie* are presumed to be gay and/or lesbian at crucial

6.2 Ed Wood and Dolores Fuller in *Glen or Glenda*
Courtesy of BFI Stills, Posters and Designs

junctures, and Daniel/Ephigenia in *Mrs Doubtfire* is brandished a 'deviant' by the divorce courts.

Glen or Glenda is a touching (if farcical) indictment of the social prejudice implicit in cross-dressing comedies. In a sequence such as the one showing a bearded man relaxing in satin leisure wear and earrings accompanied by a voice-over asking 'what would happen if this individual were to appear on the street?', Wood is confronting us with our dismissal of such an image as comic. Half-way through the film there is a protracted fantasy/nightmare sequence (for which the term 'expressionistic' is apposite if a little grandiose) which represents the confrontation between the cross-dresser and an oppressive society. Leaving to one side the Nosferatu-esque devil who appears to symbolise Glen's conscience whilst he remains closeted, this medley of scenes contains two important points: first, that most individuals in private have exotic sexual fantasies, and second that society is too dependent on gender binaries. Thus women in transparent robes squirm on sofas, being flagellated or tied up, and Glen imagines being hounded by a group comprising of men, women and the devil, whilst the voice-over taunts him with chants about the differences between girls and boys. The nightmare subsides as Glen/Glenda emerges triumphantly through the crowd dressed in his/her ubiquitous angora sweater, tight office skirt, heels and jewellery. Ed Wood realises this is a utopian fantasy, but in this moment, as the conservative hoards disperse, Glenda embodies the notion of the 'third term' and challenges the absolute belief in fixed gender identities the others represent.

The comic portrayals of cross-dressing generally repress anything so transgressive. One of the most successful Hollywood cross-dressing films has been *Tootsie*, the story of out-of-work actor Michael Dorsey (Dustin Hoffman), who, in a last-ditch attempt to raise the money for his flatmate Jeff's new play, becomes 'Dorothy Michaels' and lands a female role in a leading daytime soap. An insidious film implying that men make better women than women do, *Tootsie* has, nevertheless, been championed by Garber, who argues for a 'metadramatic' element within the narrative that implies a similarly fetishistic fascination with women's clothes to that found in a film such as *Glen or Glenda*. The scenes which Garber feels substantiate this reading are those in which Michael discusses and looks through his Dorothy outfits with his bemused and worried flatmate Jeff (Garber 1993: 5–9). Despite Jeff's perceptive enquiry, 'Are you really doing it for the money, or do you like wearing those little outfits?', *Tootsie* is sadly rarely as enticingly deviant as Garber suggests.[2] Garber's interpretation stresses the enjoyment Michael derives from creating Dorothy, but this is habitually undermined by a vehement affirmation of Michael's masculinity. A sequence that demonstrates this regressive deflection away from the fluid radicality of her 'third term' category occurs when Michael (having got the soap opera part of Emily Kimberley) is caught in his underwear by his friend Sandy, having been on the point of trying some of her dresses on. As Sandy is in the shower, Michael steals into her bedroom and finds a couple of her frocks, gradually getting more relaxed and extravagant with his feminine gestures as he swishes about in front of the mirror holding the dresses up to himself. As Sandy returns to find him virtually naked, the only option open to Michael, if he is not going to be thought deviant, is spontaneously to declare his desire for Sandy (saying 'Sandy, I want you') and to sleep with her. Transvestite clothes are thus used as a comic prelude to the reinstatement of Michael's true sex and heterosexuality.

It is significant that transvestites often express narcissistic love through the distantiating desire for what some of them identify specifically as 'the Other', because it is during this exchange that a 'third', independent identity is created. There are several documented cases which signal this very clearly, among them that of the shoemaker arrested for stealing female undergarments recounted by Krafft-Ebing, who at night 'would put on the stolen clothing and create beautiful women in imagination, thus inducing pleasurable feelings and ejaculation' (Krafft-Ebing 1899: 238–9). Michael in *Tootsie* is forever praising Dorothy, saying she is 'brighter' than he is or that she 'deserves' a better wig and nicer clothes, but, like Krafft-Ebing's case, he seldom collapses that identity into his own. (The later

Hollywood cross-dresser Daniel Hillard is similarly vain on behalf of his creation Mrs Doubtfire, and is visibly aggrieved when he hears that the Court Liaison Officer has described her as 'very unattractive'). The narcissistic 'third term' is created as the transvestite image is performed in front of the mirror, in the imagination or in a photograph. Such radicalism is clearly avoided in *Tootsie* as, by the end, the conformist distinction between Michael and Dorothy is absolute. In the final scene Michael tells Julie (the woman who, by this point, he is in love with) that Dorothy is still here: 'I've just got to learn to do it without the clothes'. Even though they walk off engaged in a 'girlie' conversation about dresses, *Tootsie*'s closure is signalled by Michael's desire to leave the deviant woman behind, and indeed to incorporate her into himself as his (socially acceptable) 'feminine side'. Being a woman, therefore, is part of being a good man.

The innate paradox of most fictional mainstream representations of cross-dressing is that, despite suggestions of imminent danger, they remain unthreatening because they subsume any disruptive potential into an analgesic farce. There are various ways in which the fundamental tension between danger and safety is manifested, the most obvious being the discrepancy between character and costume or body and clothes. In *Mrs Doubtfire*, for instance, Robin Williams's prosthetic mask literally slips at one point. The importance of the films' often manic oscillation between the character in and out of disguise is only partly to generate laughter; the device also functions as moral ballast, a reminder of the continued existence of the 'real' person under the complicating make-up. Similarly, there are the moments of danger when the cross-dressed character risks discovery (almost always involving bathrooms or beauty routines) and his/her ever increasing desire to drop the disguise. Much mainstream comedy uses the cross-dressing scenario as an obstacle to signal denial and the frustration of desire. For most of *Tootsie*, therefore, Michael's impersonation of Dorothy comes in the way of his pursuit of Julie, and Victoria's masquerade as Victor in *Victor/Victoria* temporarily prevents her from getting together with King.

The transvestite image itself is a fault line, a crack between sex and gender, a site of ambiguity and change. The incomplete transvestite image is invariably more perverse and sexual than the completed or 'closed' one, and it is precisely this which, in cross-dressing comedies, is rarely allowed to linger. The hairy transvestite reading his newspaper in *Glen or Glenda* (which the voice-over presumes the audience will laugh at), Michael Dorsey in pantyhose and girdle in *Tootsie*, Tony Curtis in male blazer and slacks plus dangling earrings in *Some Like it Hot* all represent, like Grant in *Bringing Up Baby*, the moment of transgression itself. Conventionally, therefore, the point at which the cross-dresser breaks the disguise by ripping off the wig and revealing who s/he 'really' is is reassuring for both the audience and the character coming out of disguise. The necessary concomitants of this dismantling scenario, this transvestite striptease, are the categorical instatement of difference and the simplification of the cross-dresser's gendered identity.

A rare instance, though, when perversity wins over legitimacy is the finale of *Some Like it Hot*. In this scene Daphne/Jerry (Jack Lemmon) is trying to extricate her/himself from the engagement to Osgood, an old millionaire suitor who has been in pursuit since Daphne/Jerry joined an all-female band to escape the Chicago mob. Getting increasingly desperate, Daphne offers Osgood several reasons why she will not make a suitable wife ('I'm not a natural blonde', 'I smoke', 'I have a terrible past'), but he shrugs them all off in turn. As a final resort, Daphne pulls off her wig to reveal Jerry: 'You don't understand Osgood, [voice lowers] I'm a man'. Such a blatant exposure tactic can usually be relied upon to shock and anger those characters who have been gulled by the cross-dressing (at a similar juncture in *Tootsie*, for instance, Jessica Lange slaps Dustin Hoffman), but Osgood simply smiles and replies, 'Nobody's perfect'. *Some Like it Hot* ends on the glorious image of a panicked Jack Lemmon in a frock, earrings and masculine hair confined forever to the point of transgression and doubt. Osgood is smiling because he knew all the time. When, as in *Some Like it Hot*, the segregation of the 'real' from the 'false' image fails to horrify, the destabilising chaos of the 'third' sex is foregrounded rather than repressed. The attraction of even ostensibly non-radical cross-dressing narratives is that the normalising manoeuvres never quite cancel out the abnormalising ones, that the spectator, like George in *Bringing Up Baby*, is privy to the intermittent displays of perversion whilst at the same time being instructed not to fret unduly over their implications.

This is a moment of phallic panic, when the mere possession of a penis under his dress is not enough to assure the conventional dissolution of Jerry's transvestite image. The panic signals the most terrifying fissure of all, that someone can desire the ambiguous, 'third term' body. In *Mrs Doubtfire*, Daniel Hillard experiences a similar moment of phallic panic as a bus driver who has taken a shine to Mrs Doubtfire sees an excessively hairy knee between a skirt and a droopy stocking and shows not disgust but attraction, saying he likes 'the Mediterranean look' in women because this is as 'God intended' them. Mrs Doubtfire, needless to say, hurriedly covers up the transgressive knee. *Mrs Doubtfire* is a 1990s 'progress narrative' about a newly divorced father who adopts the disguise of a 60-year-old Scottish woman and takes the position of housekeeper in his old home. Unlike *Some Like it Hot*, *Mrs Doubtfire*, though rife with subversive ambiguities, appears all but unaware of its potential deviancy, and as a result crystallises many of the debates surrounding cross-dressing in the context of ostensibly non-confrontational cinema. In its attention to elaborate make-up, *Mrs Doubtfire* recalls the very different methods of presenting the feminine of drag – theatrical cross-dressing. Misogynist cross-dressing directs the gaze of the spectator towards the woman's body and away from the man's; as Simpson comments about drag, this also entails the ridicule of the woman's body through representation:

> Much of the entertainment of drag depends upon the improbability and inappropriateness of a man in a frock, wig and 'falsies'. But this in turn depends upon not just the improbability of a man dressed as a woman but the 'improbability' of the female body itself.
>
> (Simpson 1994: 179)

Although pertaining very much to the tradition of quasi-credible cross-dressing established in films such as *Tootsie* and *Victor/Victoria*, *Mrs Doubtfire* is also part of the convention of drag in that it cites and makes strange femininity in the manner found, for example, in the gay drag films *La Cage Aux Folles* and its Hollywood remake, *The Birdcage*. Mrs Doubtfire is something of an anomaly among conventional, comic cross-dressed characters, in that she is both grotesque and her disguise intricately conceived.

The intricacy of Mrs Doubtfire's costume and appearance is principally evident in the extensive use made of prosthetic make-up. At first glance it would seem justified to formulate an equation which proves the more ardent the pursuit of credible femininity, the less male-orientated or misogynistic the impersonation. As in male fetishism's ambivalent over-valuation of the feminine, though, the methodical disguise of Robin Williams's masculinity becomes an elaborate counter-measure for containing the transvestite threat, and thus another way of displacing deviancy. The emphasis of the make-up and hair artists on the film (Greg Cannom, Ve Neill and Yolanda Toussieng) was to hide Williams 'in the manner that was needed for the plot' (Loren 1994: 91), which meant that heavy foundation and a prosthetic nose alone, as they had originally intended, was insufficient. What the make-up artists subsequently constructed were more elaborate rubber masks (both full appliances and single-piece masks for scenes in which Williams was required to change back and forth between Daniel and Mrs Doubtfire), of which forty copies were made as each could be used only once. To accompany this, a full body suit was created which extended from Williams' chin to his knees (Loren 1994: 91), and a curly wig to balance the actor's strong jaw. The whole application process took three hours every day. These would remain incidental details if it were not for the fact that this entire procedure is reproduced within the film in the sequences involving Frank (Harvey Fierstein), Daniel's gay make-up artist brother.

Like the actual make-up artists, Frank and his partner begin optimistically with minor prosthetics, creating two possible disguises, a black-bobbed Cleopatra/Louise Brooks type and a Yiddish granny. Everyone decides that they need to go a stage further, so a plaster mould is cast of Daniel's face and a latex mask made, resulting first in a Barbra Streisand-esque mistake and finally 'Mrs Doubtfire'. This last successful image is assembled for the spectator through a montage of extreme

6.3 Robin Williams as Mrs Doubtfire in *Mrs Doubtfire*
Courtesy of BFI Stills, Posters and Designs

close-ups (made-up eyes, stockings being pulled up, a skirt being buttoned), before the full-length person is revealed, the height of desexualised demureness in glasses, round-collared floral shirt, pale blue cardigan, sensible skirt and lace-up shoes. This fragmentation and assembly of the over-feminine image echoes the conventional cinematic fetishisation of the female form. This construction process is a departure from the prototype of maximising the surprise and contrast with the original masculinity by cutting sharply to the new 'dragged-up' image as occurs in both *Some Like it Hot* and *Tootsie*, and is closer to the emphasis on the transitional phase of *Glen or Glenda*. In *Mrs Doubtfire*, however, the very effort of creation distances the new image and prioritises (visually and theoretically) the disguised masculine body, for the over-falsification of the appearance paradoxically implies (in the imagination) that which it ostensibly hides. More clearly than many other films *Mrs Doubtfire* articulates through costume the function of full, faultless disguise as the mechanism for ostensibly suppressing the radical subversiveness of Garber's 'third term'. The repressive and painstakingly composed appearance (a preponderance of florals, pleated skirts and high-collars clasped tightly in prim brooches) attests to how hard it is to keep deviancy at bay. Mrs Doubtfire's appearance is thus a hysterical barricade against the dangers of ambiguity. The threat of ambiguity is signalled by Daniel himself, who, in his successful attempt to get the job, impersonates over the telephone to his wife Miranda a range of unsuitable women supposedly interested in the position of housekeeper, of whom one is a transsexual. In another scene, during which Daniel has to change rapidly into Mrs Doubtfire for the Court Liaison Officer, he loses his latex mask. As he checks his hybrid reflection in the mirror Daniel gasps, 'Aah – Norman Bates!' before deciding the only option is to bury his face in a cream gateau and pretend it is a beauty treatment. Eccentricity is infinitely preferable to psychotic perversity.

It has been posited that the reason for so many male transvestites looking 'drab' and 'old-fashioned' is that their notion of femininity is fixed by their early memories of their mothers, and that their clothes 'represent a kind of desperate conformism' and an 'attempt to pass unnoticed' (Ackroyd 1979: 23). The implication behind Ackroyd's comment is that the transvestite does not wish to

6.4 Robin Williams as Mrs Doubtfire with his family in *Mrs Doubtfire*
Courtesy of BFI Stills, Posters and Designs

be found alluring. Male to female cross-dressers in film are iconographically coded as undesirable, their clothes are excessively prudish and unrevealing, and if they dress up they are usually painfully *démodé*. They are also often set against more conventionally attractive pictures of femininity such as Jessica Lange, Geena Davis or Sally Field. Because these cross-dressed characters are in the wrong clothes 'of necessity', the conscious eroticism is exorcised from their appearance, and praise for their style (such as the compliments paid to Dorothy Michaels' 'lovely blouse' or 'cute little figure' by other women) or the fact that other men find them desirable are ironic. Garber's interpretation that Dorothy in *Tootsie* 'is more attractive, even seductive, in some ways than any other character in the film' (Garber 1993: 7) is a romanticisation of the intentions behind the image, and, in theoretical terms, a wilful misreading of the feminine iconography, which codifies Dorothy and Mrs Doubtfire as ugly and asexual in their high-necked night-gowns, curlers and A-line skirts. Garber, therefore, would seem to be responding to the attraction of the metaphoric, as opposed to the physical, appeal of the transvestite as the site of confusion, frisson and danger.

A concomitant necessity of this unthreatening appearance is the reminder (to the audience) that the masculinity of the wearer is to remain threatening. The 'phallic woman' is an imperative notion for the transvestite; the disguise of the penis, in the sure knowledge that it is retained, is the determined emphasis of much performed cross-dressing. As Stoller suggests, 'An essential part of his [the transvestite's] pleasure is to know that while dressed as a woman he has a penis' (Stoller 1985: 13), and as Garber elaborates, 'Cross-dressing is about the phallus as constitutively veiled' (Garber 1993: 390). The hidden penis (or, alternatively, hidden breasts and vagina) is also one of the eroticising features of the transvestite body which, for the spectator, remains an imagined fantasy. As one transvestite prostitute ('Jack Saul') conveys when describing cruising through a ball on the Strand, 'I do not believe there was one real female in the room, for I groped ever so many of them, and always found a nice little cock under their petticoats' (Ackroyd 1979: 61). The dormant fear which accompanies the need to check and double-check that the penis, though 'veiled', is still intact (on others, clearly, as well as on oneself) manifests itself clearly in Daniel/Mrs Doubtfire's obsessive preoccupation with his ex-wife Miranda's new suitor, the film's idealised phallus in the form of the fit, tanned, athletic Stu (Pierce Brosnan). The rivalry scenes, during which Mrs Doubtfire vandalises Stu's Mercedes, passes ribald comments concerning the inverse ratio of big cars to size of genitalia and even tries to poison him, demonstrate the ambivalence not only of the cross-dressed body but also of the cross-dressing clothes. The motivating force behind these actions is Daniel who, both veiled/protected by his costume and trapped within it, is caught in the double bind of the 'progress narrative' cross-dresser: the disguise nominally accentuates Daniel's masculinity but also renders it inexpressible.

The comedy of cross-dressing

The most transgressive incident in *Mrs Doubtfire* is, predictably perhaps, a moment of phallic revelation, involving the ultimate 'potential Waterloo' (Garber 1993: 47) of the cross-dressing film, the bathroom. One of Daniel's three children, Chris, inadvertently bursts in on Mrs Doubtfire, in cardigan, skirt and pearls, urinating standing up. The son understandably panics, and shouts to his sister Lydia that Mrs Doubtfire is 'half man, half woman'. To recuperate the situation and prevent his children from calling 911, Daniel/Mrs Doubtfire lowers the tone of his voice to reveal to them who, under his clothes, he really is. They then signal their joy and call Daniel 'dad', despite the clothes and make-up. Whilst Lydia is happy to hug 'dad' in his prosthetics and pearls, Chris refuses physical contact (as Daniel understands, 'it's a man thing'), asking warily, 'You don't really like wearing that stuff?'. It is on the level of spectatorship that the most radical cracks in *Mrs Doubtfire* are revealed, between the outward stability of the old housekeeper's image and the veiled phallus and, more pervasively, between the bland exterior of the mainstream narrative and *mise-en-scène* and the closeted skeleton of perversion. The bathroom scene is, despite its unerring attempts to function as restorative 'normalisation', a deeply transgressive interlude, when the veneer of mundanity is brutally scarred. A child sees his father, dressed as a woman with his penis out, and is pleased to have him back? Garber, at the end of *Vested Interests*, contends that cross-dressing itself is a 'primal scene', an image (conventionally of parental love-making) based in reality and constituted in fantasy, 'not only constitutive of culture, but also, by the same repressive mechanism, a deferral and a displacement' (Garber 1993: 389). Similarly the phallic disclosure in *Mrs Doubtfire* conceals as much as it reveals and fails to stabilise anything at all.

As a sign of the irresistible force of the 'progress narrative', Daniel, towards the end of *Mrs Doubtfire*, is affronted at now being branded a 'deviant' by the divorce courts, and only permitted to see his children if supervised. There are not many conventional narratives that could sustain such a gross inflection as Chris's 'primal scene', and not crack, but *Mrs Doubtfire* is devoid of overt reflectivity. This discussion began with reference to the laborious make-up procedure needed to make Robin Williams a 'convincing' older woman, and just as that approximation of the 'real' belied a subversive intent (to accentuate the masculinity so heavily disguised), so does the film's classic narrative. By emphasising its sanity, probity and conservatism, *Mrs Doubtfire* protests too much, and in effect emphasises, through distance, the perversity it is straining to conceal. By the end, the final normative act is performed as Daniel separates from Mrs Doubtfire (who has become a children's television celebrity) and is allowed, dressed as himself, to look after his kids every day after school. But even this straightening out of the cross-dresser cannot whitewash away the deviancy. In *The Adventures of Priscilla, Queen of the Desert* there is a comparable father/son relationship to the one found in *Mrs Doubtfire*, between Tick/Mitzi and Ben. Mitzi is a drag queen, a female impersonator who mimes to Abba songs, but his ex-wife (Marion) ensures that this is not concealed from their son, who winds up watching his father perform and directing his spotlight. Whilst the conformist scenario in *Mrs Doubtfire* camouflages the 'perversity' of cross-dressing, the nonconformist drag act camouflages 'respectability'. The fundamental shift that has occurred is that in a film such as *Priscilla*, cross-dressing is performance rather than 'necessity'.

There have been various national theatrical traditions, from the Greeks and Romans onwards, in which cross-dressing has become an accepted and formalised type of performance, most notably, in the modern era, in Italy, Japan, China and England (Ackroyd 1979: 89–122, Baker R. 1994: 23–95, Garber 1993: 234–66). The emphasis of many such (male) cross-dressed actors was on performance or citation of femininity, as Goethe comments of the seventeenth-century Italian opera use of castrati in female roles:

> Thus a double exposure is given in that these persons are not women but only represent women. The young men have studied the properties of the sex in its being and behaviours . . . they represent not themselves, but a nature absolutely foreign to them.
>
> (Ackroyd 1979: 98)

In China, the 'tan' actors, or female impersonators rose to prominence in the late eighteenth century, after women had been banned from the stage for moral reasons. Chinese theatre developed a tradition of female impersonation based on an ornate and rigid vocabulary of gestures, costume and make-up (Baker R. 1994: 72), and there were several distinct categories of roles for 'tan' actors, all of which demanded specific skills and emphases, from the elegant woman (or 'chingyi') to the lower-class woman (or 'huatan'). What was sought, as in Italian seventeenth-century opera, was a prescriptive enactment of femininity, a statement of and about women, not a replication. The confusion between these Chinese female impersonators and women forms the basis for the play and film *M. Butterfly*, loosely based on the true story of a diplomat (René Gallimard in the play) who falls in love with a Chinese actress who subsequently turns out to be both a spy and a man. The playwright David Henry Hwang suggests, as an explanation for his extreme naiveté, that Gallimard became so infatuated with a symbolic representation of Oriental femininity, based partly on the clichéd stereotype offered by Puccini's *Madame Butterfly*, that he did not question his lover's supposed modesty which had kept him from ever seeing his 'girlfriend' naked. The last sequence of David Cronenberg's otherwise awkward adaptation of this story encapsulates the painful improbability of the masculine citation of femininity, as Gallimard (Jeremy Irons) performs a one-person show in prison in which he applies the operatic make-up, talking as if he has become his lover, and kills himself.

Many of the comic narratives cited above utilise performance as a means of legitimising cross-dressing and the deviancy of the straight characters' behaviour. Both Michael Dorsey and Daniel Hillard are barely employed actors, not because they are bad, but because they are principled. *Tootsie* begins by cross-cutting between Michael giving acting lessons and attending auditions or rehearsing, which is when he walks out of a production over a disagreement with the director. Similarly *Mrs Doubtfire* establishes Daniel as a capable performer, in this instance in a dubbing theatre laying down the various voices to accompany a children's cartoon, who walks out because the producer disapproves of an anti-smoking line he has ad-libbed into the script. *Victor/Victoria* makes use of a similar initial premise for the stage transvestism of destitute singer Victoria Grant (Julie Andrews) who, adopting a Shakespearean 'double drag' in reverse (girl plays boy plays girl), becomes the most famous female impersonator in 1930s Paris. The difference, however (as, to a certain extent, with *M. Butterfly*), lies in the film's overtly gay backdrop used to tentatively erotic effect towards the end as King (James Garner) and Victoria have started their straight affair, but can only go out together to Brassaï-esque gay and lesbian night-clubs as Victoria is still thought to be 'Victor'.

The significant link between the historical conflation of cross-dressing with performance and gay drag is the notion of citationality, of self-consciously putting femininity in quotation marks. Drag as gay entertainment has currently been undergoing a radical reassessment, most notably in the work of Judith Butler. In her discussion of drag in *Gender Trouble*, Butler criticises Esther Newton's writing on the subject in the 1970s. A fundamental discrepancy is between Newton's comprehension of drag as governed by difference and Butler's notion of performativity and fluid identities, a debate that focuses on the relationship between the exteriority and interiority of the drag performer. Newton begins by asserting that 'The principal opposition around which the gay world revolves is masculine–feminine' (Newton 1979: 100), pursuing this into a discussion of two different levels of drag. Within the 'sartorial system', Newton suggests, this male/female binary is enacted by the clear juxtaposition of first two layers of gendered clothes, either feminine on the outside and masculine on the inside, or vice versa. The clothes that are visible are defined as 'costume' and presumed to be symbolic of a role or an act, whilst those that remain hidden reflect the wearer's 'inner identification' (100–1). The 'second level' of female impersonation juxta-poses the (stable, gendered) body with one set of gendered costumes, which

> poses an opposition between one sex-role sartorial system and the 'self', whose identity has to be indicated in some way. Thus when impersonators are performing, the oppositional play is between 'appearance' which is female, and 'reality', or 'essence', which is male.
>
> (101)

Here, drag is still perceived to be a primary indicator of difference: the exterior is consciously citing a gender which remains distinct from that of the concealed body.

Arguing for a different interpretation of drag, Simpson focuses specifically on the stereotyping of femininity that in Newton's differentiation between 'appearance' and 'essence' remains implicit, commenting that 'the travesty of drag' can go beyond 'mere carnival' and

> can take the form of an *incitement to rebellion*. It can express a desire to revolt against that most tyrannical of laws, the 'natural' link between sex and gender. This drag-as-rebellion, strange to relate, can even represent a rejection of the denigration of women's bodies on the basis of lack.
>
> (Simpson 1994: 180)

Under attack here, therefore, is the propensity for misogyny in drag, the use of costume to pass negative comment on women, as occurs in both the 'progress narratives' and old-fashioned heterosexist impersonations such as Dick Emery's 'Oooh you are awful – but I like you' woman, and the drag acts of Benny Hill or Les Dawson. A film such as *The Adventures of Priscilla, Queen of the Desert* clearly positions itself not merely within the context of gay drag, but drag as anti-misogynistic. There is a brief flashback, for instance, in which one of the drag queens (Adam/Felicia) recalls an uncle's attempted sexual abuse of him being curtailed by the uncle's penis getting trapped in the plug-hole. This is not a film overly concerned with the preservation of the penis or heterosexism, nor is it a text tied to a preoccupation of fixed gender identities.

Judith Butler's radical response to most previous writings about gender questions the idea of gender identity itself. As she comments in her response to Newton, 'drag fully subverts the distinction between inner and outer psychic space and effectively mocks both the expressive model of gender and the notion of a true identity' (Butler 1990: 137). In a manner which carries forward the arguments (raised in the discussion of *femmes fatales*) about femininity as construction identified in Riviere's analysis of masquerade or de Beauvoir's dictum, 'One is not born a woman, rather one becomes one', Butler reverses the dynamics of the body/social performance relationship as they have been traditionally understood:

> According to the understanding of identification as an enacted fantasy or incorporation, however, it is clear that this idealisation is an effect of a corporeal signification. In other words, acts, gestures, and desire produce the effect of an internal core substance, but produce this *on the surface* of the body, through the play of signifying absences that suggest, but never reveal, the organising principle of identity as a cause. Such acts, gestures,

enactments, generally construed, are *performative* in the sense that the essence or identity that they otherwise purport to express are *fabrications* manufactured and sustained through corporeal signs and other discursive means.

(136)

This assessment of the body/appearance dynamic is relevant to both a discussion of drag and to clothes generally, as it emphasises (as does Garber's concept of the 'third term') the fluidity of identity and the construction of that identity simply at the moment of performance. Clothes are always performative in that they function as signs or enactments on the body to give that body the illusion of integrity and substance. They are not, however, always read as such, particularly when they become costumes for a film where, of necessity, they function as signifiers for solidifying characters who, from the standpoint of production and intention, are completed and non-fluid entities. Costume does, though, have performative potential if one transfers Butler's discussion to the act of spectatorship, as, at the point of reception, the on-screen characters are always mutable, and comprise a series of enactments and gestures which can be identified and engaged with in multifarious ways.

The Adventures of Priscilla, Queen of the Desert is the story of three characters (two drag queens – Mitzi/Tick and Felicia/Adam and a transsexual – Bernadette) travelling across Australia from Sydney to Alice Springs on a bus called 'Priscilla'. As a film it clearly desires and suggests such fluidities as Butler proposes on both the textual and the spectatorial side. Ostensibly a minimalistically plotted drag road movie, *Priscilla* offers a playful critique of gender and sexual identity on many levels, not least within the narrative framework itself which subverts and dismantles conventional mainstream structures. As if extending the recent arguments about the performativity of drag, the way in which drag performance itself is contextualised within *Priscilla* allows it no stability or normalisation. The mime/dance numbers performed by the three principal characters pertain in one sense to the logical development of the film's narrative (for example as they top and tail the film); tangentially they exist also as emblematic counterpoints to this causality as narrative interjections or moments of emblematic stasis, functioning in a comparable way to songs in musicals. This duality forces attention onto the act of performing (the costumes, the song, the dance routine), an emphasis that is underlined by the performances being directed largely to or for the camera.

Priscilla is an assembly of citations of gender and sexuality, and as a film is intensely aware of establishing the characters' very different relationships with the drag and the non-drag or heterosexual spheres. Within the film the notion of fluid and split identities is focused on the issue of naming. Names are of fundamental significance to any individual who cross-dresses. Hirschfeld, for one, identified the act within male transvestism of taking a female name as being a symbolic and important step, and one that came after years of sporadic public and private cross-dressing. As a route into her discussion of *Paris is Burning* Butler comments, 'the occupation of the name is that by which one is, quite without choice, situated within discourse' (Butler 1993: 122). In the domain of drag, however, naming can become a dynamic discursive practice which can problematise identity and definition. A name can thus exist as a point of negotiation between the private and public domains, and although that relationship is inherently mutable, the name offered at any particular moment temporarily stabilises it. In most drag scenarios the use or alteration of a name symbolises the way in which the individual or character is to be viewed at that time; for instance, Michael Dorsey's simple inversion of his name to Dorothy Michaels in *Tootsie*, because it is not too far removed, serves to underpin the femininity of his 'act' with a constant, already established masculine identity. In the case of *Glen or Glenda* the issue of naming becomes more complex: Ed Wood, playing an autobiographical role of a transvestite is, within the script, Glen/Glenda; his own name for his cross-dressing alter ego, though, was 'Shirley', and for the film's credits he goes under the name of Daniel Davis. The significance of a name to the subject can perhaps be gauged by how random or deliberate the choice is; the name 'Mrs Doubtfire', for example, is concocted on the spur of the moment from a newspaper headline. The ambiguities of the naming process can be elucidated by referring to a case of the nineteenth-century transvestite Countess Sarolta/Count Sandor outlined by Havelock Ellis. Throughout his account Ellis refers to his subject as Countess Sarolta V., despite her having passed successfully for several years as Count Sandor (as whom she had several love affairs with women, and entered into a 'marriage') and wishing to be known by that name. Ellis ignores 'Sandor' in the belief that a person's name and gender are necessarily both constant and consistent. As a counterpoint to Sandor/Sarolta there is the far more recent case of the pop singer Boy George, who states he does not consider himself to be a transvestite because he never wears female undergarments and makes the distinction: 'I call myself Boy George, not Scarlett O'Hara. . . . I'm proud to be a man' (Kirk and Heath 1984: 112).

The junctures at which characters are called by their male or female names in *Priscilla* is equally significant. Two of the queens have more than one name: 'Felicia' and 'Mitzi' are the drag names of Adam and Tick (or Tony) and all options are used at some point. Conversely, the transsexual Bernadette is only given one name in the final credits, and reacts angrily whenever Adam/Felicia, out of spite, calls her by her birth name 'Ralph'. Names in *Priscilla* are thus (quite conventionally in many respects) linked to sex, although how sex is attributed in the film is unconventionally allied to clothes and appearance, not the body. The dividing line is that Bernadette exists entirely in feminine clothes (either on or off stage) whilst the others oscillate between drag costumes and male clothes. In one scene the play on naming and identifications is of particular importance. 'Priscilla' has broken down on a deserted stretch of road and, having gone in search of 'the cavalry', Bernadette hails a straight, middle-aged couple who give her a lift back to the bus. The couple are implicitly accepting of Bernadette because, as one of them murmurs, she 'looks like a woman'. Bernadette's elegant, subdued image is deemed acceptable by the couple because it can be reconciled with the iconography of heterosexuality. As if consciously continuing this heterosexist dialogue Bernadette, when they arrive at the broken-down bus, introduces her travelling companions as Tony (rather than the usual Tick) and Adam, presumably in an attempt to normalise the situation still further. When the couple are greeted by Tony dressed in a green sequinned body, however, they hurriedly drive off, the implication here being that the discrepancy between name and appearance proves too much.

The exchange between gay camp and the traditional gender matrix is a persistent concern in *Priscilla*, and an area in which the instabilities of identity are highlighted. An important narrative strand is Bernadette's relationship with Bob, a small-town bar owner who helps the 'girls' fix their car and in return gives them a performing spot. Although they go down very badly (much more successful is Bob's wife whose particular trick is firing Ping-Pong balls from her anus), Bob falls in love with Bernadette and joins the trio on their travels, nominally as their helpful mechanic. The attraction of the drag queen for the heterosexual man has frequently been recognised, as one queen explains:

> Years ago we didn't think drag was sexual. In fact we used to whoosh to the balls in drag, rush home and change and then go out to pick up a bloke. *Now* you leave it on, 'cos you know you can pick up straight guys'.
>
> (Kirk and Heath 1984: 58)

The normative procedure in mainstream cross-dressing films is to treat same-sex attraction as a perverse mistake or the result of the confusion surrounding the 'real' gender of the cross-dresser, and to dissipate the anxiety through farce. The Bob/Bernadette relationship elides such tensions, both in the significant and ironic casting of straight 1960s sex symbol Terence Stamp as Bernadette, and in the way that the partnership is portrayed as the film's romantic interlude echoing conventional, heterosexual love scenarios, as when the couple pass a slushy night by the camp fire and decide to remain together at the end. Although one can surmise that Bob's attraction is for precisely the unconventional femininity embodied by Bernadette (precisely, therefore, the unstable figure straight cross-dressing films banish), this choice is never discussed or stated and is therefore not marginalised by being rendered radical or extraordinary.

The film's probing of normative stereotypes counters the enactment of heterosexuality by Bob and Bernadette with notably untraditional representation of Tick/Mitzi's familial relations with his ex-wife and son (Marion and Ben). In the flashback to their wedding, Tick is in a white dress and Marion is in men's clothes, a gender blending echoed later as Tick boasts to Marion that, having got trimmer, he can now fit into the frock she had given him. Both sets of relationships (Bob and Bernadette; Tick, Marion and Ben) identify themselves with and through the conventional heterosexual model and the subversive drag model simultaneously. Tick tries, in an example of male masquerade, to closet his drag side and to reconstitute himself as an 'acceptable' macho role model when re-establishing his relationship with Ben, wearing no make-up, a bland beige man's shirt and telling his son that he does not only dress up in women's clothes, but does Elvis and Gary Glitter impersonations too (ironically, invoking two glam cross-dressing icons). It is then Ben who rejects the masquerade by asking Tick if he has a boyfriend back in Sydney, and if he does performs Abba songs. A child who has no problem with his father being a drag queen operates very differently from the child who, like Chris in *Mrs Doubtfire*, whilst accepting that his father 'had' to dress as a woman, would not treat him as a father until the cross-dressing had gone. The reversal functions on a sartorial level as well, as Tick is an awkward, posturing figure in straight men's clothes, and much more expansive and relaxed in his own.

Drag queens proclaim their homosexuality through their clothes, which is the reason for the middle-aged couple accepting Bernadette and rejecting 'Tony' in costume. In *Priscilla*, the drag clothes, very romantically, become a liberation. After the father/son bonding scene (and the 'liberation' of Tick from the straight-jacket of heterosexuality), Bernadette, Mitzi and Felicia get dressed up in long, upright ostrich and peacock feather headgear, gaudily coloured cloaks, tutus, fur and walking boots and go to King's Canyon. What *Priscilla* achieves by its focus on the performance of drag through clothes is the queering of the stigmatisation identified by Newton when she says that drag queens 'represent the stigma of the gay world' (Newton 1979: 3) through what they wear. In much the same way as the relationships, characterisations and other narrative anomalies subvert rather than sanction normalisation, so do the retro-meets-Las Vegas costumes. This use of costume in *Priscilla* goes far beyond the unthreatening, gender-preoccupied cross-dressing of a traditional Hollywood product such as *Mrs Doubtfire*, and incorporates the notions of clothes as statements, as fluid constructions, as narrative interventions that open and proclaim the sorts of fissures and tensions to do with sexuality, deviancy and the vagaries of gender the Hollywood films strive so painstakingly to submerge. As Butler intimates, 'In imitating gender, drag implicitly reveals the imitative structure of gender itself – as well as its contingency' (Butler 1990: 137). *Priscilla* ignores the body/costume binary of much straight drag, vetoing the stabilising urgency that imposes the assumption that the two are correlatives, going some way towards the imitative fluidity Butler

6.5 Terence Stamp as Bernadette and Hugo Weaving as Mitzi in *The Adventures of Priscilla, Queen of the Desert*
Courtesy of BFI Stills, Posters and Designs

suggests. The film's closing rendition of *Mamma Mia* is illustrative of the imitation game, a multi-layered pastiche on the whole concept of being able to 'do' others. Mitzi and Felicia, using a series of stylised Abba gestures, wigs and sequinned 1970s clothes, are parodying an image that is constituted in fantasy rather than fact, therefore citing the Abba women in such a way as to question the very notion of an 'original'. Just as voguing comprises such detached imitative gestures that what is being imitated no longer informs the present performance, so Abba are so displaced in *Priscilla* that they are invoked simply to be de-invoked.

This chapter began by referencing *Bringing Up Baby*, a text that, in a small sense, sought to position the spectator as an important defining element in how, within the cross-dressing scenario, the performed image of a transvestite figure can be received. Within the context of mainstream comedy, cross-dressing is defined by an acknowledgement of the fixity of sexual difference: there is always a sex which is being disguised, and a gender which is being constructed. Any radical blurring of that difference occurs, this discussion contends, on the level of fantasy, for *Tootsie* or *Mrs Doubtfire* are not interested in positively evoking the subversiveness of Garber's 'third term'. If the dangers of fluidity and uncertainty are evoked, then this occurs 'against the grain' or through the cracks in the surface of the conventional text. These tensions are absent from *Glen or Glenda* and *The Adventures of Priscilla, Queen of the Desert* because the underlying intention of both is to signal the attraction of the ambivalent, transvestite image. The dependence of the cross-dressed image on duality and conflicting, contrasting and changeable genders is ultimately what renders that image radical and transgressive: it cites the instabilities of sexual difference. The intention in the following chapter is to suggest why the blurred ambiguity of the image itself makes androgyny a far more erotic form of transvestism to watch than cross-dressing, because it is not defined by an acceptance of the fixity of gender binaries, but rather by the effect of ambiguity.

7

THE EROTIC STRATEGIES OF ANDROGYNY
The Ballad of Little Jo, The Crying Game, Orlando

In Josef von Sternberg's *Morocco* the chanteuse Amy Jolly (Marlene Dietrich), fresh off the boat from France, is preparing in her dressing room for her first performance since arriving in Morocco. She assembles a by now infamously androgynous look of black tails, waistcoat, masculine white shirt and sprung top hat, nonchalantly checking her reflection before going on stage. During her opening number Amy starts to mingle with the crowd, each action and exchange resonating with an ambiguous eroticism which is overtly veiled but covertly flaunted. The androgynous Dietrich is the scenario's controlling subjective agent, as well as the object of the multiple, conflicting gazes dissecting each other across the dim club. Amy's actions denote both aloofness and availability as, for instance, she sits on a wooden railing, one foot dangling lazily off the ground, her legs provocatively apart, only to walk away from the man who touches her on the sleeve in a fleeting, subliminal response to her sexuality. In a matter of moments, Amy has become the centre of erotic attention, a threat, an alluring icon, the sensuous focus of the desires of men and women alike, the climactic dialogue being the triangular exchange with both a woman and a man, Tom (Gary Cooper). Invited over to a table for some champagne, Amy straddles the rail again and toasts a woman sitting between two men. She makes as if to leave, but then turns around, looks the woman up and down, and plucks the flower from behind her ear, finally stooping (in man's attire) to kiss her full on the lips. Upon returning to the stage, amidst laughter and applause (as if the audience cannot decide how they should respond), Amy sniffs the flower she has filched and throws it to the doting Tom, before, hands in pockets, ambling off stage.

   Much has been said about von Sternberg's fetishisation of Dietrich's image (for example, Mulvey 1975), and in this sequence from *Morocco* the direct fetishistic rapport with the spectator is correlated with the indirect patterns of desire rehearsed within the narrative. As an emblem for androgyny (and the multiple patterns of desire it enables), Amy's representation as a sexual entity is complicated

7.1 Marlene Dietrich as Amy Jolly in *Morocco*
Courtesy of Ronald Grant Archive

by its intersection with gender identity and confusion. Arguing against the tendency among feminist critics to force a conflation between gender and sexuality, Valerie Traub distinguishes between terms (such as 'sexual difference') which denote a *gender* relation and those (such as 'sexual identity') which denote an *erotic* one (Traub 1992: 94). Traub places androgyny into the first, gender-based category, and so, like Marjorie Garber who considers androgyny only briefly in *Vested Interests* as the 'blurred sex' (Garber 1993: 11), absents it from the arena of eroticism.

174

Upon considering the imaging of Dietrich (or similarly Greta Garbo in, for example, *Queen Christina*) it seems absurd to repress the eroticism of the androgynous figure, or, by implication, to have it subsumed into the confused genderisation of the hermaphrodite. In the subsequent pages of *Desire and Anxiety*, Traub goes on to contemplate the question of erotic identification, proposing that, when watching a love scene in a film, the spectator's identification and/or desire can shift during the interaction on screen. In these pages Traub is arguing against the psychoanalytic assertion that desire will follow gender identification, and as such is excluding androgyny from the identifying fluid, erotic mode. Part of the intention of this chapter is to reinstate androgyny into the desire matrix, to suggest ways in which the androgynous figure, more so than the screen representation of the cross-dresser, borders two spheres of reference (the real and the imaginary) and necessarily straddles, like Dietrich, the domains of gender and sexuality, both of which it intrinsically represents.

In the scene from *Morocco* described above the dual mechanisms of androgyny appear very apparent: whilst Dietrich is smudging the defining boundaries of her femaleness (principally through adopting the overtly masculine signifiers of dinner jacket and trousers, an easy swagger and a cigarette), she is simultaneously making herself the point of multiple erotic identification. In a discussion of how public forms of fantasy operate, Elizabeth Cowie theorises a similar duality, arguing for fantasy as both 'a series of wishes presented through imaginary happenings' and a structure, as fantasy is also 'the *mise-en-scène* of desire, the putting into a scene, a staging, of desire' (Cowie 1984: 149). Cowie's conclusion is that 'What is necessary in any public forms of fantasy, for their collective consumption, is not universal objects of desire, but a setting of desiring in which we find our place(s)' (Cowie 1990: 168); that the specifics of a scene are not as crucial as the imaginary patterns with which they connect in the spectator. Dietrich in the night-club scene from *Morocco*, like Grant in the sequence from *Bringing Up Baby* discussed at the beginning of the previous chapter on cross-dressing, has two audiences: the audience in the film and the audience in the cinema. This double observance necessarily locates Dietrich at the intersection between various conflicting looks. The object of focus for these multiple sets of eyes is not only Amy Jolly/Marlene Dietrich but a sartorially, iconographically masculinised woman; an embodiment of fluctuating, unrestrained desire. It is important that the androgynous image is not confined, in terms of what it is empowered to suggest, to either sex, but can function as a symbolic substitute for both. Whilst the androgyne is of 'blurred sex' (conveniently divided at the end of several Shakespearean comedies into the more manageable figures of 'woman' and 'man'), s/he is also of 'blurred sexuality', and thus, unlike the traditional cross-dressed figure who ostensibly masks his/her sexuality and desire, an agent of discovery and danger. It is significant that cross-dressing comedies such as *Tootsie* and *Mrs Doubtfire* conform to the Shakespearean model and, at the end, split the potentially transgressive transvestite figure in two. Dietrich as Amy Jolly is a catalyst for erotic identification in others, both men and women, precisely because her performance of gender is slippery, ill defined and mutable. The androgyne is a potent figure of fantasy because s/he, as Cowie's model suggests, pertains to both the real and the imaginary, and it is a coalescing of the two which generates the eroticism of the image.

The question of images needs to be stressed and reiterated because, too often, the androgyne (if s/he is not to be confined to the more corporeal definitions of the hermaphrodite, the mixed gender body) is theorised into absurdity or abstraction. One such absurdity is the correlating of the ultra-feminine New Look, pioneered by Dior in 1947, with androgyny, a claim made by Wilson (1985: 46) and backed up by Cook (1996: 58–9). Androgyny would appear to have little in common with such champions of the full-skirted, tight-waisted New Look as Grace Kelly, Queen Elizabeth II or Jane Wyman, but similarly to be more physical than the abstract notions attributed to it. The androgyne, for example, has been conceptualised as a pre-sexual Platonic ideal, a romantic trope or 'figure of a privileged language in which sign is transparent to idea' (Weil 1992: 2), an image representative of 'purity' or 'universality' and a figure perceived as 'superior' to either sex which 'incarnates totality and hence perfection' (Singer 1977: 44). Such flights into intangible, symbolic fantasy capture only half of the power of an image such as Dietrich's in her early films with von Sternberg (or, much later, Tilda Swinton in *Orlando*). Dietrich is also, more concretely, a woman whose features are accentuated by their juxtaposition with masculine clothes; the crucial question is why is this attractive? One woman, who wrote to Robert Stoller querying his assertion that there is no such thing as a female transvestite, gives an indication as to why, when she describes herself as having no desire to pass as a man but likes the confusions that ensue when she wears 'unequivocally male clothes'. The woman concludes, 'One perversity, perhaps, is that I like the idea of looking like a rather feminine male' (Stoller 1985: 140–1). Whereas cross-dressing is a collision between genders which are nevertheless identifiable, androgyny is a fusion that can encompass these shifts and permutations. Despite signalling danger and transgression, the cross-dressed or 'dragged-up' body still utilises the difference between the sexes for effect, whether through camouflage or exaggerated citation. It is therefore mistaken to attach the term 'androgyny' to even a radical cross-dressed image, as Anthony Slide does when referring to the delicious comic deviancy which concludes *Some Like it Hot* (Slide 1986: 125). On the androgynous body is enacted ambiguity, the diminution of difference, and what is manifested is a softening of the contours – between corporeality and metaphor, male and female, straight and gay, real and imagined.

The erotic strategies of androgyny

In her essay 'Notes on camp' Susan Sontag identifies two ostensibly incompatible forms of camp: androgyny and 'the exaggeration of sexual characteristics'. Of androgyny Sontag comments:

> the most refined form of sexual attractiveness (as well as the most refined form of sexual pleasure) consists in going against the grain of one's sex. What is most beautiful in virile men is something feminine; what is most beautiful in feminine women is something masculine.
>
> (Sontag 1964: 108)

Sontag contrasts this with a similarly camp exaggeration and relish for 'personality mannerisms': the 'flamboyant femaleness' of Jayne Mansfield or Gina Lollobrigida or the 'exaggerated he-manness' of Victor Mature (109). It is significant that Sontag does not juxtapose androgyny with drag but with a hysterical re-emphasis of gender grounded in a consciousness of sexuality.

The impetus to dilute difference in the creation of an alternative allure is also one which has increasingly preoccupied fashion. Through the 1960s and 1970s several designers pursued unisex themes, Nino Cerruti, for example, causing something of a stir when he produced his collection of interchangeable 'his and hers' clothes in 1967, and Giorgio Armani (who trained under Cerruti) adapting the cut of his men's trousers for his first women's collections. Ralph Lauren's hugely influential *Annie Hall* look similarly advocated the wearing of not just masculine but male clothes by women, and the pages of *Vogue* in 1977 testify to the immediate impact of the style Lauren created for Diane Keaton. Whilst Armani's conflation of men's and women's collections has been primarily about expanding the designer's ethos of comfortable chic through the creation of what could loosely be termed androgynous styles for women's office and evening trouser suits, Lauren's gender-blending clothes play around with the possibilities of hiding femininity in order to accentuate it through loss. There was something paradoxically feminine about the Keaton-inspired fashion which pervaded every type of women's clothes shops in the late 1970s. By not being fitted and not accentuating the feminine curves the distance between the masculinity of the clothes and the femininity of the body became magnified, although Lauren himself often made overt reference to hidden femininity by juxtaposing masculine tweed jackets, for example, with lace-embroidered blouses, a 'symbolic qualification', according to Fred Davis, that 'in effect advises the viewer not to take the cross-gender representation at face-value' (Davis F. 1992: 42).

The designer who has best articulated the eroticism of androgynous clothes has been Yves Saint Laurent who, since the first version of his 'Smoking' evening jacket for women in 1966, has produced various male-inspired women's looks. Unlike Lauren's *Annie Hall* style constructed around genuine menswear items (ties, waistcoats, huge jackets and trousers), Saint Laurent, like Cerruti and

Armani, adapted men's styles for women. Saint Laurent's ethos was that a woman was no less feminine in a pair of trousers than she was in a skirt, but he also sought to emphasise and not downplay femininity, commenting, 'A woman who dresses like a man – in tuxedo, blazer or sailor suit – has to be infinitely feminine in order to wear clothes which were not meant for her' (Duras 1988: 227–8). In this, Saint Laurent follows on from Marlene Dietrich's ironic, complex appropriation of men's clothes, and was indeed directly influenced by her for his 1975 version of the women's pin-stripe suit. He accentuated the femininity of these masculine looks by adding details that were quintessentially feminine, such as the silk blouse underneath the 1975 double-breasted suit, or the translucent blouse under the 1966 'Smoking' which flaunted the eroticism of androgyny. The most recent examples of the marketing of androgyny as overtly sexual are Calvin Klein's early 1980s underwear collections and his 1990s jeans and perfume advertisements, in which gender differences are minimised and androgyny becomes synonymous with pubescence and precocious sexuality. His androgynous boxer shorts, Y-Fronts and boys' vests are still present, if in diluted form, in today's women's underwear styles. The current sick waif styles dominate both male and female fashions, with the tighter, effeminising cut of men's clothes (trousers, shirts and jumpers) suggesting that androgyny in dress no longer means simply the appropriation of men's styles for women. The wilder examples of feminine men's fashions, such as Jean-Paul Gaultier's experimentations through the 1980s and 1990s with the male skirt, when compared to the work of Saint Laurent, clarifies the distinction between androgyny and cross-dressing. Saint Laurent or Klein are enticed by the sensual possibilities of gender blurrings, whilst Gaultier (like Marjorie Garber) is interested in the intellectual transgressive potential of cross-dressing.

The element missing from the ways in which cinema images cross-dressing is eroticism, the expression of desire through the image itself. A critic such as Garber is excited by the transgressive potential of the cross-dressed body, but this does not necessarily mean that eroticism is being enacted on the surfaces of that body. Dietrich's androgynous, blurred identity is importantly symbolic of dangerous sexuality rather than deviancy, and as such encompasses the domains of gender and sexuality that Traub segregates. This chapter will focus on the residual tensions the androgyne brings to the surface, and the sexualisation of the androgynous image in three modern films that are informed by the eroticism of ambiguity, *The Ballad of Little Jo*, *The Crying Game* and *Orlando*. All three films enter into complex negotiations with both gender and sexuality, and display a preoccupation with constructing characters as neither male or female, 'but as both or either' (which Annette Kuhn believes to be characteristic of recent art cinema as a whole; see Kuhn 1994: 232–3).

Maggie Greenwald's *The Ballad of Little Jo* is loosely based on the life story of

Jo Monaghan who, after having an illegitimate child and being banished from home by her father, acquired a set of cowboy's clothes and began life as a man. In the film, Jo joins the gold trail, but is advised to get a steady job and so becomes a sheep minder, finally buying a homestead and a flock of her own. During her lifetime two men find out about her 'real' sex (Percy and 'Tinman' her lover), but neither tell, so the first the community knows about Little Jo's secret is from the village undertaker. *Little Jo* works, at the outset, as a 'progress narrative' in the tradition of *Tootsie* or *Mrs Doubtfire*. Jo changes her clothes when fleeing from two potential rapists; she crashes wet and bedraggled into a clothes store and buys a set of men's clothes, only because the dresses are not ready to wear. The most obvious statement being made through Jo's transvestism is the rejection of the frailty associated with femininity and the adoption of a male disguise as social protection. Women dressing as men is frequently viewed as a political act, not merely an expedient one. Robert Stoller bizarrely claims that men's clothes have no erotic value, so the wearing of them could not possibly provoke sexual desire, whilst Janice Raymond deduces that 'a woman putting on a man's clothes is, in a sense, putting on male power and status, whereas a man putting on women's clothes is putting on parody' (Raymond 1996: 217).[1] Both are reductive alternatives, upholding the views that a woman putting on men's clothes is an act unrelated to pleasure, and that men's clothes carry significant symbolic status that women's do not. Similarly Otto Weininger, in the early 1900s, claimed that 'A woman's demand for emancipation and her qualification for it are in direct proportion to the amount of maleness in her'; that it is a woman's masculinity (which, for Weininger, is her 'external bodily resemblances to a man') which makes her politically aware and assertive (Weininger 1906: 64). In this, Jo Monaghan's narrative is typical, for, despite it being against the law to dress 'improper to your sex' in nineteenth-century America (as the woman in the clothes shop reminds her), Jo does, through doing so, find the privileges afforded a middle-class man, including property ownership and the right to vote.

From the earlier allusion to Marlene Dietrich, it appears that eroticism plays some role in female transvestism, and there are cases and instances within *Little Jo* where desire and attraction (both for the masculine clothes and the androgynous image) contradict the strictly political assumptions about women adopting male dress expressed above. Of the cases of women transvestites who questioned the validity of Stoller's contention that they simply do not exist, one woman's story is of particular significance because it attests to the mutual existence, in female transvestism, of power and fetishistic motivation. This woman ('Case 3') has an attraction to that distinctly unisex item of clothing, Levi jeans. Levi's (importantly even the more recent 'girl cut' models) made this woman both extremely sexually aroused, in a way that no other item of either men's or women's clothing could, and gave her a sense of empowerment by making her feel 'emotionally strengthened, assertive, confident and totally unafraid' (Stoller 1985: 142). Among jean brands, Levi's particularly have become ubiquitous symbols for androgyny and sexuality; one just has to think of the iconography and scenarios in their UK advertising campaigns, not just the by now infamous *Laundrette*, but also *Eddie Cochran*, in which Eddie's date puts on a pair of stone-washed jeans for a party.

Although using different particular items, there is a similar ambiguity in the use of Jo's masculine clothes in *The Ballad of Little Jo*, that they are at once functional and an eroticising agent. This conflict between necessity and sexuality is accentuated at the moment of Jo's switch: the juxtaposing of flashbacks showing Jo at the 'height' of her femininity during her fleeting affair with the family portrait photographer who gets her pregnant, and the current change to a credible man. The manner in which the changing room scene is filmed intentionally emphasises the femininity being eroded not the masculinity being gained. The close-ups of Jo undoing her corset, or caressing and unplaiting her luscious hair even as she hacks it off, function as metaphors for loss not acquisition or growth. The French photographer Brassaï considered the lesbian transvestism he observed in 1930s Paris clubs to be likewise a 'sacrifice' *en route* to the unattainable goal of becoming a man, appearing particularly moved at the loss of feminine hair, which is deemed 'woman's crowning glory, abundant, waved, sweet-smelling, curled' (Brassaï 1976). Jo's transformation is completed by a final act of masochism as she scars her face with a cut-throat razor. This is not, though, a scene concerned with conveying the suppression of femininity as traumatic deprivation. Immediately prior to 'Little Jo' emerging as a young man in search of rubies and gold, there are two brief, shadowy shots of Josephine reflected in an uneven mirror, her image fractured and blurred. If this is intended to be a sad farewell, the images are hardly evocative of a perfection about to be lost; rather they suggest an aroused fascination with the impure, ill-defined androgyne about to be gained. In this, *The Ballad of Little Jo* functions quite differently from films such as either *Mrs Doubtfire* or *Priscilla* in terms of its use of transvestism. The conventional cross-dressing images discussed in the previous chapter represented a process of multiple elisions, one of the most fundamental being the denial or eroticism of the ambiguous. Although danger and transgressiveness were symbolised, desire within (not just of) the image was repressed.

Before examining the film's deployment of fetishism in its representation of the androgynous body, one facet of *Little Jo* that links it firmly with the established cross-dressing tradition is a preoccupation with the 'phallic woman'. A common way in which mainstream cinema undermines female potency as it becomes threatening is to reinstate archetypal femininity. Following her mesmerising performance in tails, trousers and top hat, Dietrich's next appearance in *Morocco* is in a very short black dress, making the focus her legendary legs. In iconographic terms, Amy Jolly goes both ways, oscillating between sadism and masochism, threat and containment. Garber has noted that the male cross-dressing perfor- mance in an exclusively male arena 'is a way of asserting the common privileges of maleness' (Garber 1993: 60), a means whereby the possession of the phallus can again be related to biological difference and the possession of the penis. What, then, of the female cross-dresser in the all-male context of the Western? As a means of explaining the centrality of the phallus as metaphor in Western culture, many feminists (and others) have turned to Lacan's distinction between the penis and the phallus, the latter existing exclusively in the Other as a signifier which 'can only play its role as veiled' (Lacan 1958: 82), the symbolic and unattainable representation of desire. The obsessive fetishisation, however, of the signified which is never shown (and which, in the assignation of sexual difference, is inevitably reduced to that anatomical difference which 'comes to *figure* sexual difference' [Rose 1982: 42]) perpetually leads back to a reconsideration of the penis as phallus, frequently in the realm of metaphor, as in the Western.

The gun is a common symbol for that which remains veiled and, as in Howard Hawks' Western *Red River* (see the scene in which John Ireland and Montgomery Clift admire each others' guns), stands for desire as much as for the penis. For the Western's 'phallic woman' (or the impotent, castrated 'penisless man' as Stoller would have her [Stoller 1968: 196]), the possession of a detached phallic symbol is a survival imperative. Even as she climbs onto the stage singing, in a dress and married to Bill, Calamity Jane has a gun hidden in the folds of her skirt ('just in case any more actresses roll in from Chicagee!'). Bill, though, ever mindful of his role and safety, passes the gun to a well-wisher in the crowd and rides off with the gunless Calam. The fundamental difference between Calamity Jane and Little Jo is that whilst the former is a tomboy, the latter is a woman passing as a man, and as such the phallic symbols Jo utilises are intrinsically more threatening by being disguised as closer to what is assumed to be a male body. Little Jo literally learns how to be a man through mimicry of the gestures and attitudes shown by the men around her, and one lesson is teaching herself how to shoot accurately, which she does whilst tending sheep over her first winter alone. The proximity between symbol and presumed penis later becomes crucial as Jo wants to get rid of the aggressive cattle company owner trying to buy her land: in a gesture copied from many past Westerns, she slowly opens her jacket to reveal the handle of a centrally positioned revolver peeping out over the waistband of her trousers.

The possibility of equating the phallus with the penis is overtly dependent on a masculine appearance, a prefiguration which Jo, in her male ensemble of wide-brimmed hat, rough tweed jacket, trousers and collarless shirt, readily conforms to. The violence of the male reactions at the end of the film to the discovery that Little Jo was in fact female stems from her dead body symbolically confronting them with their own potential for lack. If anyone can possess the phallus, so can

7.2 Suzy Amis as Little Jo in *The Ballad of Little Jo*
Courtesy of BFI Stills, Posters and Designs

a woman. It is likewise symbolic that Frank, a lifelong friend of 'Little Jo', literally reassembles Jo's male image, clothing the corpse in her man's clothes and balancing it on a horse for a final photograph. This ambivalent act gestures both acceptance and disavowal. An interesting comparison can be made with Havelock Ellis's case of Count Sandor (cited briefly in the last chapter), who was brought to court by his father-in-law in 1889 for having married his daughter Marie under false pretences, namely that he was in fact a woman, the Countess Sarolta. A great deal of the father-in-law's obsessive testimony dwells on Sandor's false (metonymic as opposed to metaphoric) penis: the stuffed handkerchiefs that gave the 'appearance of sexual organs', the 'something like an erect member' he thought he saw, and the pretence at urinating like a man behind trees. All his wrath is thus directed at being duped by Sandor's male impersonation. Of no concern is the obviously quite content Marie who, as Ellis reveals at the end of the case history, 'retains her love for the *Countess*, whom she calls the grandest of *women*, and she longs to be her companion for life' (my italics; Ellis 1897: 279–87). Whilst undergoing questioning, Sandor refused to cooperate with the doctors until they addressed 'her' as a man. Was the satisfaction Marie derived from her partner perhaps not in some way related to the eroticism of this smudged duality?

In *The Ballad of Little Jo* the comparable moment of discovery is similarly charged with sexual attraction and aggression rather than repellence. Percy, Jo's unbalanced mentor and the first to discover her 'true' sex, tries to rape her on finding out; but Tinman, the frail 'Chinaman' she has working for her when she has acquired her own homestead, falls in love with the person he realises is not 'Mr Jo'. Whilst Jo and Tinman are building the wooden extension to the hut for him to live in, Jo falls and Tinman catches her, feeling her female body through her clothes. During the subsequent sex scene, the emphasis, both in terms of the camera work and costuming, is on sensuousness; the extreme, caressing close-ups on skin, for example, and the juxtaposition of that skin with the rough, cotton male underwear they both have on. In the realm of comic, misogynist drag, a woman gently unbuttoning female underwear because she desires the man it adorns is a virtually inconceivable scene, but here the dynamics permit such eroticism. In iconographic and narrative terms, this is due to the moment of Tinman's discovery prompting a fusion rather than a severance between the polarities male and female. Jo and Tinman are significantly similar, and so unrepresentative of categorical difference: they wear the same vest/long-john ensembles, Tinman has a long, feminine plait running down his bare back and they both have prominent scars. The man Jo falls in love with, therefore, is as feminised as she is masculinised, and both of them are androgynous. In social terms, theirs is a reciprocal bonding in which they share roles and transgress traditional gender boundaries: Jo is the boss, Tinman cooks, and they are both outsiders. Jo is not attractive to the spectator or Tinman because, after all, she can

gender-specific end, and dressing as a man is not merely part of being a woman. The other characters besides Jo and Tinman display an anxiety about the potential loss of sexual difference, expressed most vehemently in Frank's gesture of dressing the dead Jo up in her man's clothes. To 'prove' Jo was a fraud, he sends this and the old picture of Josephine, the rich society girl, to a newspaper, and a shot of the two images set side by side ends the film. But what does this imposed ending prove? Far more alluring than the neat division between male and female is the gender blending suggested by the buttoned long johns and the undecorated calico dress; the eroticism of the space in between.

It is, perhaps, a considerable leap from a commercially unsuccessful woman's Western such as *The Ballad of Little Jo* to Neil Jordan's much more successful and sensationalist *The Crying Game*, but the films share a common preoccupation with the fluidities and complexities of sex and gender identities and a similar desire to eroticise the androgynous body, although *The Crying Game* approaches the questions of androgyny through the notion of passing. At the time of its release, much of the controversy and debate surrounding *The Crying Game*, the story of an IRA man who falls in love with the transvestite lover of the soldier he helped kidnap, centred on a scene the film-makers implored critics and audiences not to divulge which shows the male transvestite (Dil) being undressed by a man who, until that moment, does not realise his date is not a woman. The significance of this sequence, which occurs roughly half-way through the film, is that, contrary to cross-dressing tradition, the spectator has not (in theory at least) been granted the privilege of advance knowledge, and is as surprised as the other character, Fergus, when Dil's secret is revealed. There was subsequently a proliferation of 'had you realised?' conversations, and several articles and reviews dwelt on how it is barely credible that Fergus had not previously spotted the difference (see, for example, Simpson 1994). What causes Fergus to retch, and audiences to convince themselves that they had not been outwitted, is fear of the individual who successfully passes (in this instance as a woman), and the assumption that such a figure is manifest of a subversive threat. The common reaction suggests that, whilst most people remain happy with the character they know is cross-dressing, and can likewise relish the exotic eroticism of the androgyne, such pleasure is a correlative of certainty, of knowing how the transgressive body evolved and what (gendered, sexed) elements it contains.

The Crying Game is a multi-textured film from a director who has regularly been concerned with the trauma of the changing body and the psychological and emotional transmutations and uncertainties that accompany metamorphosis, as demonstrated in other films such as *The Company of Wolves* or *Interview With a Vampire*, both of which deal with a similar correlation between mutation and sexualisation. In keeping with Jordan's other films, the moment at which the transgression and tension between fantasy and reality becomes visible in *The Crying*

Game is a primary erotic catalyst. Dil has invited Fergus (going by the name of Jimmy) back to her flat for a second time, they kiss, and Fergus waits on the bed as Dil goes into the bathroom to change. On returning, dressed in only a light, silky robe, Dil lets Fergus touch and undress her. As Fergus unties the gown, the camera (matching Fergus's point of view) pans down Dil's body to reveal its flat chest and male genitals, like the androgynous coquettishness of Donatello's David, flaunted with a calm knowingness. Dil assumes Fergus knew, Fergus did not, and his reaction is to hit Dil, throw up and say he's sorry, before rushing out. This response marks, with violent confusion, the erosion, in seconds, of his subjective potency. The shock of viewing Dil's masculinised femininity also necessitates in the spectator an intellectual fragmentation of the integral image. The androgynous body becomes a chaotic assembly of syllables that seem meaningless in their current order: long hair, make-up, penis, tattoo, painted fingernails, hairless body. It is at this point of exposure that the process of normalising reassembly begins, starting with the reconstruction of prior events fuelled by the nagging worry that one should have known.

The (not terribly insightful) way to destroy the film has been to destroy the illusion, to cast cynical aspersions on the idea that Dil could have 'fooled' anybody. As Mark Simpson comments in parentheses, Dil, 'it must be said, is an obvious transvestite to anyone who has not lived a sheltered life' (Simpson 1994: 172). But this is to miss the point that *The Crying Game* is an extended interplay of inconsistent, fluid identities. The ironic mechanisms operative within *The Crying Game* offer a critique, not just a heterosexual validation, of 'passing'. Dil is consistently presented against a backdrop of shifting identities, and loses much through being viewed in isolation. Fergus, in hiding after the botched kidnap of Jody, goes by the name of Jimmy when in London; Jude, the female IRA member, changes disguise or look three times; Jody (the soldier who is kidnapped and dies) confides to Fergus about Dil, but never reveals she is a transvestite. And then there is the ironic, complex use of ostensibly straightforward love songs: three versions of 'The Crying Game', one by a woman (used for Dil's mime in the Metro), two by men, and 'Stand By Your Man' sung by Lyle Lovett, a straight, male new-wave Country singer. Dil is therefore contextualised by this procedure of distanciation and irony, exemplified by the first conversation with Fergus in the Metro conducted through the detached, choric figure of Carl the barman who performs the role of interpretative go-between. On a superficial level this extremely self-conscious exchange is an exclusory game at Fergus's expense, as Dil and Carl absent Fergus (whilst simultaneously engaging him) by referring to him in the third person as if he is not there ('D'you see that Carl? He gave me a look'; 'That *was* a look'). The conversation also, however, functions as a metaphor for Dil: the insistence on performative naming procedures (the substitution by Carl of the indirect 'she' and 'he' for any direct forms of address) paralleling the

7.4 Jaye Davidson as Dil in *The Crying Game*
Courtesy of BFI Stills, Posters and Designs

citationality of Dil's androgyny. *The Crying Game* examines the naming and gesturing procedures that go into delineating the 'I', the apparent subject, and Dil, at the centre of this, repeatedly constitutes her androgyny by citing and disavowing herself (miming to 'The Crying Game', referring to herself as 'she').

In *Bodies That Matter* Judith Butler feels compelled to clarify the idea of performativity and to wrest it from the clutches of those who interpreted the term, after *Gender Trouble*, as a license for a citational free-for-all, attesting that, 'a performative "works" to the extent that *it draws on and covers over* the constitutive conventions by which it is mobilised' (Butler 1993: 227), and that 'femininity', for instance, is 'not the product of a choice, but the forcible citation of a norm' (232). With regard to *The Crying Game*, the importance of these differing statements concerning the interest and potential radicalism of any gender-blending or gender-subverting act lies in how they perceive the relationship between the performative and a pre-existent structure of signification. The issue that concerns *The Crying Game* is 'passing', the valuation of the perfect rendition of 'realness', a visual homogeneity irretrievably disrupted after Fergus's (and our) 'primal scene'. If one focuses almost exclusively (as Garber does) on the transvestite *act*, then 'passing' will be conceived of as radical whether or not it is discovered because its transgression resides in the performance itself. If, however, spectatorship and the critical distanciation between act and reception are prioritised (as suggested in part by Butler), 'passing' is not radical unless recognised as such or discovered and brought into the realm of knowledge and discourse. What is paradoxically interesting about *The Crying Game*, therefore, is the discovery of the failure of Dil's impersonation.

In a very basic sense, the man or woman who successfully 'passes', who perfects 'realness' and cannot be told apart from that which is being cited, is the theoretically perfect androgyne who has fused genders to disguise his/her own sex. In the documentary *Paris Is Burning*, Jennie Livingston's film about New York African-American and Latino drag balls, there are several categories within which the contestants can compete, 'realness' being the one which is treated at greatest length. 'Passing' indicates being able to effect 'realness' in various different contexts: skin colour, sexuality, gender. For the spectator of this film, however, 'realness' is left as a theoretical category because the documentary contextualisation impels us to recognise that these are all performances (the narrativisation tells us what we are looking at/for and so cites the 'realness'). The performances that 'work' are those which defy 'reading': the act of exposing the failures of the constructed appearance and thus its artifice. As Butler remarks when discussing *Paris Is Burning*, 'the impossibility of reading means that the artifice works, the approximation of realness appears to be achieved, the body performing and the ideal performed appear indistinguishable' (Butler 1993: 129). Is there validity, however, in a fictional film couching a radical discussion of passing and the fluidities of identity within a character who passes successfully? There are cinematic examples which have answered this question very differently, as in the uncredited transvestite performance of Debra Winger in *Made In Heaven* or Linda Hunt's (credited) cross-gendered performance as a male character in *The Year of Living Dangerously*. The real point of interest as a spectator in these situations is being able to 'tell', the efforts of the make-up and costume departments notwithstanding, otherwise the inconsistency is only compelling in retrospect.

For those watching *The Crying Game* who do not 'guess' that Dil is a transvestite before this is revealed, there is in the pre-exposure performance a transparency, a coincidence between 'what appears and what it means' (Butler 1993: 129). Dil's identity is, as it were, read from the outside in – although the inverse is assumed, because of the conventionalised reading of clothing as indicative of the sex and gender of the body it adorns. There are also no deliberate mistakes, trips or the hitching up of uncomfortable pantyhose to give the spectators an opportunity to 'read' the image. After the exposure scene, the relationship between clothes and body is inevitably destabilised, in a way that enables Dil's appearance to be 'read', despite the clothes and the overall image remaining ostensibly the same. The complexities of meaning rebound off the consistency of the visual look in the second half of the film, and the discrepancies are named rather than elided, impelling the spectator/Fergus to speculate as to how the two ever seemed indistinguishable.

The issue of passing, of not being vulnerable to reading, is fundamental to trans-sexualism, gender blending and third sex identities. Jan Morris has commented, 'The whole point is lost, it seems to me, when people become obsessed with the idea that they have to prove to the world, by making *visible* changes in them-selves, that they have undergone a process of psychological adaptation' (Singer 1977: 52). This desire for invisibility (the emphasis on the 'psychological' and the concomitant denial of the corporeal) is further a desire for anonymity within one or other of the traditional genders. A very different view is proffered by Kate Bornstein in *Gender Outlaw*, in which gender fluidity (as opposed to Morris's fixity) is argued for as a radical means of transgressing boundaries and subverting the very notion of boundaries as stable divisive structures. As Bornstein remarks, 'It's hard to cross a boundary that keeps moving' (Bornstein 1994: 52). If a radical statement is intended, a public declaration of dissidence, what is the point of keeping the motions of that transgression (the gender fluidities) invisible, wrapped in the secretive veils of passing? This is not intended as an argument against passing *per se* as a personal activity, but against the belief that passing can undermine gender if it remains hidden. Gender is a social construction, its normative rules understood and fabricated in a social context; if its dictates are to be subverted, snubbed or violated, radicalism behind closed doors or zipped-up strides is a meaningless public gesture that *only* becomes interesting and oppositional if found out or shown as in *The Crying Game*. If no narrative use had been made of Dil's transvestism, if the danger, the boundary crossings, the tensions had been elided, where is the polemic? This is why knowledge of who 'she really is' is critical to a comprehension of Dil's androgyny and other gender and sex negotiations going on in *The Crying Game*, because the finding out precipitates an awareness of transgression.

Despite the violence of his reaction, Fergus remains attracted to Dil through the latter half of the film. Although Fergus cannot contemplate sex, they continue to kiss and date through an increasingly complex film. In a scene that appears soon after Fergus finds out Dil is a man, Fergus cuts Dil's hair, an exchange that parallels their first meeting when Fergus went to Millie's hairdressers to get his hair trimmed by Dil. Fergus then forces Dil to put on Jody's cricket clothes, which have been standing eerily in Dil's flat dressing a mannequin. The explanation offered by Fergus for his actions is 'I want to make you into something new'. The symbolism of Jody's clothes is complicated. It is evident from the opening scenes in Ireland that, whilst guarding Jody, Fergus falls in love with him, and that this love is a strong motivation for going in search of Dil. Simpson argues that 'Dil stands in for Jody' (Simpson 1994: 172), a substitution illustrated by the swap in costume and Fergus's frequent fantasies of Jody bowling (in his cricketing 'whites'). The intrusion of the latter (in soft focus and slow motion) as Fergus climaxes having been given his first blow-job by Dil, underlines the identification. The act of putting Dil in Jody's clothes also carries with it the more generalised symbolism that, having been repulsed by Dil as a man in women's clothes, Fergus is now reinstating a more conventional, gender-affirming compatibility between clothes and sex, so collapsing the differences that were the source of his initial trauma. The differences cannot be eradicated completely, however, and in Fergus's continuing love for Dil and the perpetuation of a relationship between them, he also manifests an attraction for the blurred space occupied by the androgyne, the figure who is eroticised because s/he is both genders and neither. During the revelation scene, this attraction to the ambiguous body is represented through the literal blurring (on the level of style and *mise-en-scène*) of the initial sexual exchanges between Fergus and Dil that predominantly take place behind veils. In the latter part of the film, when dressed in Jody's cricket clothes, Dil retains the allure of the androgyne by failing to pass as a convincing man, instead embodying the inverse complexity of the manly-woman. Dil's androgyny is created through the play between passing and not passing and between the changes of clothes and appearance and the consistency of Dil's bodily image, as if 'knowing' Dil's sex increases rather than quells the eroticism of his body.

In the non-eroticised cross-dressing narrative, the affirmation of the corporeal identity of the previously ambiguous figure (when that character is categorically 'proven' to belong to one of the two traditional genders), is a crucial piece of exposition. After such a revelation, the sexual response to the cross-dresser is usually directed at the divulged 'real' sex. In *Victor/Victoria*, once King Marchand, hiding in the bathroom cupboard, sees that the female impersonator Victor is a woman, this permits him to unproblematically look at and desire her as such. In the case of the androgyne, sexual attraction is grounded in unease and doubt. As Annette Kuhn comments about Fergus finding out the 'truth' about Dil in *The Crying Game*, 'this visually guaranteed knowledge neither puts an end to Fergus's resolve to keep his promise to Jody, nor forces any transformation in sexual identity or orientation on his part' (Kuhn 1994: 233). A comparable discovery to King's in *Victor/Victoria*, therefore, complicates rather than simplifies the matter of attraction. So far this discussion has focused on the desirability of the veiled, blurred androgyne, the enticement of the 'wistful and cool androgyne look [which] can be more haunting than the obviously all-male or all-female seductive-ness' (Zolla 1981: 55). Such an image is attractive precisely because, on a visual level, it destabilises gender identity and sexual difference. Both Woolf's novel *Orlando* and Sally Potter's film adaptation start from an alternative premise to the other films previously discussed in these two chapters, which is to treat with indifference the notion of sexual difference. Orlando is a mythic figure who lives across centuries but does not increase substantially in age, and who, at the age of 30, changes, without warning, from a man to a woman and remains one from that point on. The eroticism of androgyny in Potter's *Orlando* is not grounded in the blending or blurring of subjective identification and identity according to sexual difference, but in a disinterest with that very mode of classification. The film is thus proposing a radical reassessment of the relation between the gendered image and its interpretation. Kari Weil in *Androgyny and the Denial of Difference* suggests, 'The androgyne is at once a real, empirical subject and an idealised abstraction, a figure of universal Man' (Weil 1992: 2). In Orlando's teasing contemplation of the female body in the mirror there lies the paradox informing the film's similar interpretation of androgyny as both an abstraction and a corporeal state.

A prerequisite of *Orlando* the film is that Orlando's androgyny must be located in a body which is present, visible and non-abstract. It is not, however, made hugely significant that the pure, androgynous body is in this instance female, as Tilda Swinton's femininity whilst playing the role is disregarded rather than disguised as Debra Winger's is, for instance, in *Made in Heaven*. Sally Potter has referred to the decision not to add any facial hair and other male characteristics to Swinton's appearance because, in cases of women disguising their femininity in order to perform male roles, 'you spend your time as a viewer looking for the glue, the joins between the skin and the moustache', electing instead to assume that everyone would know that it was a woman playing a man and so to acknowledge that and 'try to create a state of suspended disbelief' (Donohue 1993: 10). She was also against casting two actors to represent the male to female switch in *Orlando* because the film 'would have lost exactly that sense of seamless individuality across genders. This really is a story about a person who happens to be a man then happens to be a woman' (Potter 1993: 17). This 'happens to be' attitude is the indifference to sexual difference signalled at the outset of this discussion, and is an attitude that permeates *Orlando* from the opening narration: 'There can be no doubt about his sex, despite the feminine appearance that every young man of the time aspires to'. This playful disinterest is also applied to Swinton as Orlando, for instance the repetition of 'he' over a close-up of her female face, a disjuncture that names that difference until Orlando turns to the camera and interjects to replace the 'he' with, 'that is – I'. This 'I', as opposed to the tense juxtaposition between 'he' and 'she' which drives most narratives preoccupied with gender, lies at the heart of *Orlando*'s radical, utopian androgyny: an androgyny less about transgressing genders than leaving them behind. As Swinton comments:

> I'm beginning to think that gender politics in principle have become a distraction. What I mean by that – a contentious statement – is that what we're *really* concerned with now, whether we know it or not, are more pressing questions of mortality.
>
> (Swinton 1993: 20)

Many of Swinton's comments about her involvement (from a very early stage) with the project are imbued with such sobriety, which rather belies the film's light ironic touch. One obvious irony (also prevalent in the novel) is the adherence to a vision of androgyny as existing outside sexual difference whilst having Orlando represented throughout (either physically or in the imagination) by a woman.[2] Woolf's understanding of androgyny is expanded upon in *A Room of One's Own*, which she wrote in 1928 contemporaneously with *Orlando*. In *A Room of One's Own* Woolf declares, 'It is fatal for anyone who writes to think of their sex . . . to be a woman or a man pure and simple; one must be womanly-manly or man-womanly' (Woolf 1928a: 102). Fixed gender, in Woolf's estimation, is repressive, a barrier to the communication of ideas which she envisages filter through the quaintly 'resonant and porous' androgynous mind 'without impediment' (97). What differentiates the far less academic *Orlando* from *A Room of One's Own* is the absence of fear of the body and sexuality, perceptible in the abstracted arguments of the latter. Elaine Showalter, for one, rejects Woolf's genderless utopianism, calling her androgyny an evasive 'flight' from her own femininity and repressed sexuality (Showalter 1977), and pinning her dislike on the fact that Woolf refuses to write about her own 'female experience'. For her discussion of androgyny from Woolf onwards, Weil rather unexpectedly hijacks the writings on sexual difference of Luce Irigaray, whose firm advocacy of an ethics of sexual difference Weil perceives as removing 'the dream of androgyny from its circumscription by the patriarchal fantasy of one, undifferentiated sex, replacing it with a vision of a meeting (not a joining) of two, positively different sexes, governed by (at least) two different standards and value systems' (Weil 1992: 169). Irigaray's feminist adherence to the importance of sexual difference, it would seem, has little to do with androgyny, as she declares the wish to dispense with sexual difference to be a 'call for a genocide more radical than any form of destruction there has ever been in History' (Irigaray 1993: 12). Later in the same essay Irigaray posits that any possibility of equality between men and women must stem directly from a 'theory of gender as sexed' (13). Irigaray's views on difference have altered very little from the mid-1970s, when she wrote *Speculum of the Other Woman*, to the 1990s. In 'Writing as a woman' [1987], she is still fighting for a culture of the subject to 'progress toward a culture of the sexed subject and not towards a thoughtless destruction of subjectivity' (Irigaray 1993: 58). Like Showalter, therefore, Irigaray believes subjectivity to reside in the affirmation not the dissolution of the sexes. To Woolf, however, and this is made particularly clear in *Orlando*, her female experience is characterised by the capacity to reject fixed, corporeal boundaries rather than embrace them; to both be and disavow her womanhood.

In the film adaptation of *Orlando* the rigidities of 1970s and 1980s gender-aligned feminism are rejected, Sally Potter even refusing to attribute the term 'feminist' to her work, saying, 'I can't use the word any more because it's become debased. My simple observation is that if I use it, it stops people thinking. They close down' (Florence 1993: 279). When asked why the theme of androgyny is pertinent to the 1990s, Potter replies that the questioning of sexed identities, precipitated by two decades of the women's movement, 'has led to a sense that we really don't know any more what it is to be a man and what it is to be a woman', believing, as a result, Woolf's hypothesis that 'we're born simply as human beings . . . and that mostly it's how we're perceived by others that makes the difference, rather than what we are' (Potter 1993: 16). This social, public perception of Orlando is examined and expressed through the film's fluctuating costumes, which alter according to gender and historical period whilst the body wearing them (Swinton's) remains the same. Weil, in her analysis of Woolf's androgyny, argues for *Orlando* as a performative text (Weil 1992: 157), basing her interpretation on the novel's oft-quoted passage about clothes: 'Thus, there is much to support the view that it is clothes that wear us and not we them; we may make them take the mould of arm or breast, but they mould our hearts, our brains, our tongues to their liking' (Woolf 1928b: 132). In the subsequent paragraph, however, Woolf proposes an alternative reading, arguing:

> The difference between the sexes is, happily, one of great profundity. Clothes are but a symbol of something hid deep beneath. It was a change in Orlando herself that dictated her choice of a woman's dress and of a woman's sex.
>
> (132)

The film's costumes (designed by Sandy Powell) reflect the ambitious ambiguity of the relationship between clothes and the body proposed by Woolf, existing between performativity and essentialism, between utopian androgyny and sexual difference. The performative potential of clothes is realised through the reactions of other characters (the servants of the house and Harry) who know Orlando as both a man and a woman, and do not know how they should respond when s/he changes sex. In a film version which is as much a critique of the English class and colonial system, the lack of surprise which Orlando's servants feign upon seeing their master in women's clothes after the ambassadorial trip abroad indicate how easy it is to make people accept and believe the gendered images they are offered.

In line with the strict colour-coding imposed by the film's designers Ben van Os and Jan Roelfs (which in turn is a realisation of Woolf's own colour-based delineations between the various periods), Powell's compatible costumes are citational interpretations as opposed to realistic reproductions. As articulated by Potter, 'the premise for *Orlando* is that all history is imagined history' (Florence 1993: 277); the clothes, like Orlando, exist on the cusp between the abstract and the real. The costumes likewise oscillate between being overtly resonant of gender and androgynous, although the costumes are not (until, arguably, the final sequence) in the traditional mould of androgynous dress, which self-consciously camouflage difference, such as Dietrich's costumes in *Morocco*. Orlando's female period costumes are excessively restrictive caricatures of a feminine appearance, and in no way ambiguous. The pre-twentieth-century women's clothes obviously restrict Orlando's movement, and function as the metaphoric site for the traditional struggle between the freedom she craves and the role society has allotted her, particularly during the middle section of the narrative dominated by the fight for power, property and identity. The first time we see her in female clothes, the social distinction between men and women is directly symbolised through Orlando being pulled and laced into a tight bodice. The recurring action representing the tension between the personal and the social is Orlando hitching up her voluminous eighteenth- and nineteenth-century skirts and trying to run, an uneasy movement which ironically recalls the opening sequence of the film in which the male Orlando, late to greet Elizabeth I to his family home, is able to gallop towards the house with unfettered strides. The most remarkable of these sequences straddles the historical transition from 1750, when Harry proposes to Orlando and is turned down, to 1850, when she falls on the ground and meets her future lover Shelmerdine who has been thrown by his horse. Orlando's action of raising her skirt off the ground to facilitate movement is consistent throughout the sequence, as she runs from Harry and into the narrow pathways of a maze where, over one edit, she is transported from one century to the next.

Orlando's masculine costumes, on the other hand, are not only more physically liberating but also less obviously genderised. Many of Orlando's outfits when a man are overly elaborate and effeminate, like the huge bowed neckerchief he wears when affecting the style of a seventeenth-century poet, or the heavy, curled wigs worn a hundred years later. Androgynous clothes (or clothes that intentionally disguise sexual difference) occur in the film at traumatic or critical junctures. Just such a moment of significant change occurs as Harry arrives unexpectedly in Constantinople to escort Orlando back to England. Harry is shocked to find Orlando wearing an ivory turban and Turkish robes, although Orlando has happily rid himself of the heavy western wigs and cumbersome clothes, and is loathe to reinstate them. Likewise, Orlando's transition from man to woman is marked by an engulfing black robe which leaves only Swinton's face visible. (In the novel Orlando puts on 'those Turkish coats and trousers which can be worn indifferently by either sex' [Woolf 1928: 98], thereby emphasising the androgynous intention). The contemporary sequence that concludes the film adopts the most clearly conven-tionalised androgynous costume, as the female Orlando wears a heterogeneous mixture of old-fashioned biking leathers (brown leather jacket, jodhpurs and long, laced boots) and modern white shirt. This last image, offering a bridge to the present, is expressive of the narrative's utopianism: that gender is irrelevant and that clothes are perfection when they too become a timeless hybrid of genders, periods and styles.

This is not a compromise but an ideal, and one that is rooted in the unimpor-tance of Orlando's 'real' sex. This returns the discussion to the problem of the corporeal representation of an intellectual conceit. Androgyny is so much more exciting and sexual than its physical counterpart the hermaphrodite that it must, as a notion of desire, exist beyond the limits of the body, but maybe it is only in its intellectualisation that the androgyne is able to transcend gender, or in the pre-sexual state as suggested by Freud and Lacan. Perhaps, on the other hand, androgyny is simply an impossibility. Many critical assessments of Woolf's notion of androgyny alight on its lack of eroticism, the absence of physicality and desire (Heilbrun 1973), which, whilst a justified stance to adopt when considering *A Room of One's Own*, is an inaccurate representation of *Orlando*. The novel, once described by Sackville-West's son Nigel Nicolson as 'the longest and most charming love letter in history', is full of moments of Sapphic desire and longing, to use Woolf's phrase, which the film, in a notably 1990s manner, inflates into an eroticised, sensual, more heterosexual portrait of androgyny.

In both novel and film Orlando's change from man to woman is an easy, painless process, Woolf writing bluntly, 'It is enough for us to state the simple fact; Orlando was a man till the age of thirty; when he became a woman and has remained so ever since' (Woolf 1928b: 98). In the film version Orlando, waking from one of his great sleeps, lies in bed, his face framed by the opulent finery of

7.5 Tilda Swinton as Orlando in *Orlando*
Courtesy of Ronald Grant Archive

his long curled wig and lace linen and caressed by a bleached golden light. As the wig is slipped off, Orlando's long, red, feminine hair tumbles out, signalling the juxtaposition and the fusion of the two sexes. The representation of the scene celebrates the ease of the transition; Orlando's calm, fluid movements reflected by the slow, sweeping camera, for example. The increased sensuality creates a liberating moment, as when the light catches the sparkle of the water and the lint against the dark background as the now female Orlando bathes her face. Whereas the revelation of a character's 'real' sex in a cross-dressing narrative is a moment of crisis and trauma, here Orlando serenely contemplates her poised, balletically posed nakedness in the full-length mirror and displays a muted surprise as she finds there is 'no difference, no difference at all – just a different sex'. As Potter comments on Orlando's transition, 'I think that most notions of sexual difference are really about mystification, and that it's much simpler than that' (Potter 1993: 16). In more tortuous ways, both *The Ballad of Little Jo* and *The Crying Game* conveyed that the point of demystification (of showing the sex of the body) can also be the point of greatest eroticism, which is what sets the androgynous texts apart from the cross-dressing comedies in which the horror of the trauma proves insurmountable.

The eroticisation of Orlando's change of sex is reinforced by the 1850 sequence with Shelmerdine, in which androgyny is shown not to belong exclusively to either the female or more particularly the lesbian domain, as is suggested by Woolf. The attraction between Orlando and Shelmerdine is at first a mutual acknowledgement of the self in the Other. As they both speculate what kind of a member of the opposite sex they would be ('If I were a man . . . '; 'If I were a woman. . . . ') they articulate a desire for the ambiguity and fluidity of the androgyne which they both, to an extent, possess, Orlando by virtue of her unstable gender, Shelmerdine by his appearance, with his Romantic opened shirt and tousled long hair. The likeness between Orlando and Shelmerdine (or Jo and Tinman) dispenses with the necessity for absolute difference, as androgyny comes to encompass both the corporeal and the cerebral. Their ambiguous, shared desire is then represented, when they are in bed, through the abstraction of the body. A slow close-up pan runs along the contours of Orlando's outstretched body, from her leg, along her hip, waist, ribs and shoulders to her half-concealed face. The proximity of the camera to Orlando's pale, blue-lit skin, the contrast of her white, hilly contours against the black void of the background, make the body (the most obviously gendered sign of all) into an abstract, unrecognisable image. In the duality of this single moment, the notion of a sexed androgyny becomes crystallised as both essence and ideal, an image onto which the meanings imbedded within the narrative can be imposed and through which the multiple desires of the spectator can be realised. In 'The face of Garbo' Roland Barthes makes a classic distinction when saying, 'The face of Garbo is an Idea, that of [Audrey] Hepburn, an Event' (Barthes 1957: 64); in a sense androgyny that is both abstract and real elides these differences. The radicalism of *Orlando*'s representation of androgyny is that its abstract and real connotations (that it both pertains to the body, language and sex and possesses a symbolic potency as it transcends all these) are locked into the same image. The abstract and the real become the same.

Abstraction is the key to the film and its representation of an androgynous self 'that lies beyond gender' (Glaessner 1992: 14). As Potter states elsewhere, the book *Orlando* does not so much explore sexual identities as dissolve them, a 'melting and shifting' she wanted to convey in the film (Florence 1993: 283). Preventing this view of a transcendental subjectivity from becoming tautological is the dogged attachment to the physical, resulting not in a denial of sexual difference but in a de-emphasising of its significance. The corporeality at the heart of *Orlando* also avoids the biologically anomalous form of the hermaphrodite, the body forever inscribed with the fear of incompleteness. Jonathan Dollimore comments that 'androgyny typically envisages a unity ostensibly beyond sexual difference, but in fact inseparable from it; androgyny especially has too often been a genderless transcendent which leaves sexual difference in place' (Dollimore 1991: 262). This chapter has posited that such a reaffirmation of difference is what marks the cross-dressed body not the on-screen androgyne, whose ambiguity cannot be so easily made to conform to the old binary system. The androgynous body is never complete because it is innately unstable; it always possesses the capacity for mutability and transformation, and, unlike the cross-dressed body, does not hold onto the notion of its single, 'real' sex. Contrary to much writing about androgyny that considers it to be an impossible idealisation or a non-sexual state, most cinematic representations of the androgyne stress the eroticism of his/her ambiguity. This sexualisation pertains directly to the acts of watching and desiring the ambiguous body, and so is an intrinsic component of the act of spectatorship itself.

One of the aims of this book has been to explore the multiple ways in which clothing interacts with the body in the formation of identity. The relationship between these two elements is at its most fluid when approaching the androgynous image, because established correlations between how one looks and how one is looked at here become unworkable. The arguments posed have had as their basis issues of gender construction through and by clothing, and it is in the realm of androgyny that such categories are most manifestly questioned and undermined. As the conversation between the female Orlando and Shelmerdine attests, one can imagine oneself into a gender, or indeed imagine oneself to be genderless; so costume or clothes are no longer merely forms of consolidation and social communication, but also testaments to fantasy and desire.

NOTES

1 CINEMA AND HAUTE COUTURE

1 See also Leese 1976, Prichard 1981.
2 See also the numerous accounts Edith Head, Hollywood's foremost costume designer, gives of her trade and the differences between costume and fashion design, for example, Head 1959 and 1983. Head is particularly informative about her numerous collaborations with Alfred Hitchcock and on the way the costume designer's role is to realise the symbolism, the ideas about colour co-ordination in the *mise-en-scene*, the character interpretation that the director has formed before the production process begins.
3 Greer, who became the head designer at Paramount, had worked at both the New York and Chicago branches of Lady Duff Gordon's house. After the First World War he went to Paris and worked under, among others, Poiret and Molyneux before returning to America and working in cinema and establishing his own couture house in 1927. Adrian was invited to Hollywood after Valentino and Rambova had seen his costumes for the 1923 Irving Berlin musical *Music Box* in New York. His first feature was *The Hooded Cobra*, which was never released, but he is probably most famous for his work in creating the looks of Greta Garbo and Joan Crawford.
4 For a discussion of the influence of Gilbert Adrian's 'Letty Lynton' dress on women's ready-to-wear fashions in 1932 see also Herzog and Gaines 1984. At one party in 1951 seventeen replicas of Liz Taylor's off-the-shoulder ballgown from *A Place in the Sun* were seen, although Edith Head, the film's costume designer, has on occasion inflated the number to thirty-seven (Head 1983: 97–8).
5 For a discussion of the relationship between women spectators and stars see Chapter 6, Stacey 1994.
6 Robert Gustafson claims that the 'Sabrina neckline', square across the chest and held up by two bows on either shoulder, was in fact far from original, having been 'sold for years' in various catalogues and magazines (Gustafson 1982: 14).
7 Shopping films is still part of the costume designer's remit. Ellen Mirojnick, who designed *Fatal Attraction* and *Wall Street*, defends the practice and comments, 'Just because you shop a film doesn't mean it's not designed!' (quoted in Troy 1989: 51).
8 One such copy of Chanel's cape is Helen Storey's 'Death in velvet' dress for her 1994 collection.
9 During the final credits the collaboration of Yves Saint Laurent is also mentioned.

Notes

10 The anti-romantic view of how alien clothes can function against a woman is exemplified by *Rebecca*. Whenever Joan Fontaine experiments with different looks she is mocked or ordered to go and change.

11 See Greenberg 1991, Miner 1992.

12 The Saint Laurent dress is pictured in Duras 1988: 154–5, 183; the Roehm dress in Milbank 1989.

13 This was the most revealing dress Grace Kelly wore in films, and interestingly, in most publicity shots the shoulders are splayed still further to make the top even more *décolleté*. (See also Engelmeier 1990: 147.)

14 In January 1962 Yves Saint Laurent established his own fashion house, and after his inaugural show *Life* magazine proclaimed his to be 'the best collections of suits since Chanel' (quoted in Duras 1988: 226).

15 Although Chanel is not credited at the end of *Trop Belle Pour Toi!* (whilst Saint Laurent, who provided Gerard Depardieu's suits, is), the Chanel office confirmed to me that Bouquet wears exclusively Chanel designs throughout the film.

16 See also Peter Lehman, '*American Gigolo*: the male body makes an appearance of sorts'; Patricia Mellencamp, 'The unfashionable male subject'; William Luhr, 'Gender representation in Paul Schrader's *American Gigolo*'; Robert T. Eberwein, 'Framing and representation in *American Gigolo*', in Ruppert (ed.) 1994: 8–40.

17 Nino Cerruti has designed costumes for *The Witches of Eastwick*, *Fatal Attraction*, *Reversal of Fortune*, *Indecent Proposal*, *In The Line of Fire* and *Prêt-à-Porter*, among others.

18 Armani usually sues if his name is used in dialogue as a short-hand for a certain type of man.

19 Cerruti dressed Kim Basinger, Marcello Mastroianni, Rupert Everett, Tim Robbins and Danny Aiello.

2 DESIRE AND THE COSTUME FILM

1 Andrew Higson, for example, notes that in the conventional heritage film 'Camera-work generally is fluid, artful and pictorialist, editing slow and undramatic. The use of long takes and deep focus, and long and medium shots rather than close-ups, produces a restrained aesthetic of display' (Higson 1996: 233–4). This sort of style is very different from the sensuous fetishism of *The Age of Innocence*.

2 *Witness* is not strictly speaking a 'costume film' in that its setting is contemporary America. But because the strict Amish sect eschew modernity and wear traditional clothes, Kelly McGillis' costume (particularly in the eyes of the 'modernised' Harrison Ford) take on a particular, archaic eroticism.

3 Sara is consistently represented as deviant: she is, for example, an orphan, poor, solitary and is clearly in love with Miranda.

4 Later on it is Edith who, refusing to climb any further, runs back down the rock screaming; another indication (if one interprets the rock as somehow related to sexual initiation) that she lacks the maturity of the others. As they approach the rock Miranda tells her fellow schoolgirls to look up at it, but Edith the unready looks down.

5 'Brattoilette', in *Wiener Caricaturen*, 22 March 1890; quoted in Kunzle 1982: 12.

6 This is the reverse of the Truffaut three-edit sequence in *Tirez sur le Pianiste* which Scorsese has said he puts into every film.

7 Freud and others have declared, for example, that male fetishists are in fact disgusted

by the sight of the female sex organs, and thus want to maintain that distance. See Freud 1927.

8 Although Janet Patterson stresses the authenticity of Baines's costume she and Campion decided that his clothes should, more generally, denote an internationalism and a desire to travel (Patterson 1993 and Campion 1993: 9).

9 This shot would not have been so ambiguous if in fact Ada had died. It is her mind's fantasy of the perfect tragic (and feminine) death.

10 Brand also discusses another case from this century of a woman who uses a pair of home-made velvet underpants as a fetish, but uses them only as foreplay (113–120). For a further discussion of female fetishism see Gamman and Makinen 1994.

11 For a further discussion of the importance of touching in *The Piano* see Bruzzi 1995.

3 THE INSTABILITIES OF THE FRANCO-AMERICAN GANGSTER

1 Breward notes, however, that there is evidence to disprove men's assumed disinterest in fashion, even in the nineteenth century when there was already 'a variety of forms possible in the cutting and decoration of the staples of jacket, waistcoat and trousers' (172).

2 See Introduction: xiv–xv.

3 Melville was particular about all the details in the film, for instance the white editing gloves that all his killers wear, and the bird. Melville used a female bullfinch 'because it is just black and white, without the male's orange breast' (Nogueira 1971: 136), which fitted in with his plans 'to make a colour film in black and white' (130).

4 Not only are their subject matters similar, but both are adapted by Nicholas Pileggi and Martin Scorsese from two of Pileggi's books and have similar casts, Joe Pesci playing a virtually identical character in *Casino* to the one he played in *Goodfellas*.

5 Several writers on fashion, including Quentin Bell whose *On Human Finery* was hugely influenced by Veblen, have assumed that aesthetic and utilitarian perfection in clothing can be attained and then 'restless change' will cease to be necessary.

4 THE SCREEN'S FASHIONING OF BLACKNESS

1 See also Grant D. McCracken, 'The trickle-down theory rehabilitated', in Solomon 1985: 39–49.

5 CLOTHES, POWER AND THE MODERN *FEMME FATALE*

1 In fact Rosalind Coward also ignores the dramatically increased concern among men with appearance, body shape and desirability, pressures which she attributes only to women (154). Simply looking at the sales of men's lifestyle magazines and the growing number of exclusively male fashion shops indicates that the balance is shifting.

2 Among these films it is, ironically, a *noir* without a duplicitous female at its core – Otto Preminger's *Laura* – which most explicitly deals with femininity being a male construction, as Laura's image is embellished in her absence by the men around her, and collides with rather than consolidates her actual character.

Notes

3 For instance in Walker 1992, Krutnik 1991, Hirsch 1981.

4 The mutilation of women's feet was not peculiar to China. If one examines, for instance, the various European versions of the Cinderella fairy-tale, a similarly extreme deformation of the female foot is taking place. In one particularly violent version from Russia, a girl chops off her feet in order to fit into the glass slipper, comforting herself with the thought that as a princess she will never have to walk again.

5 James Laver cites the long 1930s evening dress as an example of a style which undercut the erotic potential of women's legs and instead emphasised the back (Laver 1945: 150–2). A more recent example would be the 'maxi' which was introduced in 1969.

6 The title of the original book is *Single White Female – Seeking the Same*.

6 THE COMEDY OF CROSS-DRESSING

1 A woman in these functional, controlling and notably unfussy clothes almost invariably signifies no-nonsense strength, another almost contemporaneous example being the representation of Max de Winter's sister in Hitchcock's *Rebecca*.

2 It is therefore surprising that Garber does not remark upon a scene which is particularly interesting in this respect. Before going on a weekend with Julie, the woman he is secretly in love with, Michael is getting Dorothy's clothes together and casually asks Jeff, 'Do you know where my night-gown is? You know, the pink one, the one with the flowers?' Now what is Michael, who has to this point only appeared as Dorothy fully dressed in social, daytime situations and always changes into mufti back at home, doing with a night-gown obviously not bought especially for the weekend? And why does Jeff respond as if he is asked this sort of thing all the time?

7 THE EROTIC STRATEGIES OF ANDROGYNY

1 For further discussions of the political power aspects of women dressing in men's clothes, see Gamman and Makinen 1994, Wheelwright 1989.

2 *Orlando* the novel was similarly written with a woman in mind (Woolf's lover Vita Sackville-West), and photographs of Sackville-West are used in the text as representations of Orlando.

FILMOGRAPHY
Title, director, date, costume designer

Adventures of Priscilla, Queen of the Desert, The (Stephan Elliott, 1994)
Costume designers: Lizzy Gardiner, Tim Chappel

Age of Innocence, The (Martin Scorsese, 1993)
Costume designer: Gabriella Pescucci

American Gigolo (Paul Schrader, 1980)
Costume designer: Alice Rush
Additional wardrobe: Giorgio Armani (Richard Gere)

Ballad of Little Jo, The (Maggie Greenwald, 1993)
Costume designer: Claudia Brown

Belle de Jour (Luis Buñuel, 1967)
Costume designer: Hélène Nourry
Additional wardrobe: Yves Saint Laurent (Catherine Deneuve)

Boyz N the Hood (John Singleton, 1991)
Costume designers: Darryle Johnson, Shirlene Williams

Casino (Martin Scorsese, 1995)
Costume designers: Rita Ryack, John Dunn

Cleopatra Jones (Jack Starrett, 1973)
Costume designers: Giorgio di Sant'Angelo (Tamara Dobson). Tommy Welsh (men's costumes)

Cook, the Thief, His Wife & Her Lover, The (Peter Greenaway, 1989)
Costume designer: Jean-Paul Gaultier

Crying Game, The (Neil Jordan, 1992)
Costume designer: Sandy Powell

Disclosure (Barry Levinson, 1994)
Costume designer: Gloria Gresham

Do the Right Thing (Spike Lee, 1989)
Costume designer: Ruthe Carter

Doulos, Le (Jean-Pierre Melville, 1962)
Costume designer: not credited

Filmography

Glen or Glenda (Edward D. Wood Jr., 1954)
Costume designer: not credited

Goodfellas (Martin Scorsese, 1990)
Costume designer: Richard Bruno

Kika (Pedro Almodóvar, 1993)
Costume designer: Jose Maria Cossio
Additional Wardrobe: Jean-Paul Gaultier (Victoria Abril), Gianni Versace, Yves Saint Laurent

Last Seduction, The (John Dahl, 1993)
Costume designer: Terry Dresbach

Leon (Luc Besson, 1994)
Costume designer: Magali Guidasci

Mrs Doubtfire (Chris Columbus, 1993)
Costume designer: Marit Allen

New Jack City (Mario Van Peebles, 1991)
Costume designer: Bernard Johnson

Orlando (Sally Potter, 1992)
Costume designer: Sandy Powell

Piano, The (Jane Campion, 1993)
Costume designer: Janet Patterson

Picnic at Hanging Rock (Peter Weir, 1975)
Costume designer: Judy Dorsman

Prêt-à-Porter (Robert Altman, 1994)
Costume designer: Catherine Letterier
Additional Wardrobe: Cerruti 1881 (Simone Lo's collection and others), Xuly Bet (Cy Bianco's collection), Vivenne Westwood (Cort Romney's collection), Jean-Paul Gaultier, Issey Miyake, Christian Lacroix, Sonia Rykiel, Gianfranco Ferré for Christian Dior (featured as themselves), Agnès B., Giorgio Armani, Azzedine Alaïa, Chanel, Jean-Charles de Castebajac, Paul Smith, Chantal Thomass, Yohji Yamamoto, Yves Saint Laurent, Comme des Garçons

Pretty Woman (Garry Marshall, 1990)
Costume designer: Marilyn Vance-Straker.
Additional wardrobe: Cerruti 1881

Pulp Fiction, (Quentin Tarantino, 1994)
Costume designer: Betsy Heimann
Additional wardrobe: Agnès B.

Rear Window (Alfred Hitchcock, 1954)
Costume designer: Edith Head

Reservoir Dogs (Quentin Tarantino, 1992)
Costume designer: Betsy Heimann

Filmography

Sabrina (Billy Wilder, 1954)
Costume designer: Edith Head
Additional wardrobe: Hubert de Givenchy (Audrey Hepburn)

Samouraï, Le (Jean-Pierre Melville   1967)
Costume designer: not credited

Shaft (Gordon Parks, 1971)
Costume designer: Joe Aulisi

Single White Female (Barbet Schroeder, 1992)
Costume designer: Eileen Kennedy

Superfly (Gordon Parks Jr., 1972)
Costume designer: Nate Adams
Additional wardrobe: Hill & Reed

Tootsie (Sydney Pollack, 1982)
Costume designer: Ruth Morley

Trop Belle Pour Toi! (Bertrand Blier, 1989)
Costume designer: Michele Marmand-Cerf
Additional wardrobe: Chanel (Carole Bouquet), Yves Saint Laurent (Gerard Depardieu)

Untouchables, The (Brian de Palma, 1987)
Costume designer: Marilyn Vance-Straker
Additional wardrobe: Giorgio Armani

Voyager (Volker Schlöndorff, 1991)
Costume designer: Barbara Baum
Additional wardrobe: Giorgio Armani (Sam Shepard)

Waiting to Exhale (Forest Whitaker, 1996)
Costume designer: Judy L. Ruskin

ADDITIONAL FILMS

A bout de souffle (Jean-Luc Godard, 1959)
Asphalt Jungle, The (John Huston, 1950)
Assassin (John Badham, 1993)
Basic Instinct (Paul Verhoeven, 1992)
Black Widow (Bob Rafelson, 1987)
Blanche Fury (Marc Allégret, 1948)
Bloodline (Terence Young, 1979)
Body Heat (Lawrence Kasdan, 1981)
Breathless (Jim McBride, 1983)
Daughters of the Dust (Julie Dash, 1991)
Diary of a Chambermaid, The (Luis Buñuel, 1964)
Dillinger (Max Nosseck, 1945)
Double Indemnity (Billy Wilder, 1944)
Driver, The (Walter Hill, 1978)
Duel in the Sun (King Vidor, 1946)

Filmography

Fatal Attraction (Adrian Lyne, 1987)
Funny Face (Stanley Donen, 1957)
Golden Braid (Paul Cox, 1990)
Gun Crazy (Joseph H. Lewis, 1950)
Hand That Rocks the Cradle, The (Curtis Hanson, 1992)
Hollywood Shuffle (Robert Townsend, 1987)
Hot Spot, The (Dennis Hopper, 1990)
Jassy (Bernard Knowles, 1947)
Killing, The (Stanley Kubrick, 1956)
Killing Zoë (Roger Avary, 1995)
Letty Lynton (Clarence Brown, 1932)
Little Caesar (Mervin LeRoy, 1930)
Made In Heaven (Alan Rudolph, 1987)
Married To The Mob (Jonathan Demme, 1988)
Mother's Boys (Yves Simoneau, 1993)
My Brilliant Career (Gillian Armstrong, 1979)
Nikita (Luc Besson, 1990)
Out of the Past (Jacques Tourneur, 1947)
Palmy Days (A. Edward Sutherland, 1931)
Pépé le Moko (Julien Duvivier, 1937)
Place in the Sun, A (George Stevens, 1951)
Postman Always Rings Twice, The (Tay Garnett, 1946)
Presumed Innocent (Alan J. Pakula, 1990)
Rosa Luxemburg (Margarethe von Trotta, 1986)
Scarface (Howard Hawks, 1932)
She's Gotta Have It (Spike Lee, 1986)
Sister My Sister (Nancy Meckler, 1995)
Some Like it Hot (Billy Wilder, 1959)
Sommersby (Jon Amiel, 1993)
Tirez sur le Pianiste (François Truffaut, 1960)
Tonight or Never (Mervin LeRoy, 1931)
23h58 (Pierre-William Glenn, 1993)
Witness (Peter Weir, 1985)
Year of Living Dangerously, The (Peter Weir, 1982)

BIBLIOGRAPHY

Ackroyd, Peter (1979) *Dressing Up, Transvestism and Drag: The History of An Obsession*, London: Thames and Hudson

Appiah, K. Anthony (1993) '"No bad nigger": blacks as the ethical principle in the movies', in Marjorie Garber, Jana Matlock and Rebecca L. Walkowitz (eds) *Media Spectacles*, London and New York: Routledge

Armani, Giorgio (1986) 'A certain style', *Vogue* 143, 3: March

Armes, Roy (1966) *French Cinema Since 1945, Volume 2: The Personal Style*, London: Zwemmer

Ash, Juliet and Wilson, Elizabeth (eds) (1992) *Chic Thrills: A Fashion Reader*, London: Pandora

Aspinall, Sue (1983) 'Sexuality in costume melodrama', in Sue Aspinall and Robert Murphy (eds) *BFI Dossier No. 18: Gainsborough Melodrama*, London: BFI Publishing

Baker, Houston A., Jr. 'Spike Lee and the commerce of culture', in Manthia Diawara (ed.) *Black American Cinema*, London and New York: Routledge

Baker, Roger (1994) *Drag: A History of Female Impersonation in the Performing Arts*, London: Cassell

Barthes, Roland (1957) 'The face of Garbo', *Mythologies*, London: Paladin, 1973

—— (1963) *The Fashion System* (tr. Matthew Ward and Richard Howard), Berkeley and Los Angeles: University of California Press

—— (1973) 'Erté, or A la lettre', *The Responsibility of Forms: Essays on Music, Art and Representation* (tr. Richard Howard), Oxford: Blackwell

Beetham, Margaret (1996) *A Magazine of Her Own?: Domesticity and Desire in the Woman's Magazine, 1800–1914*, London and New York: Routledge

Bell, Daniel (1960) 'Crime as an American way of life: a queer ladder of social mobility', *The End of Ideology* New York: Free Press

Bell, Quentin (1947) *On Human Finery*, London: Hogarth Press

Bergan, Ronald (1989) 'Food for thought', *Films and Filming* 420: October

Bergler, Edmund (1953) *Fashion and the Unconscious*, New York: Robert Brunner

Bogle, Donald (1994) *Toms, Coons, Mulattoes and Bucks: An Interpretative History of Blacks in American Film* (3rd edn), Oxford: Roundhouse

Bornstein, Kate (1994) *Gender Outlaw: On Men, Women and the Rest of Us*, London and New York: Routledge

Bouquet, Carole (1990) *Interview* 20, 2: February

Bowen, Peter (1994) 'Pedro on the verge of a new film', *Filmmaker* 2, 3: Spring

Bibliography

Brand, Clavel (1970) *Fetish*, London: Luxor Press

Brassaï (1976) *Sodom and Gomorrah: The Secret Paris of the 1930s* (tr. Richard Miller), London: Thames and Hudson

Breward, Christopher (1995) *The Culture of Fashion: A New History of Fashionable Dress*, Manchester: Manchester University Press

Brownmiller, Susan (1984) *Femininity*, London: Paladin

Bruzzi, Stella (1993) 'Jane Campion: costume drama and reclaiming women's pasts', in Pam Cook and Philip Dodd (eds) *Women and Film: A Sight and Sound Reader*, London: Scarlet Press

—— (1995) 'Tempestuous petticoats: costume and desire in *The Piano*', *Screen* 36, 3: Autumn

Butazzi, Grazietta and Molfino, Alessandra Mottola (1986) *Italian Fashion: From Anti-Fashion to Stylism*, Milano: Electra Spa

Butler, Judith (1990) *Gender Trouble: Feminism and the Subversion of Identity*, London and New York: Routledge

—— (1993) *Bodies That Matter: On The Discursive Limits of 'Sex'*, London and New York: Routledge

Campion, Jane (1993) *Sight and Sound* 3, 10: October

Carter, Ernestine (1980) *Magic Names of Fashion*, London: Weidenfeld and Nicolson

Case, Brian (1987) 'Fitting The Frame' *Time Out* 871, 28: April

Chenoune, Farid (1993) *A History of Men's Fashion* (tr. Richard Martin), Paris: Flammarion

Christie, Ian (1994) Interview with Martin Scorsese, *Sight and Sound* 4, 2: February

—— (1996) Interview with Martin Scorsese, *Sight and Sound* 6, 1: January

Cook, Pam (1994) Review of *The Age of Innocence*, *Sight and Sound* 4, 2: February

—— (1996) *Fashioning The Nation: Costume and Identity in British Cinema*, London: BFI Publishing

Cosgrove, Stuart (1989) 'The zoot suit and style warfare', in Angela McRobbie (ed.) *Zoot Suits and Second-hand Dresses: An Anthology of Fashion and Music*, London: Macmillan

Coward, Rosalind (1993) *Our Treacherous Hearts: Why Women Let Men Get Their Way*, London: Faber

Cowie, Elizabeth (1984) 'Fantasia', in Parveen Adams and Elizabeth Cowie (eds) *The Woman in Question*, London and New York: Verso, 1990

—— (1993) '*Film Noir* and women', in Joan Copjec (ed.) *Shades of Noir: A Reader*, London: Verso

Craik, Jennifer (1994) *The Face of Fashion: Cultural Studies in Fashion*, London and New York: Routledge

Cripps, T. S. (1978) *Black Film as Genre*, Bloomington and London: Indiana University Press.

Dargis, Manohla (1994) 'Quentin Tarantino on *Pulp Fiction*', *Sight and Sound* 4, 11: November

Darwin, Charles (1871) *The Descent of Man and Selection in Relation to Sex*, London: John Murray, 1909

Davis, Fred (1992) *Fashion, Culture and Identity*, Chicago and London: University of Chicago Press

Davis, Mike (1990) *City of Quartz: Excavating the Future in Los Angeles*, New York and London: Verso

Dawson, Graham (1991) 'The blond bedouin: Lawrence of Arabia, imperial adventure and the imagining of English-British masculinity', in Michael Roper and John Tosh (eds) *Manful Assertions: Masculinities in Britain Since 1800*, London and New York: Routledge

Bibliography

Dawson, Jeff (1995) *Tarantino: Inside Story*, London: Cassell

de Beauvoir, Simone (1949) *The Second Sex*, London: Picador, 1988

Diawara, Manthia (1993) 'Black American cinema: the new realism', in Manthia Diawara (ed.) *Black American Cinema*, New York and London: Routledge

Doane, Mary Ann (1991) *Femmes Fatales: Feminism, Film Theory, Psychoanalysis*, London and New York: Routledge

Docter, Richard F. (1988) *Transvestites and Transsexuals: Towards a Theory of Cross-gender Behavior*, New York and London: Plenum Press

Dollimore, Jonathan (1991) *Sexual Dissidence: Augustine to Wilde, Freud to Foucault*, Oxford: Oxford University Press

Donohue, Walter (1993) 'Immortal longing', *Sight and Sound* 3, 3: March

Duras, Marguerite (1988) *Yves Saint Laurent: Images of Design, 1958–88*, London: Ebury Press

Dyson, Michael Eric (1993) 'Between apocalypse and redemption: John Singleton's *Boyz N the Hood*', in Jim Collins, Hilary Radner and Ava Preacher Collins (eds) *Film Theory Goes to the Movies*, London and New York: Routledge

Ekins, Richard and King, Dave (eds) (1996) *Blending Genders: Social Aspects of Cross-dressing and Sex-changing*, London and New York: Routledge

Ellis, H. Havelock (1897) *Studies in the Psychology of Sex, Volume 1: Sexual Inversion* (2nd edn), London: The University Press

Engelmeier, Regine and Peter (eds) (1990) *Fashion in Film*, Munich: Prestel-Verlag

Faludi, Susan (1992) *Backlash: The Undeclared War Against Women*, London: Chatto and Windus

Florence, Penny (1993) Conversation with Sally Potter, *Screen* 34, 3: Autumn

Flügel, J.C. (1930) *The Psychology of Clothes*, London: Hogarth

Foucault, Michel (1976) *The History of Sexuality: Volume One*, Harmondsworth: Penguin

Fowler, Alistair (ed.) (1991) *The New Oxford Book of Seventeenth Century Verse*, Oxford: Oxford University Press

Freud, Sigmund (1905) 'The sexual aberrations', *On Sexuality*, Penguin Freud Library, Vol. 7, London: Penguin, 1991

—— (1911) 'A hat as a symbol of a man (or of male genitals)', *The Interpretation of Dreams*, Penguin Freud Library, Vol. 4, London: Penguin, 1991

—— (1914) 'On narcissism: an introduction', *On Metapsychology*, Penguin Freud Library, Vol. 11, London: Penguin, 1991

—— (1923) 'The ego and the id', *On Metapsychology*, Penguin Freud Library, Vol. 11, London: Penguin, 1991

—— (1927) 'Fetishism', *On Sexuality*, Penguin Freud Library, Vol. 7, London: Penguin, 1977

Friday, Nancy (1973) *My Secret Garden*, London: Virago

—— (1980) *Men In Love*, London: Hutchinson

Fried, John (1995) 'Pulp friction: two shots at Quentin Tarantino's *Pulp Fiction*', *Cineaste*, 21, 3: July

Frosh, Stephen (1994) *Sexual Difference: Masculinity and Psychoanalysis*, London: Routledge

Fuchs, Cynthia J. (1993) 'The buddy politic', in Steven Cohan and Ina Rae Hark (eds) *Screening The Male: Exploring Masculinities in Hollywood Cinema*, London and New York: Routledge

Furnival, Jane (1990) 'Chic to chic' *Screen International* MIFED, 20

Gaines, Jane (1990) 'Costume and narrative: how dress tells the woman's story', in Jane

Gaines and Charlotte Herzog (eds) *Fabrications: Costume and the Female Body*, London and New York: Routledge

Gaines, Jane and Herzog, Charlotte (eds) (1990) *Fabrications: Costume and the Female Body*, London and New York: Routledge

Gamman, Lorraine and Makinen, Merja (1994) *Female Fetishism: A New Look*, London: Lawrence and Wishart

Garber, Marjorie (1993) *Vested Interests: Cross-dressing and Cultural Anxiety*, London: Penguin

Glaessner, Verina (1992) 'Fire and ice', *Sight and Sound* 2, 4: February

Goodridge, Mike (1994) 'Looking the part', *Screen International* 986, 2: December

Grant, Richard E. (1996) *With Nails*, London: Picador

Greenberg, Harvey Roy (1991) 'Re-screwed: *Pretty Woman*'s co-opted feminism', *Journal of Popular Film and Television*, 19, 1: Spring

Gustafson, Robert (1982) 'The power of the screen: the influence of Edith Head's film designs on the retail fashion market', *The Velvet Light Trap* 19

Haggard, Claire (1990) 'Dressing Up in Public', *Screen International* MIFED Issue, 20: September

Harper, Susan (1987) 'Historical pleasures: Gainsborough costume melodrama', in Christine Gledhill (ed.) *Home Is Where The Heart Is: Studies in Melodrama and the Woman's Film*, London: BFI Publishing

—— (1994) *Picturing the Past: The Rise and Fall of the British Costume Film*, London: BFI Publishing

Hart, Lynda (1994) *Fatal Women: Lesbian Sexuality and the Mark of Aggression*, Princeton: Princeton University Press

Hayward, Susan (1993) *French National Cinema*, London and New York: Routledge

Head, Edith (with Jane Kesner Ardmore) (1959) *The Dress Doctor*, Boston and Toronto: Little, Brown and Co.

—— (1983) (with Paddy Calistro) *Edith Head's Hollywood*, New York: E.P. Dutton Inc.

Heard, Gerald (1924) *Narcissus: An Anatomy of Clothes*, London: Kegan, Paul, Trench, Trubner & Co.

Heath, Stephen (1986) 'Joan Riviere and the masquerade', in Victor Burgin, James Donald and Cora Kaplan (eds) *Formations of Fantasy*, London: Methuen

Hebdige, Dick (1979) *Subculture and the Meaning of Style*, London and New York: Methuen

Heilbrun, Carolyn (1973) *Towards a Recognition of Androgyny*, New York: W.W. Norton

Herzog, Charlotte (1990) '"Powder Puff" promotion: the fashion show-in-the-film', in Jane Gaines and Charlotte Herzog (eds) *Fabrications: Costume and the Female Body*, New York and London: Routledge

Herzog, Charlotte and Gaines, Jane (1984) 'Puffed sleeves before tea-time: Joan Crawford and women audiences', *Wide Angle* 6, 4

Higson, Andrew (1993) 'Re-presenting the national past: nostalgia and pastiche in the heritage film', in Lester Friedman (ed.) *British Cinema and Thatcherism: Fires Were Started*, London: UCL Press

—— (1996) 'The heritage film and British cinema', in Andrew Higson (ed.) *Dissolving Views: Key Writings on British Cinema*, London: Cassell

Hill, Henry (1990) Interviewed in *Premiere* 4, 25: December

Hirsch, Foster (1981) *The Dark Side of the Screen*, New York: A.S. Barnes

Hirschfeld, Magnus (1935) *Sexual Anomalies and Perversions: Physical and Psychological*

Development and Treatment (a Summary of the works of the late Magnus Hirschfeld), London: Torch Publishing Co. Ltd.

Hollander, Anne (1993) *Seeing Through Clothes*, Berkeley: University of California Press

hooks, bell (1992) *Black Looks: Race and Representation*, London: Turnaround

Irigaray, Luce (1993) *Je, Tous, Nous: Towards a Culture of Difference*, London and New York: Routledge

Irvine, Susan (1995) 'Fashion's big close-up', *Vogue* April

Jacobs, Laura (1994–5) 'Haute couture: the director's cut', *Modern Review* 1, 18: December–January

James, Darius (1995) *That's Blaxploitation! Roots of the Baadasssss 'Tude*, New York: St. Martin's Press

Jermyn, Deborah (1996) 'Rereading the bitches from hell: a feminist appropriation of the female psychopath', *Screen* 37, 3: Autumn

Kaplan, E. Ann (ed.) (1992) *Women in Film Noir*, London: BFI Publishing

Kaplan, Louise J. (1993) *Female Perversions: The Temptations of Madame Bovary*, London: Penguin

Keenan, Brigid (1977) *The Women We Wanted To Look Like*, London: Macmillan

Keyser, Les (1992) *Martin Scorsese*, New York: Twayne Publishers

Kirk, Kris and Heath, Ed (1984) *Men In Frocks*, London: GMP Publishers Ltd.

Krafft-Ebing, Dr R v. (1899) *Psychopathia Sexualis: With Especial Reference to Antipathetic Sexual Instinct, A Medico-forensic Study* (10th edn), London: Rebman

Krutnik, Frank (1991) *In A Lonely Street: Film Noir, Genre, Masculinity*, London and New York: Routledge

Kuhn, Annette (1985) *The Power of the Image: Essays on Representation and Sexuality*, London and New York: Routledge

—— (1994) *Women's Pictures* (2nd edn), London: Verso

Kunzle, David (1982) *Fashion and Fetishism: A Social History of the Corset, Tight-lacing and Other Forms of Body-sculpture in the West*, New Jersey: Rowman and Littlefield

Lacan, Jacques (1948) 'Aggressivity in psychoanalysis', *Ecrits: A Selection*, London: Routledge

—— (1949) 'The mirror stage as formative function of the I', *Ecrits: A Selection*, London: Routledge

—— (1954–5) *The Seminars of Jacques Lacan, Book II*, Cambridge: Cambridge University Press

—— (1958) 'The meaning of the phallus', in Juliet Mitchell and Jacqueline Rose (eds) *Feminine Sexuality*, London: Macmillan

Lapsley, Robert and Westlake, Michael (1992) 'From *Casablanca* to *Pretty Woman*: the politics of romance', *Screen* 31, 1: Spring

Laver, James (1945) *Taste and Fashion: From the French Revolution to the Present Day* (rev. edn), London: George G. Harrap

—— (1969) *Modesty in Dress: An Inquiry into the Fundamentals of Fashion*, London: Heinemann

—— (1995) *Costume and Fashion* (rev. edn), London: Thames and Hudson

Leader, Darian (1996) *Why Do Women Write More Letters Than They Post?*, London: Faber and Faber

Leese, Elizabeth (1976) *Costume Design in the Movies*, Isle of Wight: BCW Publishing Ltd.

Lee, Spike (1989) (with Lisa Jones) *A Companion Volume to the Universal Pictures Film 'Do the Right Thing'*, New York: Fireside

Bibliography

Light, Alison (1989) '"Young Bess": historical novels and growing up', *Feminist Review* 33: Autumn

Lindsay, Joan (1968) *Picnic at Hanging Rock*, Harlow: Longman, 1991

Loren, Christalene (1994) 'Quick cuts: a lady in disguise', *Cinefex* 58, June

Lurie, Alison (1981) *The Language of Clothes*, London: Heinemann

McArthur, Colin (1972) *Underworld USA*, London: Secker and Warburg

McDowell, Colin (1987) *McDowell's Directory of Twentieth Century Fashion* (rev. edn), London: Frederick Muller

——— (1992) *Dressed to Kill: Sex, Power and Clothes*, London: Hutchinson

Mackrell, Alice (1992) *Coco Chanel*, London: B.T. Batsford Ltd.

Madhubuti, Haki R. (1990) *Black Men: Obsolete, Single, Dangerous? Afrikan American Families in Transition: Essays in Discovery, Solution and Hope*, Chicago: Third World Press

Maiberger, Elise (1989) '*The Cook, the Thief, His Wife & Her Lover*', *British Vogue*, June

Malcolm X (with Alex Haley) (1968) *The Autobiography of Malcolm X*, London

Melly, George (1970) *Revolt Into Style: The Pop Arts in the 50s and 60s*, Oxford: Oxford University Press

Mercer, Kobena (1994) *Welcome to the Jungle: New Positions in Black Cultural Studies*, London and New York: Routledge

Merelman, Richard M. (1995) *Representing Black Culture: Racial Conflict and Cultural Politics in the United States*, New York and London: Routledge

Metz, Christian (1975) 'The imaginary signifier', *Screen* 16, 2: Summer

Middleton, Peter (1992) *The Inward Gaze: Masculinity and Subjectivity in Modern Culture*, London: Routledge

Milbank, Caroline Rennolds (1985) *Couture: The Great Fashion Designers*, London: Thames and Hudson

——— (1989) *New York: The Evolution of American Style*, New York: Harry N. Abrams, Inc.

Miner, Madonne (1992) 'No matter what they say, it's all about money', *Journal for Popular Film and Television* 20, 1: Spring

Molloy, John T. (1980) *Women: Dress For Success*, London: W. Fousham & Co. Ltd.

Mulvey, Laura (1975) 'Visual pleasure and narrative cinema', in Bill Nichols (ed.) *Movies and Methods II*, Berkeley: University of California Press, 1985

Murphy, Kathleen (1990) 'Made men', *Film Comment* 26, 5: September/October

Neale, Steve (1983) 'Masculinity as spectacle', in Steven Cohan and Ina Rae Hark (eds) *Screening the Male: Exploring Masculinities in Hollywood Cinema*, London: Routledge, 1993

Newton, Esther (1979) *Mother Camp: Female Impersonators in America*, Chicago and London: University of Chicago Press

Nogueira, Rui (ed.) (1971) *Melville on Melville*, London: Secker and Warburg

Nowell-Smith, Geoffrey (1987) 'Minnelli and melodrama', in Christine Gledhill (ed.) *Home Is Where the Heart Is: Studies in Melodrama and the Woman's Film*, London: BFI Publishing

Patterson, Janet (1993) *Sight and Sound* 3, 10: October

Philips, Mike (1996) 'Chic and beyond', *Sight and Sound* 6, 8: August

Place, Janey (1992) 'Women in film noir', in E. Ann Kaplan (ed.) *Women in Film Noir*, London: BFI Publishing

Polhemus, Ted (1988) *Body Styles*, Luton: Lennard Publishing

——— (1994) *Street Style: From Sidewalk to Catwalk*, London: Thames and Hudson

Potter, Sally (1993) Interview, *Cineaste* 20, 1: July

Bibliography

Pritchard, Susan Perez (1981) *Film Costume: An Annotated Bibliography*, Metuchen, NJ and London: Scarecrow Press Inc.

Raymond, Janice (1996) 'The politics of transgenderism', in Richard Ekins and Dave King (eds) *Blending Genders: Social Aspects of Cross-dressing and Sex-changing*, London and New York: Routledge

Reid, Mark A. (1988) 'The black action film: the end of the patiently enduring black hero', *Film History* 2, 1

Rich, B. Ruby (1992) 'Art House Killers', *Sight and Sound* 2, 8: December

Riviere, Joan (1929) 'Womanliness as masquerade', in Victor Burgin, James Donald and Cora Kaplan (eds) *Formations of Fantasy*, London: Methuen, 1986

Romney, Jonathan (1996) Review of *Casino*, *Sight and Sound* 6, 3: March

Rose, Jacqueline (1982) 'Introduction – II', in Juliet Mitchell and Jacqueline Rose (eds) *Feminine Sexuality: Jacques Lacan and L'Ecole Freudienne*, London: Macmillan

Rosow, Eugene (1978) *Born to Lose: The Gangster Film in America*, Oxford: Oxford University Press

Rubinstein, Ruth P. (1995) *Dress Codes: Meanings and Messages in American Culture*, Boulder: Westview Press

Ruppert, Jeanne (ed.) (1994) *Gender: Literary and Cinematic Representation*, Gainesville: University Press of Florida

Rutherford, Jonathan (1988) 'Who's that man?', in Rowena Chapman and Jonathan Rutherford (eds) *Male Order: Unwrapping Masculinity*, London: Lawrence and Wishart

Schatz, Thomas (1981) *Hollywood Genres: Formulas, Filmmaking and the Studio System*, New York: Random House

Scorsese, Martin (1990) Interviewed in *Cinema Papers* 81: December

Scorsese, Martin and Cocks (1993), Joe *The Age of Innocence: A Portrait of the Film Based on the Novel by Edith Wharton*, New York: Newmarket Press

Showalter, Elaine (1977) *A Literature of Their Own*, Princeton NJ: Princeton University Press

Silk, Catherine and Silk, John (1990) *Racism and Anti-racism in American Popular Culture: Portrayals of African-Americans in Fiction and Film*, Manchester and New York: Manchester University Press

Silverman, Kaja (1986) 'Fragments of a fashionable discourse', in Tania Modleski (ed.) *Studies in Entertainment*, Bloomington: Indiana University Press

Simmel, George (1904) 'Fashion', *On Individuality and Social Forms*, Chicago: University of Chicago Press

Simpson, Mark (1994) *Male Impersonators: Men Performing Masculinity*, London: Cassell

Singer, June (1977) *Androgyny: Towards a New Theory of Sexuality*, London and Henley: Routledge, Kegan and Paul

Singleton, Janet (1988) 'After *Super Fly*: the rise and fall of an anti-hero', *Black Film Review* 4, 2: Spring

Slide, Anthony (1986) *Great Pretenders: A History of Male and Female Impersonation in the Performing Arts*, Lombard, Illinois: Wallace-Homestead

Smith, Gavin (1994) Interview with Quentin Tarantino, *Film Comment* 30, 4: July–August

Smith, Paul (1995) 'Eastwood bound', in Maurice Berger, Brian Wallis and Simon Watson (eds) *Constructing Masculinity*, London: Routledge

Sontag, Susan (1964) 'Notes on camp', *A Susan Sontag Reader*, London: Penguin, 1983

Spencer, Margaret Beale, Cunningham, Michael and Swanson, Dena Phillips (1995) 'Identity as coping: adolescent African-American males' adaptive responses to high-risk environments', in Herbert W. Harris, Howard C. Blue and Ezra E. H. Griffith (eds) *Racial and Ethnic Identity: Psychological Development and Creative Expression*, London and New York: Routledge

Stacey, Jackie (1988) 'Desperately seeking difference', in Lorraine Gamman and Margaret Marshment (eds) *The Female Gaze: Women as Viewers of Popular Culture*, London: Women's Press

—— (1994) *Star Gazing: Hollywood Cinema and Female Spectatorship*, London: Routledge

Steele, Valerie (1985) *Fashion and Eroticism: Ideals of Feminine Beauty from the Victorian Era to the Jazz Age*, New York and Oxford: Oxford University Press

Stoller, Robert (1968) *Sex and Gender, Volume 1: The Development of Masculinity and Femininity*, London: H. Karnac Books Ltd.

—— (1985) *Observing The Erotic Imagination*, New Haven and London: Yale University Press

Strauss, Frédéric (1996) *Almodóvar on Almodóvar*, London: Faber and Faber

Straayer, Chris (1992) 'Redressing the "natural": the temporary transvestite', *Wide Angle* 14, 1: January

Swinton, Tilda (1993) Interview in *Cineaste* 20, 1: July

Tarantino, Quentin (1993) Interview in *Empire* 44: February

Tasker, Yvonne (1993) *Spectacular Bodies: Gender, Genre and the Action Cinema*, London and New York: Routledge

Taubin, Amy (1992) 'The men's room' *Sight and Sound* 2, 8: December

—— (1993) 'Dread and desire', *Sight and Sound* 3, 12: December

Traub, Valerie (1992) *Desire and Anxiety: Circulations of Sexuality in Shakespearean Drama*, London and New York: Routledge

Troy, Carol (1989) 'Can you imagine them making love?: Ellen Mirojnick and the inner game of costume', *American Film* 14: 8, June

Tulloch, Carol (1993), 'Rebel without a pause: black street style and black designers', in Juliet Ash and Elizabeth Wilson (eds) *Chic Thrills: A Fashion Reader*, London: Pandora

Vance-Straker, Marilyn (1991) 'See that girl with the red dress on', *Hollywood Reporter* 315, 47: 21 January (Supplement)

Veblen, Thorstein (1925) *The Theory of the Leisure Class: An Economic Study of Institutions*, London: Unwin

Vincendeau, Ginette (1992) 'France 1945–65 and Hollywood: the *policier* as international text', *Screen* 33, 1: Spring

Walker, Michael (1992) 'Introduction', in Ian Cameron (ed.) *The Movie Book of Film Noir*, London: Studio Vista

Warshow, Robert (1948) 'The gangster as tragic hero', *The Immediate Experience: Movies, Comics, Theatre and Other Aspects of Popular Culture*, New York: Doubleday, 1962

Weil, Kari (1992) *Androgyny and the Denial of Difference*, Charlottesville and London: University Press of Virginia

Weininger, Otto (1906) *Sex and Character*, London: William Heinemann, 1910

Wharton, Edith (1920) *The Age of Innocence*, London: Virago, 1993

Wheelwright, Julie (1989) *Amazons and Military Maids: Women Who Dress as Men in Pursuit of Life, Liberty and Happiness*, London: Pandora

Williams, Terry (1990) *The Cocaine Kids: The Inside Story of a Teenage Drug Ring*, London: Bloomsbury

Wilson, Elizabeth (1985) *Adorned in Dreams: Fashion and Modernity*, Berkeley and Los Angeles: University of California Press

Bibliography

Wolfe, Tom (1977) 'Funky chic', *Mauve Gloves & Madmen, Clutter & Vine*, New York

Wollen, Peter (1995) 'Strike a pose' *Sight and Sound* 5, 3: March

Wollen, Tana (1991) 'Over our shoulders: nostalgic screen fictions for the 1980s', in John Corner and Sylvia Harvey (eds) *Enterprise and Heritage: Crosscurrents of National Culture*, London and New York: Routledge

Woolf, Virginia (1928a) *A Room Of One's Own*, London: Penguin, 1945

—— (1928b) *Orlando*, London: Penguin, 1993

Zolla, Elémire (1981) *The Androgyne: Fusion of the Sexes*, London: Thames and Hudson

INDEX

Index

Index

Index

Index

Index